CHRISTIAN MORAL REASONING

Christian
Moral Reasoning:

An Analytic Guide

Garth L. Hallett

BJ
1249
.H29
1982

UNIVERSITY OF NOTRE DAME PRESS
NOTRE DAME – LONDON

199417

Library of Congress Cataloging in Publication Data

Hallett, Garth.
    Christian moral reasoning.

    Includes bibliographical references and index.
    1. Christian ethics — Catholic authors. I. Title.
BJ1249.H29 1982   241   82-13436
ISBN 0-268-00740-3
ISBN 0-268-00741-1 (pbk.)

Contents

Acknowledgments

FRIENDS AND COLLEAGUES, sharing their expertise and insights, have done much for this book. I wish to mention with special gratitude those who read and commented on the entire work at various stages of its composition: Donald Abel, Vincent Burns, Roger Couture, William Davish, John Elliott, Louis Gendron, Arnold Hogan, Gerard Hughes, T. Michael McNulty, Dominic Maruca, James Mattea, Francis Oppenheim, Sean O'Riordan, Gene Outka, Sister Mary Emil Penet, Jules Toner, and the helpful unknown reader for the University of Notre Dame Press.

Note on References

REFERENCES IN PARENTHESES within the text (e.g., V, A or X, G, 2) indicate a chapter, section, and perhaps subsection of this book.
Scriptural quotations are from The New English Bible.

Introduction

I UNDERTOOK THIS STUDY because I sensed a lack in existing literature. No work I knew of, whether for layperson or professional, examined systematically and fairly thoroughly the broad topic here explored: Christian moral reasoning. Yet such an inquiry is central for the whole of Christian ethics, to an extent realized today more than ever before. Indeed, it is arguable that a grasp of the Christian approach to moral issues, illustrated by varied case studies, is a better preparation for life than a fuller set of answers whose legitimation and application are left unclear, and that therefore in a general course of Christian ethics the emphasis should shift from content to method.

The book I have provided in response to this common need should prove useful, in differing ways, to specialists and nonspecialists alike. The ample footnotes are intended for both and should obviate the need for reading lists. Nonspecialists will find familiar matters explained and others curtailed for their sake. Specialists, on the other hand, are more likely to appreciate certain theoretical features of the study.

It is distinctive, for example, in the way it unites two currents of thought which for long flowed separately. Analytical philosophers focused on issues of meaning and method but largely ignored the religious dimensions of morality. Christian theologians for their part showed little interest in the analytic inquiries of philosophers. Recent attempts at rapprochement have been numerous but have generally been piecemeal. Even the more systematic studies that have appeared since I set to work differ importantly from this one. Gerard Hughes' *Authority in Morals*, for instance, is less comprehensive, while Alan Donagan's *The Theory of Morality* is less theological.

The work is distinctive, furthermore, in its specific orientation. Its key term and central query are borrowed from Ludwig Wittgenstein, whose well-known interest in meaning led him to distinguish between "criteria" (or defining traits) and "symptoms" (or mere clues to the thing so defined). When applied to ethical expressions, the term "crite-

1

ria" serves as well to mark off the expressions' descriptive content from their emotive and dynamic features. In relation to these nondescriptive aspects, on the one hand, and to symptoms or clues, on the other, criteria play a decisive role. Indeed there is no more crucial question in all of Christian ethics than this: By what criterion or criteria should a Christian define "right" and "wrong"?

Until this question is clarified, few others can properly be addressed. No guidelines for closer analysis, no procedures for judging specific actions, can be reliably proposed so long as the criterial issue is left unresolved. One might as profitably debate, say, whether the weekend will be overcast or bright without agreeing on the sense of "overcast" and "bright." In discussions of the weather, to be sure, we can usually assume agreed-on meanings for our words. But not in ethics. Not in ethics generally, nor in Christian ethics specifically.

The focal issue, therefore, that structures this study is the following: By what consistent criterion are right and wrong to be assessed? What sense should Christians give that pair of terms? Chapters 1 to 5 prepare an answer; chapter 6 delivers it; chapters 7 to 10 trace its implications. More precisely, the inquiry proceeds as follows.

Part one is preparatory. It argues three needs and indicates three directions the book will therefore take: first, the need for much careful moral reflection by Christians as by others (chapter 1); second, the need, on most occasions, for a purely objective evaluation of acts, abstracting from subjective considerations such as motive and intention (chapter 2); third, the need to accord a central place to the study of moral criteria in view of their decisive importance (chapter 3).

To some this stage-setting may seem excessive. However, each chapter of this part seeks to surmount a major obstacle. Many Christians have viewed moral reasoning with a jaundiced eye. Many Christian ethicians strongly contest the legitimacy of abstracting from subjective considerations. And no one to my knowledge, whether philosopher or theologian, has systematically set out the central role of criteria in morality. If, then, a study of Christian moral reasoning is to be taken seriously by Christian readers, and a consistent objective focus is to be accepted by Christian ethicians, and the strong stress here placed on criteria is to be understood, let alone endorsed, the way must be prepared with some care.

In part two the search for a Christian criterion of right and wrong gets under way with a survey of the whole history of Christian moral reasoning. Though the evidence to be sifted is so varied and vast, and no major strand of reasoning can be ignored, still the aim of the survey allows some selectivity; order is achieved, and a final verdict prepared, through the following division. Chapter 4 first documents the Christian tendency to decide moral issues by the balance of values and disvalues, pro and con; chapter 5 then scrutinizes tendencies in real or apparent conflict with such value-balancing.

From these systematic samplings part three can then identify the chief contenders for the status of Christian criterion and adjudicate between them. This it does in chapter 6, deciding in favor of a broadly teleological norm. That is, the criterion of maximal value over disvalue, implicit in value-balancing like that of chapter 4, seems basically correct; it must, however, extend, as chapter 5 reveals, to moral values as well as nonmoral, and to acts themselves as well as to their consequences. Thus the fact, for instance, that an action is just or unjust in itself may tell decisively for or against it despite (though not regardless of) its consequences.

The broad norm stated by chapter 6 does not specify what values should shape our moral verdicts or how. So chapter 7 starts to fill in the missing details. Sifting the same evidence as before, it identifies various values Christians have stressed in their reasoning, notes and resists a tendency to reduce the many values to few or only one, and weighs the possibility of ordering these many hierarchically so as to replace a system of precepts with a guiding system of values.

The verdict on this project being negative, part four proceeds in a less systematic, yet ordered, manner to fill in further particulars. Chapter 8, on analytic issues, aims at surer value-balancing. Chapter 9, on procedural questions, examines especially some alternative ways of discovering God's will. For the single Christian criterion of right and wrong may set procedural limits but does not dictate a single method for distinguishing right from wrong. Various techniques are compatible with insistence on maximal value over disvalue. Chapter 10, finally, drawing on the data and conclusions of chapters 4 through 9, compares Christian moral reasoning with non-Christian.

From this introductory sketch it can be seen that the book as a whole converges on, then diverges from, a central point: the choice of a Christian criterion in chapter 6. Thus its structure can be represented graphically as follows:

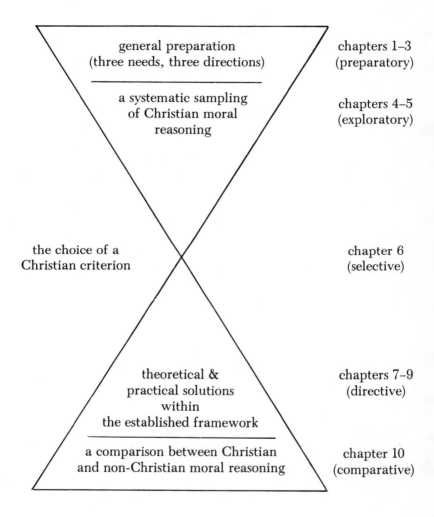

The meaning of this diagram can be grasped still more fully by turning to the final retrospect. Its first pages, in particular, complement the present overview.

PART ONE

Fixing the Focus

To exist as a man means to act. And action means choosing, deciding. What is the right choice? What ought I to do? What ought we to do? This is the question before which every man is objectively placed. And whatever may be the results of his examination of the question as a question, it is the question to which he never ceases even for a moment objectively to give an answer. — Karl Barth

1
The Need for Moral Reasoning

AT THE START OF a book concerned with wise decision and right action, it is fitting that I propose reasons for a person's undertaking to read a work such as this and for persevering, despite some arduous and perhaps arid stretches, to the end. The chief reasons may be summed up by distinguishing between two kinds of deliberation — deliberation about acts and deliberation about standards by which acts are judged — and saying that Christians, like other people, have need of both kinds. This is no truism. For serious questions have been raised not only about the "how" of Christian moral reasoning but also about the "whether": Should it be done at all?

When reasoning has a bad press, it is perhaps futile to reason in its behalf. It is somewhat as though a journalist were to stand up for the honor of his profession, writing a lengthy column in defense of columnists. However, there are some whose mistrust of intellect is not complete or universal and who may therefore consent to listen when reason pleads a role for reason. Those who need no convincing on this score may move ahead to chapter 2, if they wish. Yet the present vindication is not purely polemical. From a dialectical discussion there may emerge a clearer view of reason's proper place — of its limits as well as of its just claims.

A. Deliberation about Acts

In the popular opinion of the time Peter the Hermit, not Pope Urban II, was the real instigator of the First Crusade (1096–1099). According to this version Christ, using Peter as his intermediary, commanded Urban not merely to help Eastern Christians resist a common threat but to preach a holy war for the deliverance of Jerusalem. And that, at any

7

rate, is what Peter proceeded to do, with such eloquence and fame for sanctity that soon a vast throng was trooping at his heels. Without discipline and without plan, they swarmed across the Bosporus and advanced toward their goal. But not very far. Falling upon the pilgrim host, only a quarter of whom, at most, were men able to fight, the Turks massacred all save a couple thousand stragglers before they even reached Nicaea.

The main fighting force under the Western barons and the Greek Taticius was better organized and had greater success. Yet its efforts were similarly flawed from the beginning. "The sole object, motive, and justification of this adventure — which in time grew vast enough to involve more or less deeply the conscience of the whole of Catholic Christendom — was the mirage of the Holy City, Jerusalem. It is Jerusalem alone which still gives this long succession of sufferings, atrocities, wars, feudal squabbles, and frequently disastrous military enterprises a glory which even the centuries have not dimmed. And yet at the end of the eleventh century, when Christianity had endured for a thousand years and the Moslems dominated Syria for four hundred, there was no need for the men of France, Flanders, and Provence to go out and fight for Jerusalem."[1]

Indeed their very success proved calamitous. Successive generations felt obliged to maintain the positions won or to regain those later lost, with the result that one disastrous expedition followed another. Thus most historians, and most Christians acquainted with the facts, would agree that the crusades as a whole were a mistake. Would that Peter the Hermit had not preached, and preached so effectively! Would that no shout had arisen: "God wills it!" Not only were individual campaigns undertaken with insufficient planning, based on inadequate information, but too little thought was given from the start to the desirability of such an undertaking for such a purpose.

To pleas for fuller reflection, the standard answer has doubtless always been that it cools the crusading ardor of those who want to get things done. The important thing for a Christian, after all, is to do God's will, not to talk about it. And indeed: How much enthusiasm would Peter the Hermit have aroused and how many would have rallied to his banner had he talked strategy or debated the wisdom of his proposal? Surely far fewer than those forty thousand who perished near Nicaea.

So their blood has a lesson to teach us: Better no crusade than a crusade ill conceived; better no action at all than action made energetic through the suppression of thought. Instance after historical instance — the Inquisition, Philip's armada, the "white man's burden," America's "manifest destiny," the holy war to "make the world safe for democracy," the campaign for prohibition, Senator McCarthy's crusade against communism, Vietnam — reiterate the message. In these and countless similar cases, as in the first crusades, sincere Christians have believed they were doing God's will. And perhaps they sometimes were. But a review of the record may make us reflect somewhat longer before we too raise the cry "God wills it!"

The same lesson applies to our personal crusades, as well as to large-scale undertakings. One thinks, for instance, of an early case in point: "Paul tells us that prior to his conversion he had been a member of the strict Jewish party of the Pharisees. He had studied the ancestral law in the school of Gamaliel and had been extremely zealous in his effort to keep its requirements. And when the new sect of the followers of Jesus arose and proclaimed as the long-awaited Messiah an itinerant preacher from Galilee who had scandalized the religious leaders of the day by his highly critical attitude toward the Law and the Temple, Paul devoted himself zealously and effectively to the suppression of this heresy in and about Jerusalem."[2] Doubtless many of the heretics were sincere, and some painful scenes ensued. Still, there could be no doubt where his duty lay.

As he would later state the situation, he had zeal for God, but not according to knowledge. He was so sure he was right that the only way God could reach him was to knock him to the ground. So the message of Paul to all such knights on horseback would seem to be: "Hold your horses!" Before you ride off furiously to the battles of the Lord, reflect a bit longer and make sure they are his.

Against such advice it may be objected that Christians, like most people, require the spur more than the rein, and that more needed crusades have been forgone than needless ones launched. How slow Christians and Christian churches have been to combat slavery, or support democratic regimes, or promote social justice, or urge women's rights, or question questionable wars and methods of warfare. However, such examples reinforce the present point: the need for more reflection, so as to discern more surely what really is God's will, and not too readily equate it either with some current crusade *or* with traditional ways and views. In Christopher Dawson's view such was, for instance, the main criticism Matthew Arnold leveled against the religion of his day: "The burden of his complaints is always that *religious people would not think* — that they made religion a matter of strong emotion and moral earnestness so that it generated heat and not light. And that at the same time they were complacent and uncritical in their attitude to their own bourgeois culture: so long as men went to church and read the Bible and abstained from gambling and drunkenness and open immorality, it did not matter that they were at the same time helping to turn England into a hideous and disorderly conglomeration of factories and slums in which the chapel and the gin palace provided the only satisfaction for man's spiritual and emotional needs."[3]

Many another example could be cited: It was because he thought more not less than others that John Ford questioned saturation bombing even as the bombs fell during World War II; it was because he was more prayerfully reflective than most that John Woolman gently insisted with his Quaker brethren that they reconsider slavery; and so on, back to Gamaliel (Acts 5:33-39). However, a Christian will want to look beyond a Ford or a Woolman to their Master, as the Gospels portray him. "Is it permitted to do good or to do evil on the Sabbath," Jesus asked, "to save life or to kill?" (Mk. 3:4). No answer came. "Do you take me for a bandit," he later inquired, "that you have come out with swords and cudgels to arrest me? Day after day I was within your reach as I taught in the temple, and you did not lay hands on me" (Mk. 14:48-49). Again, no answer, no explanation. "If I spoke amiss, state it in evidence; if I spoke well, why strike me?" he asked the soldier (Jn. 18:23). But again, no reply is recorded. Such contrasts are instructive. The Pharisees in the synagogue were sure of God's will, the mob in the garden took decisive action and did not merely talk, the soldier reacted with spontaneous indignation. But Jesus questioned and reasoned. So should Christians.

And they should keep on questioning in search of clarity. That is perhaps the more important point. For frequently the first serious question is the last. It is considered sufficient, for example, to have noticed that there is a problem for Christians in basing an economic system on the profit motive. ("Profit motive" and "altruism," juxtaposed, seem to clash as clearly as did "infidel" and "holy places.") The enemy having been thus identified, it appears evident that he must be driven from the field. The time has come for crusading. However, have we really identified the enemy by this facile allusion to "profit motive"? Selfishness takes such varied forms (greed, yes, but also hedonism, laziness, pusillanimity, vainglory, thirst for position and power), and so does private gain. Even economic advantage takes in far more than the label "profit" suggests (fringe benefits, dividends, services, legacies, bonuses, home improvements, tax exemptions, etc.) and, regardless of type, is sought for such varied motives, both selfish and altruistic. So what, precisely, do we wish to reduce or eliminate, and how, and why, with what alternative system in view, designed still for human beings?[4]

Often such counterquestioning is regarded as evidence that a person has already taken sides. For dialectical probing in dispassionate search of the truth is unfortunately rare. It is as though one could reflect too much or too seriously on major issues, and reasoning were to be countenanced as long as it provides clear answers but discouraged the moment it complicates matters. But on that assumption reason loses its proper function and becomes subservient, not to the will of God, but to the blind will of man. A cause thus withdrawn from scrutiny, no matter how holy in appearance, is already suspect. For God is not a lover of darkness — not even when from the darkness the cry goes up more fervently, "God wills it!"

"Every moral life," wrote John Dewey, "has its radicalism; but this radical factor does not find its full expression in direct action but in the courage of intelligence to go deeper than either tradition or immediate impulse goes."[5] Reason without will is sterile, but will without reason is blind.

B. Objections

To this claim it may be objected: (1) that even with reason the will is blind; (2) that better natural guidance is available; or (3) that divine guidance is available and alone reliable.

(1)   The first objection may stem from an identification of "reason" with some distrusted form of reasoning: a utilitarian calculus, void of faith and blind to transcendent values, or rationalistic deduction via syllogisms. But once such simplisms are set aside, the task of reason is not superseded; rather, its true complexity and urgency emerge.

But also its difficulty. So such a defense sets the stage for a more serious charge. "Life is not long," declared Doctor Johnson, "and too much of it must not pass in idle deliberation how it shall be spent; deliberation, which those who begin it by prudence, and continue it with subtility, must, after long expence of thought, conclude by chance. To prefer one future mode of life to another, upon just reasons, requires faculties which it has not pleased our Creator to give us."[6] The sage may seem to exaggerate. But how strong a case can be made for his verdict will appear in the course of this treatise. A shortcut to the same conclusion is to recall that no individual event can be cited in disproof of divine providence; for human intelligence, unable as it is to situate any occurrence within the total weave of history, is therefore incapable of assessing its overall significance or worth. But the same holds for our own decisions and acts, even the surest: were we omniscient, we might appraise them otherwise.

(2)   The only rejoinder, therefore, is to ask: Are we more likely to

choose well with reasoning than without? Are the chances improved by thinking things out as best we can? Some would say they are not — and not merely because the libido is at work, or class interest, turning reasoning into rationalization. They hold, as Sidgwick put it, "that what is intuitively perceived is the rightness or wrongness of individual acts, — a view which obviously renders ethical reasoning practically superfluous."[7] As we shall see, this inference is faulty, for reasoning might prepare the intuition. But the assessment fits well enough a statement like Bishop Butler's: "The inquiries which have been made by men of leisure after some general rule, the conformity to, or disagreement from which, should denominate our actions good or evil, are in many respects of great service. Yet let any plain honest man, before he engages in any course of action, ask himself, Is this I am going about right, or is it wrong? Is it good, or is it evil? I do not in the least doubt, but that this question would be answered agreeably to truth and virtue, by almost any fair man in almost any circumstance. Neither do there appear any cases which look like exceptions to this; but those of superstition, and of partiality to ourselves."[8]

Now surely this assertion goes too far; for honest, intelligent people are repeatedly puzzled concerning their obligations. But it contains a kernel of truth, which Norris Clarke states as follows: "The . . . notion of deeply felt commitment to the good as the inner dynamo of the moral conscience and the whole moral life may help also to illuminate one aspect of conscience that has always filled me with wonder and not a little puzzlement. This is the spontaneous, intuitive, non-analytic character of its judgment in so many cases, even quite complex ones, in which it comes out with clear-cut judgments — 'This is right; do it; that's no good, avoid it' — even though we find it very difficult to justify or organize these in any explicit analyzable reasoning. The answer is perhaps the peculiar intuitive connaturality or affinity with the good which results from the radical commitment to the good itself as absolute ideal. . . . St. Thomas himself gives an important place to such knowledge by connaturality — the term itself is his — in the knowledge of God, of morality, and of spiritual things in general — a place which is often overlooked in our traditional treatises both of epistemology and of ethics."[9]

Connaturality — the good person's kinship with the good, facilitating recognition of it — is often touched on but seldom explained, and its relation to reason therefore remains unclear. How, precisely, does a good person's goodness help him or her to discern what is good? Granted, reason is then not warped by "partiality to ourselves"; reasoning does not become rationalization. But surely more than this is meant.

Father Clarke suggests a fruitful line of reflection when he speaks of "a certain intuitive feel or flair for discovering the good wherever it is found that is beyond the reach of step-by-step analytic reason." His words recall a more general phenomenon: the antennae people develop when they have an absorbing interest. Consider, for example, the special sense observed in many collectors—for instance a collector of butterflies and moths. Let dull wings flutter ever so slightly in the undergrowth as he passes, and he spots the movement instantly from the corner of his eye. No calculation, just instant alertness and attention, though he is perhaps engaged in conversation or his thoughts are wandering elsewhere. Others would note nothing, but he has already whirled to have a closer look. His eyes are special eyes: trained, attuned, at the service of his interest.

Now the truly good person has a propensity for value in all its forms: the good, the true, the beautiful. So his eye catches what others miss. Without calculation he registers instantly the slightest stir of wings.

Yet that does not mean he can do without reasoning, or would wish to. Consider again the parallel with the collector. A boy with little learning but keen interest will discover far more specimens, it is true, than a detached specialist poring over books in his study. But of course the boy will become a specialist if he can. He will want to know more about his specimens. And he will want to know where others can be found, which he may have missed because he did not know their habits or habitat. And so it is for the good man. He will want to know more about the action, the principle, the institution, the problem under consideration. Desirous of value, he will wish no value to escape him. Intent on the good, he will be concerned about possible errors, oversights, or confusions. Indeed, his natural bent will be to learn all he can about the good and its pursuit, regardless of what utility the knowledge may have.

All of us do in fact base our actions on available information and at least minimal calculation. We do not wave aside the person who tells us the highway we intend to use will be closed the day we intend to use it, or that our candidate has Mafia connections, or that cigarettes endanger one's health. We do not reply that information is irrelevant since it can never be complete, and reasoning futile since it may always err. So why draw a line, and where? At what point does fuller information or more thorough deliberation become irrelevant or inappropriate (save for reasons of time, as in IX, B, 6)? As Father Clarke himself concludes: "To know what angle of vision to take on a problem, what set of relevant value perimeters to situate it within, what horizon of consequences to include in one's vision — all this can be done well only by a mature judgment."[10]

(3)   Connaturality, then, does not replace reasoning but stimulates and guides it. In the teaching of Karl Barth, on the contrary, it sometimes appears that little room is left for deliberation. "My human decision," he writes, "in face of the divine command does not consist in a decision of the question whether this or that is the good, whether the command wills this or that of me, whether I am to do this or that — this question would be just about as intelligent and relevant as the question whether there is a God. . . . No, my decision — the human ethical decision — is whether in my conduct I shall correspond to the command which encounters and confronts me in the most concrete and pointed way. . . . The question cannot be whether He speaks, but only whether we hear."[11]

Such assurance leaves one perplexed. When saint opposed saint, or a Lincoln opposed a Lee, is it really so certain that both saw clearly what to do and one resisted the light? Surely a survey of the historical scene provides no such certainty. And as for our own inner experience, it is true that our failure to perceive a divine command may result from our failure to listen; but if in fact we frequently hear no command, how can we know one is given?

Barth replies: "The fact that the decision of God which claims and judges us in His command is a specific decision is something we must affirm because this is how matters stand according to the witness of Holy Scripture, and therefore the witness of God's revelation of His real relationship to us and our real relationship to Him. It is in this way, concretely, that man is commanded in Holy Scripture, and from this we may infer that it is in this way, concretely, that we ourselves are commanded."[12] In confirmation Barth adduces an impressive list of specific, personalized orders — from the divine injunction in Genesis, "Be fruitful and increase, fill the earth and subdue it" (Gen. 1:28), to the risen Lord's instructions, "Go and take word to my brothers that they are to leave for Galilee" (Mt. 28:10). Time and again the source is sure, the message unmistakable, the only response obedience or disobedience.

Now the first, rather obvious fact to note is that a catalog of non-commanded acts in the Old and New Testaments would occupy many more pages than Barth's collection of commanded ones. His list contains only commands because that is what he went looking for. And the commands are all from God because such, once again, were the objects of his search (the Macedonian's appeal to Paul, or the Baptist's directives to his hearers, would have to be listed elsewhere). So what can we conclude from all this selective evidence? Certainly that Scripture often represents God as intimating his will in this definite way. Probably that some such directives were issued. But even if we supposed that all these orders were actually given (for instance, the Old Testament injunctions to slaughter and exterminate) and that they were as specific as portrayed (for instance, the blueprints of the temple and the ark), we could at most infer that this being God's way with men — on those occasions — he doubtless so acts even today — on some occasions. We have no reason to allege, generally, a paternalistic providence which makes all the decisions and tells us what to do, in detail, all the time, in unmistakable terms.

Neither does experience warrant such a thesis. We might, for example, inquire whether Barth himself received clear intimations from the start concerning the evils of National Socialism and only later heeded them. If, instead, he heard no command because he "turned a deaf ear," did not that consist largely, even principally, in his not praying, reflecting, inquiring, discussing as earnestly and fully as he might have? For did not fuller reflection and experience lead to his change of attitude?

If it is maintained, nonetheless, that deliberation is infidelity and inquiry a sin, then the warning of H. D. Lewis seems in place: "Instead of making for harmony and patient understanding of one another's problems, the abjuration of ordinary ethical thinking in favour of reliance on immediate revelation has just the reverse effect. It breeds dissent and encourages a fanatical dogmatism."[13]

So, too, is it in the more popular variant: once rule out reason in favor of the "heart" alone, and one gets the heart — the whole heart, and all hearts. The whole heart: the passion along with the sympathy, the rage along with the compassion, the intolerance along with the pity, the pride along with the mercy. And all hearts: so heart against heart with no meeting of minds, the mind having been suppressed. And if to the heart's strong promptings one adds an intuitive conviction of doing God's will, the resulting mixture may be potent, yet sadly mistaken: a Saint Bernard then preaches another crusade or persecutes an Abelard.

Dewey could be assessing precisely this last case, so apt are his remarks: "Our moral failures go back to some weakness of disposition, some absence of sympathy, some one-sided bias that makes us perform the judgment of the concrete case carelessly or perversely. Wide sympathy, keen sensitiveness, persistence in the face of the disagreeable, balance of interests enabling us to undertake the work of analysis and decision intelligently are the distinctively moral traits — the virtues or moral excellencies."[14] One is reminded of Saint Thomas: "In all matters of moral virtue, practical wisdom [*prudentia*] serves as guide."[15]

C. Deliberation about Standards

From the need just urged, to reflect on our acts, it does not follow automatically that we need to reflect on our standards of action, at least very urgently or at any great length. Thus if the reader glances through the involved discussions in this book he or she may well exclaim: "How can all this be necessary, to lead a moral life or to make our daily decisions?!" After all, "men sought food before they studied the science of nutrition, reproduced without benefit of genetics, trained their children before child psychology, formed families and cities without sociology, spoke without linguistics, claimed their due without law courts, and lived moral lives without a formal study of ethics."[16]

Even C. D. Broad, partial as he was to the use of reason and specifically to the examination of ethical standards, wrote at the end of a long survey: "Quite simple people, there is no reason to doubt, often act rightly in quite complicated situations. How could they possibly do so if the problem is so involved as we have made it out to be? The answer to this objection is to compare right action with playing a ball rightly at tennis or cricket, and to compare the theory of right action to the mechanical and hydrodynamical theory of the action of the racket or bat and the flight of the ball. The good player responds, without explicit analysis or calculation, to a highly complex situation by actions which an observer possessed of superhuman powers of analysis and calculation would deduce as the solution of his equations. We can no more learn to act rightly by appealing to the ethical theory of right action than we can play golf well by appealing to the mathematical theory of the flight of the golf-ball. The interest of ethics is thus almost wholly theoretical, as is the interest of the mathematical theory of golf or of billiards. And yet it may have a certain slight practical application. It may lead us to look out for certain systematic faults which we should not otherwise have suspected; and, once we are on the look out for them, we may learn to correct them. But in the main the old saying is true: *Non in dialectica complacuit Deo salvum facere populum suum* [God did not choose to save his people through dialectics]."[17]

At the point Broad reaches, the ethical expert is still accorded a slight advantage, and the study of ethics retains some utility. But the same line of thought is often carried further, in the direction Aquinas suggested when he wrote: "Many are good at counsel, yet lack the good sense to form a sound judgment."[18] Thus Broad's comparison may receive a stronger twist: "Some excellent athletes are quite ignorant of the complex processes that go on inside themselves when they perform. And, needless to say, the somewhat elderly professors who know most about such things would perform very poorly were they to risk their dignity on the athletic field. Even given the same basic muscular and nervous apparatus, the person who knows might not surpass the 'natural athlete.'"[19]

Austin Fagothey gives content to the comparison when he explains: "Rules cannot be given for prudence itself, because all rules must have some universality and prudence deals with the single instance. How to break bad news gently, when to ask one's employer for a raise, whether to punish a fault or to let it pass this time, whom to pick out as the right man for the right job, how to arrange the troops for battle in a particular terrain, what legislation will best promote the common good and conciliate all interests — all such matters, great and small, are governed by prudence. The widest possible observation and experience of human behavior are the only teachers of prudence. It has little correlation with book learning. Some pick it up readily, some otherwise intelligent persons are slow to catch on, some geniuses are deficient in it."[20]

All this is true as far as it goes, but were the matter left there, it might appear that a study like the present one does not possess even the slight utility Broad accorded it. So I shall point out, as a start, that the eventual success of a Washington, despite his lack of professional training, is no argument against military academies. It just puts things in perspective. Nor does the success of a Rockefeller, who got no further than high school, demonstrate the futility of business schools. And as for knowledgeable athletes versus natural athletes, anyone acquainted with developments in the Olympic Games knows that theory does pay off. Other things being equal, the "examined life" is more successful than the unexamined, whether in war, business, or sport.

Continuing the comparison with business, suppose we were to paraphrase Broad: "Quite simple businesspeople, there is no reason to doubt, often act rightly in quite complicated situations. They buy the right stocks, open the right store in the right place, charge the right prices in relation to their competitors. How could they possibly do so if the problems are as involved as the business schools make out?" The absurdity of this parallel query is evident, and so is the inappropriateness of an answer such as Broad suggests. The interest of business schools is not "almost wholly theoretical."

With little knowledge of theory but sufficient intelligence, reflection, and experience, a person may find his way, even in complex matters, but with theory he may proceed more surely and avoid disasters which others incur for lack of sufficient theory. In economics clearly it is a matter of practical importance whether a Keynes is right or wrong.

And though an economic theory's validity is debated and established by experts, the nonexpert — businessperson, planner, or legislator — must understand the theory if he is to relate it to the current situation and take appropriate action. Similarly, it is a practical matter whether an Aquinas, say, or a Kant is right about moral standards. And even if the man in the pews could leave the experts, or church authorities, to pick a theory for him, he would still have to understand the theory in order to apply it.

That theory has practical import in ethics as in economics is borne out by conflicts traceable to theoretical disagreement. Such abound. The illustrations in just this present study are too numerous to name (see, e.g., IV, G; V, A, D, E, F, H; VI, A, B; VIII, A). No mere discrepancy in calculations accounts for the divergences among Christians concerning censorship, contraception, civil disobedience, remarriage, abortion, social justice, premarital sex, and so on. Christian differs from Christian, and church from church, largely for theoretical reasons. It is therefore to fundamental standards of Christian moral reasoning that we must direct our attention in order to resolve such conflicts and determine more surely the genuine will of God.

2

The "Acts" to Be Assessed

A HUMAN PERSON MAY also be a legal person, but the two notions, "human person" and "legal person," do not coincide; and a treatment of personality which overlooked the difference would quickly come to grief. It may easily be imagined what a morass we would enter if we asked all the same questions about Barbara and Bob that we ask about General Motors or the Metropolitan Museum (legally recognized subjects of rights and duties), or vice versa. To extricate ourselves we would have to specify what type of person, in what sense of the word "person," we intended to discuss. Now something similar obtains in ethics. Chapter 1 urged that Christians reflect on their acts. But the word "act," like the word "person," has different senses, determining different classes of things. So if we are to avoid serious confusions, we had better say straight off, first, what type of acts, in what sense of the term, we intend to consider; second, what mode of inquiry will therefore be appropriate, within the stated focus. This chapter's two sections perform this double service.

A. Varieties of "Action"

Acts 22 provides a helpful paradigm of the viewpoint that will be ours. At the moment of his conversion Paul there asks: "Lord, what shall I do?" The same query comes constantly to a sincere Christian's mind: "Lord, what shall I, or we, do?" And for him as for Paul the apposite reply would not be, "Follow me," "Obey me," "Love your neighbor," "Do God's will." He would gladly do all these things, but he doesn't know, concretely, how to. The guidance he seeks is the kind Paul received: "Get up and continue your journey to Damascus." In the requisite sense he was told what he should *do*.

This example and this contrast suggest already, in a general way, what kinds of acts we shall consider, in what sense of "act," and the course our discussion will therefore take: By "Christian moral reasoning" we shall mean reasoning directed to questions like Paul's, similarly understood. To further highlight this focus, I shall now contrast it more fully and systematically with other perspectives and other senses of "act." A handy passage for this purpose appears in successive editions of Viktor Cathrein's once-popular text: "There are actions which are right or wrong intrinsically and of their nature, so independently of any external precept. . . . Such, for example, are all acts which help a man toward his final end, as the love of God, or which withdraw him from it, as hatred, contempt of God, blasphemy, etc. . . . Likewise actions which of their nature hinder social life, as murder, theft, etc. clash with man's *social* nature."[1]

Love of God, hatred, blasphemy, murder, theft — how disparate these specimens will turn out to be when put beneath the lens! It is as though one were to classify as items of a kind the area of a triangle, the area of a cube, the area of an epidemic, and the area of a person's special interest, on the ground that they all are "areas." Yet, varied though the collection is, not a single sample is an action in the sense indicated by Paul's question or required by our present concerns. To see why, let us examine these "actions" one by one, starting from the first.

(1)   I think it would be better — more in keeping with the everyday employment both of "act" or "action" and of "love" and "hatred" — to call love and hatred attitudes or dispositions. This point is often made in another setting to avoid a different confusion: "Christian love . . . is not a particular emotion, or sort of emotion, or mood (which is but the foretaste or aftertaste of an emotion), but a bent, set or attitude of the whole mind, whose various operations it controls. In its human reference it is a settled, stable, steady concern with and for other people. The sign or test of its presence is not any one specific emotion."[2]

Nor is it any one specific action, even of the mind. True, there are acts of love or hatred, as there are acts of gratitude or revenge. But gratitude and revenge are not acts, and neither are love and hate. Yet a long speculative tradition has so repeatedly and unquestioningly referred to love, hate, faith, knowledge, belief, and the like as actions, that those brought up in this tradition react with incredulity to any contrary suggestion. I recall one such person who, when asked whether his belief in the location of New York City was an action he had been performing day and night for the last forty years, roundly replied that it was. Supposedly, then, the same would obtain for all the other cities and towns he knew and all he knew about them; and not just for cities and towns,

but for rivers, mountains, nations, seas, and planets; and not just for ge-
ography and astronomy, but for every other discipline known to him,
whether speculative or practical, sacred or secular; and not just for universal knowledge, but for his personal lore as well: all the people he had
known, things he had done, events he had witnessed.

It is not my intention here to call in question this marathon in the
mind or to request elucidation of the term "act" when extended to such
cases. It will suffice for present purposes to point out that such "actions"
are not objects of deliberation, so are not our concern. A person does not
debate within himself, for example, whether he should continue his belief in New York City or take a break for a day or two, as he does with his
work. He does not consider how rapidly or thoroughly or attentively to
perform the act, or when to start and when to stop, as he does with regard to a tennis match or his jogging in the park. And he need never fear
that such acts as these, if multiple, will therefore vie with one another
and require a choice between them. A person cannot visit New York,
Tokyo, and London on the same day, but he can readily believe in their
existence, and in that of countless other places, all in a single instant.
Innumerable such "acts" can persist concurrently without the slightest
conflict. And without distraction or confusion: for they do not divide
his attention, since they do not require attention, but continue indefinitely on their own. And if one day he learns that his belief was false or
that the man he admired is a hypocrite, he need not deliberately discontinue the belief or admiration; that, too, will take care of itself. For
these varied reasons such "acts" fall outside our inquiry. For what we
want to know is how a Christian should *choose* between alternative, *incompatible* actions, which he will then deliberately *discontinue* or deliberately *undertake*.

Accordingly we are interested in both sides of dichotomies like
these: "What shall I do: *stay home* or go to the game? *keep silent* or tell
the truth? *let him drown* or jump in the freezing river?" In a narrower
sense, to be sure, staying home, keeping silent, or allowing a person to
drown is not *doing* anything but is failing to act. Yet each of these passive alternatives is something we can weigh, choose for or against, then
deliberately continue or discontinue. And the reasoning for or against
the passive option resembles — indeed coincides with — the reasoning for
or against the active one (going to the game, speaking up, attempting
the rescue).

(2)   Unlike love or hatred, blasphemy (the next item on Cathrein's list)
would commonly be called an act. But it is not the mere saying of certain words. The speaker's attitude or intention is included. Thus (to re-
vert to our original comparison) blasphemy relates to the mere words

"God be damned" as a volume relates to a surface area. It takes in more, adds another dimension. And as a volume might be of interest to an excavator but not to a surveyor, so too the act of blasphemy may be of interest to a penitent or a confessor but not to someone asking, "Lord, what shall I do?" It incorporates too much.

To understand why, it is necessary first to notice that the motivation here in question is motivation in the primary, conscious, pre-Freudian sense of the term. It is this that makes the act a sin. It is this that ethicians have stressed. And it is this that they have insisted should be kept constantly in view. So it is important to note that a person, deciding what to do, need not and for the most part does not reflect on his conscious motivation, but on reasons for or against various lines of conduct.[3] If he is moved to action by these considerations rather than those, such is his motivation; he does not choose to be motivated one way or the other. And if the objective reasons that move him are good ones, he is subjectively moral; that too follows on objective deliberation and choice, not on self-scrutiny. For subjective morality as for objective, the requisite focus is objective. Anyone who decides to do what is right for the objective reasons that make it right is subjectively in order, though he give not a thought to himself or his intentions.

He is, let us suppose, a Samaritan on his way to Jericho along the wilderness road and comes upon a bleeding victim of the region's notorious robbers. He senses the inconvenience this discovery may entail. But the man's need is evident. Others have already passed him by. If left unaided, he may die. And his groans invite pity. So with concern for the other man's plight but none for his own intentions, present or prospective, he proceeds to do the things that earn our admiration in the gospel narrative (Lk. 10).

It is conceivable, perhaps, that he would transpose all these considerations from the objective into the subjective key. Instead of simply reflecting on the victim's condition, needs, and prospects, and weighing them against the inconvenience of caring for him, he might ask himself: "By which of these aspects shall I be motivated? Which shall become my subjective why?" But this appears an odd and needless complication and is hardly a condition for our approving both him and his deed unreservedly.

Intentions and motives become constitutive, so have to be heeded, when innocence or guilt is assessed. Preparing for confession, say, a person needs to note the dispositions with which he acted. Only thus can he ascertain in the requisite sense what he has done, what actions he has performed (e.g., deliberate blasphemy). But within the perspective of decision ("What *shall* I do?" "What action *should* I perform?"), terms like "action" and "do" generally shift their sense. Intention and motivation drop from consideration. And such, on the whole, is the perspective here adopted: "concern with antecedent rather than consequent conscience, i.e., with prospective decision-making rather than with retrospective judgment-passing."[4]

(3)   Continuing in Cathrein's list, we come to the words "murder" and "theft." As used by him and by many another they clearly add a moral qualification to the description of the act: Murder is the *illegitimate* taking of human life, theft is the *illegitimate* taking of property. So to say that a person should not murder, or should not steal — that these acts are "intrinsically wrong" — is an empty tautology, enlightening no one on how he or she should act. When Paul, for example, asked what he should do, he did not want to know whether he should do right or wrong. Nor does a contemporary Christian, when he desires to know whether he should inflict capital punishment, or engage in combat, or help himself to some occult compensation. Telling him he should not murder or steal is no help at all; it does not describe the course of action to follow — does not, in an important sense, tell him what he should *do*. Only pronouncements on *killing* or on *taking others' goods* would do that.

In retrospect we can now observe that no action of this kind, or in this sense, appears in Cathrein's list. There are attitudes like love, behavior-with-intention like blasphemy, behavior-with-evaluation like murder and theft, but no sheer behavior such as aborting a fetus, premarital intercourse, sending arms to El Salvador, legalizing marijuana, divorcing and remarrying, fixing prices, registering for the draft. Yet actions like these typically fill our sights when we take aim ahead and estimate what we shall or should do.

It is important to grasp these distinctions and to note when they occur, but it is neither important nor always possible to fit each action-verb into a single slot. Think of "cheat." Sheer behavior? Behavior-with-intention? Behavior-with-evaluation? Behavior-plus-intention-and-evaluation? I have heard all four answers given. And perhaps all four are right, at least for some speakers of the word, on some occasions.

Senses can shift from context to context and from person to person. Thus "murder" and "theft" do not invariably signal blame, as in Cathrein's text, nor does "blasphemy" always stop short at intention: on some occasions it may add a clear note of moral reprehension. None of this, however, invalidates the distinctions just drawn: it does not show they are vague and uncertain and therefore of little value. They are just more pervasive than we may have realized, and more difficult to spot, so doubly worth underscoring. Were they evident, they could be taken for granted; were they trivial and unimportant, they could be passed by. But, as the following section will further attest, such is not the case: they are neither obvious nor inconsequential.

B. Implications

Much else might be said about acts, and even about the preceding distinctions, but these observations should suffice for present purposes. Our preoccupation parallels Paul's. Moved to fervent gratitude and zeal, he needed no instruction about motivation, nor reminder to do what was right, but specifics of conduct. His inquiry had a corresponding focus: objective, prospective. So shall ours.

This is quickly said, but not so quickly assimilated. Were I simply to propose this orientation, then pursue it, the reader might fail to notice the link between the initial remarks and the subsequent practice. To highlight the connection, therefore, I shall do as before. The preceding section brought out the intended sense of "act" by contrasting it with alternative senses (all of them common, so important to note). The present section will throw the implications of this focus into sharper relief by contrasting the approach it dictates with others often encountered. (1) In *The Methods of Ethics,* plausibly termed by C. D. Broad "the best treatise on moral theory that has ever been written,"[5] Henry Sidgwick observes: "Moralists of all schools, I conceive, would agree that the moral judgments which we pass on actions relate primarily to intentional actions regarded as intentional. In other words, what we judge to be 'wrong'— in the strictest ethical sense— is not any part of the actual effects, as such, of the muscular movements immediately caused by the agent's volition, but the effects which he foresaw in willing the act; or, more strictly, his volition or choice of realising the effects as foreseen."[6]

Sidgwick here writes as though all moral judgments were basically alike. Yet if objective, prospective deliberations, for example, are the ones we have in mind, it cannot be said of them that "the moral judgments which we pass on actions relate primarily to intentional actions regarded as intentional." In that type of discussion, intention drops from consideration. Retrospective assessments, too, are often objective, and quite legitimately so: we speak, for instance, of a person's having done the right thing (objectively) for the wrong reason, or of a person's having acted wrongly (again in an objective sense) although with a good intention. These sharply focused judgments of right and wrong, abstracting from motive and intention, may be just what is called for. And the sense our moral terms have on these and similar occasions is not a lesser, imperfect one, as Sidgwick's reference to "the strictest ethical sense" would suggest, but the only one appropriate in the particular circumstances. We should not be intimidated, therefore, and adopt a "higher" sense, under the impression that we omit the essential thing if we overlook intention. What is essential on any occasion is determined by the context of discussion. And the context of the present inquiry requires that we *not* introduce the "agent's volition."

(2)   Possible consequences of following Sidgwick's lead appear in a recent document on sexual ethics prepared for the Catholic Theological Society of America. In much the same vein as Sidgwick the authors first observe: "Contemporary theologians are once again insisting that any attempt to evaluate the moral object of an action apart from motive and circumstances is necessarily incomplete and inadequate. It is the whole action including circumstances and intention that constitutes the basis for ethical judgment. This is not to say that the concrete act is not an important consideration. It is simply to insist that the genuine moral meaning of particular individual acts is most accurately discerned not solely from an abstract analysis of the biology of the act but necessarily including [sic] the circumstances as well as intention that surround the action."[7]

Here too there is no acknowledgment of varying types of discussion and their corresponding perspectives — objective or subjective, prospective or retrospective. Regardless of the inquirer's needs or the question asked, "it is the whole action including circumstances and intention that constitutes the basis for ethical judgment." To narrow one's focus and "evaluate the moral object of an act apart from motive and circumstances is necessarily incomplete and inadequate"; "the genuine moral meaning of particular individual acts" cannot be thus discerned. Accordingly, within the specific area of the study — sexuality — "a sound approach to the moral evaluation of sexual behavior must . . . recognize both the objective and the subjective aspects of human behavior as indispensable to any genuine moral judgment."[8] To focus more sharply is to falsify.

From such premises important conclusions then follow concerning "concrete norms, rules, precepts, or guidelines. These formulations attempt to distill from the experience of the Christian community the most practical and effective way that the desired values may be realized. They serve to enlighten the Christian conscience as to which particular patterns or forms of sexual behavior have proven generally to be conducive to or destructive of creativity and integration. To the extent that they refer to concrete, physical actions (e.g., masturbation, sterilization, contraception, premarital sex) without specifying particular circumstances or intention, to that extent they cannot be regarded as universal and absolute moral norms."[9]

The irony of these repeated injunctions is that they commit the kind of error they warn against. Discussing, reasoning, assessing, judging are also activities. They too have contexts. They too have purposes and goals. They too must be judged, individually, in terms of their particular setting and aim. Sometimes one focus is appropriate, sometimes another: now prospective, now retrospective; now objective, now subjective, now perhaps both together. And the sense of the words used— "right," "wrong," "act," and the like—will vary accordingly.

In answer, then, I would repeat that there is no one "genuine moral meaning of particular individual acts," for there is no single sense of "acts," nor any single perspective within which they must be judged. To ignore the context, purpose, and intended recipient(s) of the moral assessment and insist upon uniform treatment does not assure that an act's moral meaning "is most accurately discerned." Quite the contrary. If a person has Paul's problem—if he wants to know what he should do —then the appropriate answer not only may but should omit all mention of motive and intention. If addressed to that typical query and that typical inquirer, "concrete norms, rules, precepts, or guidelines" should make sure *not* to mention these subjective features.

Suppose it were urged, analogously, that no trip is complete without a goal and a motive, and that guidelines for travelers are therefore incomplete if they overlook these essential features. And imagine what odd roadmaps might result from such advice. Well, what people repeatedly need and desire is, so to speak, a roadmap, not a lecture on intentions. Tell them what to do and why, and they ask for nothing more. If they then choose to do the thing prescribed, and if they do it for the reasons indicated (that is, if the objective why becomes their subjective why), the subjective rightness of their deed is assured.[10] Hence even for their subjective needs they require no other guidance than the objective norms and their objective rationale.

Intrusion of subjective elements might prove not only confusing but positively misleading. Thus note, in the document quoted, how the scales are weighted against universal norms. They must first survive the consideration of varied circumstances with their varied configurations of objective value. Fair enough (and hard enough, as we shall see). But then they must pass a second, subjective hurdle, of varied intentions and motives. Only if subjected to this double test, objective and subjective, can a moral judgment be "genuine." Yet people's real-life needs typically require a restriction. Within the prospective viewpoint for which norms are most helpfully tailored, intention and motive need not, indeed should not, be alluded to.

(3)   Weighting more often tilts the other way, in favor of absolute norms. Cathrein, for example, lends them support when he ticks off his catalog of "intrinsically evil acts." Being intrinsically evil — and evidently so, in virtue of their definition or of the agent's malevolent will — they can be proscribed universally. However, such "acts" are not the kind for which we most need norms, nor therefore the kind most commonly at issue when the question of universality arises. It is the legitimacy of killing that we need to resolve, not that of murder. The taking of others' property occasions problems; theft does not. Thus by bundling all these acts together, without proper discrimination, Cathrein obscured the difficulty of the real-life issue. That the one kind of action can be banned unconditionally is evident; that the other kind can be is not.

Even authors quite otherwise inclined may create a like impression through similar blurring. Thus Giles Milhaven writes: "Few are the acts whose value simple direct insight suffices to establish. They would be restricted to acts such as 'love and honor and pity and pride and compassion and sacrifice.' Moreover, although moral qualities are needed to appreciate these and live them fully, they pose no intellectual problems for the educated Christian. On the other hand, for the numerous acts whose value direct insight does not suffice to establish, e.g., sexual actions, the question is frequently open or being reopened."[11]

This appears innocent enough. Some acts are clearly right or wrong, others more problematic, and we should note the difference. But how, in either case, do we know they are right or wrong? By what criterion are they either? That is the basic question for Christian moral reasoning. And Milhaven's examples, when described as he describes them, yield an all-too-ready answer. No system is acceptable, it would seem, which would require us in all cases to consider the circumstances of an act and the attendant values. For here we have instances where insight into the "act" itself provides a decisive verdict. Love, pity, compassion — these are always right, regardless of circumstances or consequences, whereas hate and pride and greed are always wrong, without regard to human benefit. The answer, though, to this knockdown proof is that "actions" such as these are not the ones generally in question when a criterion of morality is sought. Like Paul in Acts 22, and in the same sense, we want to know: "What shall we, should we, *do*?"[12]

Should similar confusion arise concerning the "intrinsic evil" of murder, theft, or the like (which, unlike love and hate, are typically labeled acts), doubtless the reader sees by now (if he did not already) how the move should be countered.[13] The act to be judged prospectively is, for instance, killing, not murder. "Murder" is killing with a moral appraisal already attached. Little wonder, then, that it is always wrong, whatever the consequences or circumstances. Yet consequences and circumstances may account, nonetheless, for the attachment of the label. Thus tautologies like "Murder is always wrong" permit no ready answer, in favor of some other, less circumstantial solution, to the crucial question: "By what general standard should Christians judge prospective acts?"[14]

To summarize now: The tendency of the typical passages quoted in this section has been either to overlook the distinction established in the first section, between the objective, prospective viewpoint and others, or to oppose it. And the thrust of the countercomments has been to maintain the legitimacy and frequent necessity of that distinction and that viewpoint. Such are the parameters of the discussion to come in parts two to four. If the reader remarks few allusions there to motive and intention or to acts such as those Cathrein cites, he will now understand why. Other acts, in another sense of the term, are our concern, for it is they, above all, that require the reflection urged in chapter 1. The following chapter will strengthen the case for this focus.

3

The Central Question
to Be Answered

To JUDGE ACTS we need standards to judge them by. And to judge them well, chapter 1 maintained, we need to reflect on the standards as well as on the acts. So having considered acts in the last chapter, we turn now to standards. Our present interest is general. We shall not yet attempt a specific, Christian answer to the question "What makes an action right or wrong?" That is a task for subsequent chapters. Instead, what we need to consider here, in preparation for that task, is how to deal with such a question.

The first requisite is attention to the question's terms: What does it mean to call an action right or wrong? What sense do we or should we give those words "right" and "wrong"? Most especially, we need to know what have been called the terms' "criteria," that is, the ultimate, defining traits governing their application. For of all the varied strands in the weave of moral discourse, such criteria are the most decisive. Section B will demonstrate their primacy, after section A has disentangled most of the strands; and section C, building on both, will then indicate the importance of criterial analysis. The sharper form our initial question will therefore have to take, in subsequent inquiry, is this: "By what criterion, or criteria, should Christians determine right and wrong?"

A. Moral Meaning

"Ethics," wrote G. E. Moore, "is undoubtedly concerned with the question what good conduct is; but, being concerned with this, it obviously does not start at the beginning, unless it is prepared to tell us what is good as well as what is conduct."[1] Moore himself, however, after testing various answers, could only report: "If I am asked 'What is good?' my answer is that good is good, and that is the end of the matter. Or if I am asked 'How is good to be defined?' my answer is that it cannot be defined, and that is all I have to say about it. But disappointing as these answers may appear, they are of the very last importance."[2]

Importance of a sort they do indeed have, as appears more clearly from Moore's explanation: "My point is that 'good' is a simple notion, just as 'yellow' is a simple notion; that, just as you cannot, by any manner of means, explain to any one who does not already know it, what yellow is, so you cannot explain what good is. Definitions of the kind that I was asking for, definitions which describe the real nature of the object or notion denoted by a word, and which do not merely tell us what the word is used to mean, are only possible when the object or notion in question is something complex."[3]

Were Moore's analysis correct, the consequences would be incalculable for the whole of ethics. Quite generally we may say that if basic moral terms are viewed in this way, as akin to color words, then their meaning will appear unproblematic, constant, and universal. Beneath the swirl of argument, of heterogeneous evidence and proofs, leading to contrasting verdicts on the most varied questions, the key moral concepts—"right" and "wrong," "good" and "evil," "moral" and "immoral"—stand fast, like rocks beneath the beating waves. *They* need no close attention: evidence, arguments, proofs, and conclusions are all that need concern us. For if good and evil, right and wrong, are as simple as red and yellow, and as evident to the mind's eye when once established, there can hardly be any problem about *them*, in themselves.

Indeed, even when a definition is given and an equivalence stated, the resulting complex notion will appear relatively unproblematic if the constituent terms are so conceived. The contemplated object is now two-toned, as it were, rather than monochrome; but the individual shades are as simple and constant as ever. Thus the concept "right," for example, will occasion little puzzlement if we define it uniformly in relation to the good, as Moore did (see V, J), and conceive the good itself as simple and invariant.

Such thinking was still more natural in centuries past, when attention focused on truth and falsehood, and meaning received less attention. Thus in Thomistic ethics, for example, the paradigmatic starting point was the adage "Do good, avoid evil," not the concepts "good" and "evil"; and the area of unclarity most emphasized was that of the secondary, specific precepts, not that of the basic concepts and the ultimate standards by which the precepts would have to be judged. Thus it was possible for the most diverse and sometimes mutually incompatible standards to be applied without any suspicion arising that the very meaning of the terms "right" and "wrong" might thereby be affected, and that disagreement in conclusions might reflect disagreement in the criteria employed. After all, if an object is said to be yellow, one time on the basis of direct observation, another time as the result of scientific inference, and a third time on the strength of testimony, this radical diversity in evidence does not affect in the least the meaning of the predicate "yellow." And the like might be said of right and wrong, good and evil, in the view of many ethicians. Moore articulated their viewpoint.

A good illustration is artificial contraception, which at first was condemned for teleological reasons, that is, reasons concerned with the purposes of marriage, which were then quite narrowly conceived. Attention focused on procreation. In more recent times other aims have been recognized, but the ban has held firm, since its basis has shifted to the "unnaturalness" of the act. A new, nonteleological criterion is now operative. Yet even critics of the traditional teaching are wont to concede that "the ways of formulating and explaining this teaching have evolved, but not the doctrine itself." The act has always been judged to be evil — whatever that may mean. After all, evil is evil, as yellow is yellow. Just the arguments and evidence differ. Such is the syndrome Moore illustrates.

He was representative, too, of traditional interest in definitions. Others — as intent as he on producing a definition of the good, the right, the ethical — fixed on some limited aspect. The good, for example, they identified with the natural, the normal, the pleasurable, or the like. Moore, recognizing the inadequacy of each such identification, concluded that the good (and hence the right and the obligatory) is something entirely different and still simpler, since it lacks even these specifications. What he thus reached was, in Wittgenstein's characterization, an artichoke without any leaves. Since no one of the leaves with which he strewed his path could be identified with the whole complex artichoke, he concluded that the artichoke itself was something else, something indescribable, indefinable.

If we examine attentively the bits and pieces discarded by Moore and others, we shall understand why it is so difficult to define evaluative terms, including moral ones. The reason is not their simplicity. Quite the contrary. Each of the following eight features, explaining the difficulty of definition, reveals new complexity. Together with a ninth, at the start of the second section, they situate moral terms at the opposite pole from color words like "yellow" and "blue."

(1)   If one person demonstrates that an artichoke has no leaves, nor

even a nub, and concludes that it must be an aethereal, "nonnatural" vegetable, someone else may infer instead that it is no vegetable at all and that the word "artichoke" designates nothing. That is how many reacted to Moore's doctrine.[4] A. J. Ayer, for instance, declared: "The presence of an ethical symbol in a proposition adds nothing to its factual content. . . . It merely serves to show that the expression of it is attended by certain feelings in the speaker."[5]

Nowadays this is generally recognized to be a simplification. But not an invention. Ethical terms do have an emotive dimension, as do evaluative terms generally. It is characteristic of them (that is, obtains often, though not always) — as it is not of "red" and "yellow" — to express approval or disapproval. When a man exclaims "What a splendid den!" his feelings are engaged; he admires or covets the layout. When a woman utters "Good dog," she's typically fond of the animal. An orator, too, when he declares a war "unjust," may speak with heat and urgency — may clench his fists, thump the rostrum, flush red in the face — but hardly when he calls an object red or yellow. Favor and disfavor, like and dislike, surround the evaluative expressions ("splendid," "good," "just," "unjust"). They may not be sheerly emotive, but they are that too.

Here, then, is one reason for the failure of the definitions Moore weighed and found wanting. They were mere neutral descriptions: the good was the natural, or the normal, or the necessary, or the pleasurable, and the like. So of each proposed content it was always possible to ask, "Is that really good?" Something was sensed to be lacking, and indeed was: the emotive dimension.

(2) Also the imperative, or persuasive. For much the same remarks, both negative and positive, as apply to Ayer's emotive analysis hold also for Rudolf Carnap's kindred claim that "a value statement is nothing else than a command in a misleading grammatical form. It may have effects upon the actions of men, and these effects may either be in accordance with our wishes or not; but it is neither true nor false. It does not assert anything and can neither be proved nor disproved."[6]

Here too a kernel of truth is to be retained: evaluative and especially moral discourse has this aspect as well as the emotive one. More characteristically than "red" and "yellow," moral terms are used to influence action. Often there is little pragmatic difference between a parent's "should" and a command, or between an encyclical's "It's wrong" and a prohibition. Here, then, is another reason for the failure of any purely descriptive definition of "good" and "evil," "right" and "wrong," "should" and "shouldn't." It omits this further dimension.

(3) From the emotive and persuasive aspects we may distinguish a

third, which I shall call the evocative. "Moral judgments," writes Charles Stevenson, "are concerned with recommending something for approval or disapproval."[7] A characteristic function of the moral terms they contain, as of evaluative expressions generally, is to evoke favorable or unfavorable sentiments in those addressed. This third dimension, too, descriptive definitions fail to capture. They are too neutral for a word like "good."

(4)   Joel Kupperman draws attention to still another dynamic aspect, closely related to the emotive, when he observes: "Ethical statements . . . normally are interpreted as pledging that the person who makes them will act, or try to act, accordingly. This is as true of statements of value as it is of statements about what is right and wrong. If someone says that aesthetic experiences are the most valuable, and then spends all of his spare time in bowling and drinking beer, resolutely avoiding concerts and poetry recitals, we say that his behaviour conflicts with his words. The question of hypocrisy arises, and we wonder whether he 'really meant' what he said."[8] No such conflict would be noted if he said that aesthetic experiences are normal, or common, or widely sought. Any such descriptive predicate, therefore, if employed to define "good" or "valuable," would give rise to Moore's objections. It would not be equivalent to the term defined.

(5)   As Moore himself later recognized, "the word 'good' is highly ambiguous: it is not only used, but correctly used, in a number of different senses."[9] No single definition could possibly capture them all.

Such differences of meaning highlight the cognitive dimension of valuation. For there lies the explanation of the shifts in sense, and not, say, in the emotive or imperative dimension. When we call a knife good and a man good, we approve in both cases, and neither command nor forbid; it is the standards applied that vary. Likewise, when we call an action bad and a painting bad, in one case we apply moral standards, in the other aesthetic; our negative attitude does not alter.[10]

(6)   Moore did not sufficiently notice that similar contrasts arise for even a single type of evaluation, for instance, ethical judgments. His ready assumption, for example, that "right" or "obligatory" simply means "maximizing the good" (see V, J), betrays inadequate reflection on moral discourse and the history of ethics. As we shall see, people's criteria of right and wrong are not basically invariant (VI, A, B), nor therefore is the meaning of "right" and "wrong" (III, B).

Thus, a further explanation of the nondefinability of evaluative terms is the fluctuation of standards, from group to group and from person to person. Even fundamental standards may be challenged, it is true, and their merits may be weighed. But this possibility does not establish the existence of still deeper criteria, implicitly acknowledged, common to all, and issuing in agreement when their implications are grasped. To say that people are capable of conversion at this basic level is not to say that their present divergences are illusory or superficial.

(7)   Stuart Hampshire notes a further dimension of diversity. When we inquire after the criteria of even one individual, he observes, "there is no reason to expect a simple answer in terms of a single formula, *e.g.* 'it is likely to increase happiness.' But to search only for definitions or verbal equivalences is to assume that there must be a single sufficient reason from which I always and necessarily derive my judgment."[11] As we shall see, Hampshire's skepticism is warranted. One and the same author is perfectly capable of altering his criteria from case to case (especially if he does no criterial analysis and attends only to solutions). Even within his personal realm of discourse, therefore, definition may be impossible.

(8)   For reasons like these the boundaries of ethical concepts are still more indefinite than most. It is hard enough even concerning concepts such as "red" and "yellow," "chair" and "table," "pamphlet" and "book," to say where one leaves off and the other begins. But if we attempt to trace precisely the borders of ethical concepts, even within a single tradition, the task is still more hopeless.[12]

Consider even a concept like "chair": "I say 'There is a chair.' What if I go up to it, meaning to fetch it, and it suddenly disappears from sight? — 'So it wasn't a chair, but some kind of illusion.' — But in a few moments we see it again and are able to touch it and so on. — 'So the chair was there after all and its disappearance was some kind of illusion.' — But suppose that after a time it disappears again — or seems to disappear. What are we to say now? Have you rules ready for such cases — rules saying whether one may use the word 'chair' to include this kind of thing? But do we miss them when we use the word 'chair'; and are we to say that we do not really attach any meaning to this word, because we are not equipped with rules for every possible application of it?"[13]

What we see is obviously relevant, indeed decisive, for our judgments concerning chairs; yet we cannot adequately define a chair in terms of what we see. We possess no such definition. So too the description of any object or act is decisive for its evaluation, yet we cannot completely characterize its goodness or badness descriptively. Still more clearly we possess no such definition. We should be slow, however, to infer from this lack either that chairs are invisible, colorless objects or that goodness is nondescriptive, as Moore did.

In retrospect, now, we have noted eight obstacles to precise definition such as Moore and others sought: (1) the emotive dimension of moral and other evaluative terms; (2) their imperative, persuasive character; (3) their evocative function; (4) their performative aspect (one takes a stand, makes a commitment, implicates oneself); (5) the variety of their uses; (6) the diversity within even a single type of application, from group to group and person to person, (7) or even from judgment to judgment for a single agent or from passage to passage within one author's writings; (8) consequent indefiniteness of border, in addition to the internal heterogeneity. None of these features, notice, characterizes "red" or "yellow," at least to any notable degree. Hence Moore's comparison is seriously misleading.[14]

B. The Primacy of Criteria

The comparison is defective, furthermore, in a ninth respect: if we examine the cognitive dimension of moral meanings, we find inner richness as well as heterogeneity. Fixing on a single employment among the shifting many, we repeatedly discover greater cognitive complexity than in a simple color concept (especially as conceived by Moore). However, this objection too requires elucidation. For how is the "cognitive dimension of moral meanings" to be understood?

One way is that suggested by Wittgenstein: "Asking whether and how a proposition can be verified is only a particular way of asking 'How d'you mean?' The answer is a contribution to the grammar of the proposition."[15] Some would contest whether value assertions are propositions, but of these, too, Wittgenstein reportedly once said "that each different way in which one person, A, can convince another, B, that so-and-so is 'good' fixes the meaning in which 'good' is used in that discussion —'fixes the grammar of that discussion.'"[16]

This should not be taken to mean that any and every shift in arguments or evidence induces a change in meaning. That is hardly the case. If, for example, one person cites thunder as evidence that it is raining and another refers instead to the patter on the roof, the sense of the word "rain" does not alter in their statement: they are not talking about different things. If, on the other hand, one person cited thunder and another pointed to kites in a cloudless sky, doubtless their semantic paths would have parted. In the ordinary sense of "rain" kites are neither constitutive of rain nor helpful clues — neither "criteria" nor "symptoms," to use Wittgenstein's handy terminology.

This distinction between symptoms and criteria has received various interpretations. The simplest, and sufficient for our purposes,[17] is

Norman Malcolm's: "What makes something into a symptom of *y* is that experience teaches that it is always or usually associated with *y*; that so-and-so is the criterion of *y* is a matter, not of experience, but of 'definition.' . . . The satisfaction of the criterion of *y* establishes the existence of *y* beyond question. The occurrence of a symptom of *y* may also establish the existence of *y* 'beyond question'—but in a different sense."[18] Thus, if you tell your doctor that you are running a fever, feel sick, and have pains in the lower-right abdomen, he may feel quite sure that your appendix is inflamed. Still, it is just an inference. But if he then operates and beholds the organ, all inference is at an end. Bedrock has been reached. To look like that *is* to be inflamed.[19]

"Symptom" is an apt term for items like nausea, fever, pains (and was apparently suggested by them). For other such extrinsic, nonconstitutive clues, "sign" is the more common designation. Thunder and lightning, for example; or black thunderheads; or soft, pattering sounds outside—all are signs of rain (and would be so called); they are not rain itself. The criteria, on the other hand, are what make rain rain, inflammation inflammation, right right, wrong wrong. For this reason, and in this sense, they are decisive evidence.

Notice, though, that an intrinsic trait which is not decisive *by itself* does not satisfy Malcolm's description of a criterion. "The criterion of *y*," he said, "establishes the existence of *y* beyond question." Again, think of rain. If there are drops, of water, falling, from clouds, then it is raining. That is what makes rain rain. It is the decisive criterion. But drops alone are not (they might be of honey or bourbon); nor is water (it might come in flakes or pellets); nor are drops of water (they might scatter from a sprinkler); nor are drops falling from heaven (they might be sprayed from a plane). In Malcolm's terminology, adopted here, the criterion is just the total bundle: drops of water falling from clouds.

A person who can recognize sure instances knows the criterion or criteria. But he need not be able to give a definition, or to state either sufficient or necessary conditions for the expression's correct application. Figuratively, he may know with surety that a given case falls within the borders without knowing precisely where the borders lie. He may be certain, for instance, that the appendix before his eyes is inflamed without being able to define "inflamed appendix." He may be in no doubt about the morality of a specific act, yet be unable to state exactly even his personal criteria of right and wrong. The impossibility, repeatedly, is not just cognitive (not a matter of ignorance) but logical: no exact definition can be given because no exact definition exists (that is, no sharp conceptual boundary).

The significance of criteria tends to be obscured in the following way, consequent on a further fact about them. Moral criteria vary more from person to person than do those of rain or inflammation. As ultimate determinants of right and wrong, some people, for example, look to the divine will; others to nature (in various senses of that term); others to causal connections; others to certain inviolable values (e.g., the sanctity of innocent human life); others still to a calculus of consequences, with very different things counting as consequences and the calculations varying accordingly. Yet even when the shift in cognitive content is radical, we need not say that the moral terms have changed their meaning. From this combination — "different criteria, same meanings" — it has sometimes been inferred that the criteria do not belong to the meanings of the terms;[20] the meanings are therefore noncognitive (emotive, persuasive, etc.), containing at most the general requirement that there be criteria.[21]

This conclusion is both invalid and deceptive. Suppose, by way of comparison, that we argued similarly with regard to human beings, excluding leg, liver, nose, scalp, stomach, and the like as parts of a person, on the ground that an individual may lose one or all of these yet remain the same person. The invalidity of the inference form "same x, different y, therefore y no part of x" would here be palpable. What may mislead us with regard to "meaning" is the shifting employment of the term from context to context. Thus we frequently speak of a word's meaning or use "in the language" and accordingly disregard idiosyncracies, however widespread (much as we speak of "the parts of the human body" and ignore personal privations or peculiarities, however common). However, we also speak, with equal frequency, of a word's meaning in a specific context, statement, work, author, or school, as we speak of the parts of some specific human being. Personal or group criteria, furthermore, may be as firmly fixed as a cornea or kidney, and their removal or replacement may require as drastic surgery. It would be misleading, therefore, to place ethical criteria with symptoms beyond the pale of meaning — as misleading as classing bodily organs under the heading "apparel."

If, moreover, a sign's meaning is not only the relatively stable element but also, "roughly, that which is of importance about the sign,"[22] then it would be doubly misleading to exclude criteria from moral meanings.[23] For criteria are the most fundamental aspect of the most fundamental aspect of ethical discourse. By right and largely in fact they determine the other cognitive features, and the cognitive determine the noncognitive. Thus criteria are basic to the second power, so to speak. Their supremacy is so important for this study and for ethics generally that we had better examine it in some detail. We shall start with the primacy of cognitive features in relation to the noncognitive, using the emotive and imperative as illustrations, and then pass to the primacy of criteria with respect to other cognitive features.

Primacy of the Cognitive

In relation to the emotive aspect: As a matter of definition, we morally approve or disapprove of an action — and do not merely like or dislike, favor or oppose it — according as we judge it conforms or does not conform to moral standards. As a matter of psychological fact, our emotions may deviate from this norm, but as Christians we agree we *should* rejoice in the right and not in the wrong.

In relation to the imperative aspect: Our orders, implicit or explicit, often do and universally should follow the same norm. Our use of moral terms to direct others should direct them to what is right, and do so rightly, according to the standards of what is right and wrong. Once again, the cognitive is primary.

Cognitive Primacy of Criteria

In relation to other motives: Within the cognitive dimension it is important to discriminate two kinds of motive, that is, two classes of considerations which motivate people to act as they do and which therefore, quite legitimately, receive the common label "motive." Some are intrinsic to the act's objective morality; others, extrinsic. On the one hand there are criteria whose fulfillment makes an action objectively right and which may also figure as motives (e.g., benefit to one's neighbor) and on the other hand there are supplementary reasons for doing what the criteria show to be right. One thinks immediately of the familiar contrast between doing what is right because it is right and doing it for a reward. However, extrinsic motivation need not be self-regarding: gratitude, love, obedience may move us to do what is right, good, just, God's will. The gratitude, love, and obedience do not make it God's will; that must be determined by other norms, prior to these traits. The criteria come first.

In relation to symptoms: A symptom of y is such through a regular connection with y and so depends on the definition of y. Conceive y differently, and the symptoms change. Suppose, for example, that I am a utilitarian and judge morality by the criterion of human happiness. The evidence I will then consult, to determine right and wrong, will be attendance figures, say, indicating what forms of entertainment people most enjoy; standings within each category of entertainment; responses to questionnaires concerning marital felicity, contentment at work, satisfaction in one's calling, and the like. For the utilitarian such statistics, standings, and responses are all "symptoms": they do not constitute or define either happiness or morality, but they do suggest how to maximize happiness, and therefore what course to pursue: subsidies to the arts or to sports, a career in music or in science, an evening at the theater or at the arena. The significance of such clues to morality alters or entirely ceases, however, if the criteria of right and wrong change. Thus, for that largely mythical (but useful) individual, the pure voluntarist, all this evidence no longer counts as evidence, for it gives no indication of the arbitrary will of God by which the voluntarist gauges the morality of prospective acts. Given that criterion, the pages of Scripture, say, replace the Nielsen ratings as relevant clues to morality. From such illustrations it appears, therefore, that criteria are not only distinct from symptoms (though the distinction is less sharp than our examples might suggest) but are also logically prior.

In relation to procedures: This being so, the whole process of ethical deliberation, whatever the form it takes (consultation of authorities, calculation of values, discernment of spirits, etc.), is governed by the underlying criteria. They determine what evidence is germane, what arguments are appropriate, and what reasoning is conclusive or persuasive. Even when other considerations are pertinent, perhaps decisive, they are so only by virtue of the constitutive criteria of right and wrong. Alter the criteria, and they too would alter.

The situation may sound complicated but is fairly standard: *what* we seek determines *how* we seek. For microbes I use a microscope and focus on a slide. For birds I use binoculars and look, say, in the trees. For stars I use a telescope and wait till dark. For sea shells I patrol the seashore and use my own two eyes. The kind of thing I seek determines the place, the time, the instrument, the procedure. And so it is when people investigate the "right" thing to do. Their common terminology should not deceive us. If their criteria differ, so does the object of their search, and with it the appropriate procedures.

Here too, however, as in the previous steps, it is necessary to distinguish between the logical ideal and human reality. For it should not be imagined that examination of an author's reasoning will always reveal his basic criteria or that, though never examined and set in order by him or anyone else, they form a coherent set. Criterial analysis is difficult and rare, at least in Christian ethics. And moral discourse is a maze in which even able thinkers lose their way, as Moore did. So it is perfectly possible for an author to argue at cross purposes, now following one standard, now a different, incompatible one, without noticing the incoherence. And what is possible for a single author, more intimately acquainted than others with his own system of thought, is still more possible for a major current or school, grouping varied representatives. As for the whole of Christian ethics through the centuries—well, the seed has grown into a great tree, and wild birds have perched in its branches. But which are the branches, which the wild birds?

C. Implications

What we need to know most particularly, I said at the start of this chapter, are the criteria of basic terms like "right" and "wrong," for of all the varied strands in the weave of moral discourse, criteria are the most decisive. Their decisiveness has now been demonstrated. It is not immediately evident, though, that they should occupy a central position, indeed even a prominent one, in a study of Christian moral reasoning. For criteria might be crucial, but criterial analysis not. Unreflective knowledge might suffice.

Thus suppose, by way of comparison, that somebody were to write a manual on weather prediction. Would he linger long on the criteria of rain, snow, wind, sleet, and the like? Would he take the elucidation of these criteria as his central task? Hardly. For although such criteria are indeed decisive for the whole process of calculation and prediction, they occasion no problems. Identical for all speakers, known with unreflective sureness, followed with consistency and ease in our talk and thought about the weather, they stand in no need of scrutiny or explicit formulation.

It is important to note how different are ethical concepts; otherwise the proposal to focus on criteria may appear unrealistic. What makes ethical criteria so special (someone is sure to ask); why reflect on them more than on others? The following five-point reply spells out the implications of sections A and B:

1. Ethical criteria differ more frequently.
2. The differences are less readily detected.
3. They are more serious.
4. They are less tractable.
5. We are less competent to deal with them.

Thus:

(1)   As section A noted, in numbers 6 and 7, ethical criteria differ more from passage to passage, person to person, group to group, than do those of terms like "red" and "yellow"—or "rain" and "snow." Repeatedly, therefore, ethical disputants need to check their bases. If they are arguing from different criteria, they cannot hope to succeed. (What

chance of agreement would there be in two people's rain predictions if one meant by "rain" what the other meant by "sleet"?)

(2)   In ethics it is more difficult to check one's bases. For the complexity of ethical terms, displayed in section A, helps to veil their workings. Thus, whereas a divergence like that just mentioned (one person meaning by "rain" what another means by "sleet") would soon catch our attention, sharper discrepancies in moral meanings may pass unsuspected and unperceived. In Plato's *Republic*, for example, when Thrasymachus contends that justice is what serves the interests of the powerful and Socrates describes it as each performing his proper task, the disputants appear to disagree concerning a common referent. It is as though they were both speaking about the weather, and one described it one way and the other described it differently. However, this impression, though widespread, is mistaken. No common criterion underlies their two accounts, so no common referent is differently described.

The lesson of such samples is alertness to criteria. Not only are they more likely to vary in ethics, but their fluctuations are more likely to escape notice unless we are specially attentive.

(3)   Furthermore, criterial divergences are more serious there, for ethical concepts, as we also saw, add emotive, persuasive, evocative, and performative aspects to the cognitive. They engage the whole person, pervade his life. Thus Thrasymachus, if he really means what he says, favors the violent self-serving of the strong, while Socrates opposes it. Their disagreement, though criterial, is far from purely verbal.

(4)   Accordingly, it cannot be resolved by mere definition of terms, as in our weather sample. If one person means by "rain" what another means by "sleet," they can note the discrepancy, hit on a common definition (for instance the standard one), and get back to the business of weather prediction. The criterial complication is but a momentary distraction, easily dealt with. Not so, however, in ethics. When criteria differ there, attention must shift to them. No verbal stipulation, smoothing communication, will resolve the problem. For more than mere terminology is at stake. If Socrates, for example, accepts Thrasymachus' formulation as the criterion of justice, or Thrasymachus his, countless concrete judgments will have to change. The one who agrees will be committed to new positions on wars, laws, governments, business, education, private conduct, and not just to new ways of stating his former views.

(5)   In ethics criterial elucidation is specially difficult, and appropriate training specially necessary. For ethical discourse being more labyrinthine, we more readily lose our way when we undertake to explore

it. Subsequent discussions will confirm this point, like the others. But think already of Moore. Though an outstanding analytic thinker, he botched the account of our moral concepts, including the most basic. As we have argued and most would agree, his comparison of "good" with "yellow" is seriously misleading.

The comparison would be still more deceptive, we can now see, if it led us to suppose that in the study of moral reasoning we may bypass or take lightly the question of criteria. Ethical discussion differs from factual, and so do its needs. Whereas it might be foolish to give much thought to the criteria of yellow, red, rain, and the like, it makes excellent sense to inquire, persistently: "By what criterion or criteria should Christians discriminate right from wrong?"

PART TWO

Varied Christian Modes of Moral Reasoning

An informative treatise on ethics — or on the ethics of a particular society or person — would contain an accumulation of examples selected to illustrate the kind of decisions which are said to be right in various circumstances, and the reasons given and the arguments used in concluding that they are right. — Stuart Hampshire

4

Value-Balancing

SEEKING SURE FOOTING for the study of morality, Sidgwick noted Aristotle's solution in the *Ethics:* "What he gave us there was the Common Sense Morality of Greece, reduced to consistency by careful comparison: given not as something external to him but as what 'we' — he and others — think, ascertained by reflection."[1] Sidgwick himself adopted a like procedure, and so shall we. For where else might Christian norms be sought than in actual Christian thinking, current and past? No solution can be presented as the Christian solution, no approach as the Christian approach to morals, if it ignores the way Christ himself thought, or Christians after him. Yet from apostolic times onward Paul's words have held true: Our knowledge is imperfect and our preaching is imperfect (1 Cor. 13:9). So we must sift our heritage — we and future generations — till perfection comes and what is imperfect passes away (v. 10). Accordingly, the present treatment is divided into a historical section (part two), furnishing samples from the distant and recent past, and analytic, systematic sections (parts three and four), reflecting on the materials thus provided.

Inquiry will first center, for reasons just explained in chapter 3, on locating a Christian criterion, or criteria, of right and wrong. It is as though, surveying a maze of waterways at the delta of some great river, we sought to determine where the main current flows. Perhaps it follows a single channel, straight to the sea; perhaps it diverges into two or three outlets, each of them navigable. What harm? In ethics, however, multiple criteria of right and wrong would be unfortunate. For alternate criteria may give conflicting answers, and then which answer should we follow? So our hope will be to find a single main channel, that is, one criterion so dominant that it alone answers the question: If we wish to be both consistent and true to our Christian heritage, what criterion of right and wrong should we adopt?

45

The terrain we shall reconnoiter here in part two, in pursuance of this aim, will be Christian moral reasoning, past and present; and our focus will be methodological. Interest will center not so much on "the kind of decisions which are said to be right in various circumstances" (to quote Hampshire's motto for this part) as on "the reasons given and the arguments used in concluding that they are right." To achieve sharpness of focus within each paradigm studied, I have indented a key text or two, where the chief point of interest comes most clearly to the fore. As a further step toward clarity, and as an aid to subsequent sorting, the samples are ordered in two series, comprising two chapters (this and the next). The first series exemplifies one prominent approach to moral issues; the second illustrates others, in real or apparent conflict with the first. Eventual sifting, at the start of part three, will adjudicate among them. Having seen how Christians *have* reached their moral verdicts, we shall be in a position to judge how they *should*.

The approach canvassed in the present chapter and exemplified by its samples I have termed value-balancing. The procedure is basically simple, as is the criterion that underlies it. One judges the right thing to do by considering the values and disvalues entailed in each alternative line of action, then comparing the alternatives to see which is preferable. The one that promises most value, or least disvalue (when prospective disvalue outweighs prospective value in all alternatives), is the one to choose. A chief purpose of the chapter is to provide concrete acquaintance with this mode of thought. Another is to suggest how widespread it is: confined to no one denomination or period or area of concern, it appears equally in the consideration of actions, rules, vocations, institutions, ways of life. Concurrently with the achievement of these two purposes, through a smorgasbord of samples, "many essential truths are at the same stroke gathered in along the way, in a manner that is nonsystematic but perhaps more stimulating for the mind, because they emerge from the long reflection that is pursued from age to age, with its advances and its failures, and from the successive occasions that it offers for discussion."[2]

Should the reader wonder how I understand the chapter's key word, "value," he may consult the samples strewn through this chapter and the next, and listed in VII, A. Or he may consult a dictionary. For I intend to employ the term in customary fashion, to indicate (concretely) that which is desirable in itself or useful for some purpose, or (abstractly) the worth thus possessed. And I see little profit in more high-powered formulae (e.g., equating value with "the good as the possible object of rational choice"[3]). If such definitions are to conform with the familiar concept, they must be understood in its light, not vice versa. And as for terminological innovations, I agree with Nicholas Rescher: "Since our interest lies with values as we have in fact come to conceive of them, it will be a good policy to stick close to the vocabulary of everyday value talk."[4]

The same may be said of "duty," "ought," "right," "obligation," and the like. In a context like the present one, vague concepts should be left broad and vague to permit free discussion among proponents of varying views. To write one's own positions into the meaning of the terms would preclude debate; to define them in terms of one's conclusions would turn the "conclusions" into mere tautologies. Thus the precision we aim to achieve, eventually, is precision of doctrine and preference, not of definition.[5] And both on the way to that goal and in the interpretation of the result, clarity will come chiefly, not from technical terminology, but from specific illustrations and their analyses. Without further preamble, therefore, let us get down to cases.

A. Jesus on Sabbath Observance

The Gospels contain much inspiration, motivation, and moral guidance, general and particular, but relatively little argumentation for or against specific acts or precepts. This parenetic emphasis (as it is called), which characterizes the rest of the New Testament as well and early Christian literature as a whole, reminds us that many of life's concerns require no casuistry. "Paul says that *agapé* is 'the full content of the moral law,' because anyone who acts under its impulses will not injure his neighbor by stealing, killing, committing adultery, coveting his goods, or in any other way."[6] Many matters require little deliberation.

Yet concrete problems inevitably arise which demand closer attention. And already in gospel times the issue of Sabbath observance occasioned some notable examples of moral reasoning. Just how closely these arguments correspond to the original words of Christ we cannot say with assurance. However, in the present context it does not seem too important to discriminate between the Jesus of history and the Jesus of early faith. Either is prime evidence of Christian moral reasoning, and I see no reason to suppose that numerous Gospel texts, all conveying a similar impression, do not mirror Jesus' own basic viewpoint. So let us consider a typical text, as evidence not of the historical Jesus or of the Jesus of faith, but of both together: Jesus of Nazareth as the Gospels picture him.

He went on to another place, and entered their synagogue. A man was there with a withered arm, and they asked Jesus, "Is it permitted to heal on the Sabbath?" (They wanted to frame a charge against him.) But he said to them, "Suppose you had one sheep, which fell into a ditch on the Sabbath; is there one of you who would not catch hold of it and lift it out? And surely a man is worth far more than a sheep! It is therefore permitted to do good on the Sabbath." Turning to the man he said, "Stretch out your arm." He stretched it out, and it was made sound again like the other. But the Pharisees, on leaving the synagogue, laid a plot to do away with him. (Mt. 12:9-14)

Bruno Schüller suggests, as do others, that we have here an instance of value-balancing: "The value of cultic worship may be higher; but the care of a sick person, the restoration of his health, is more basic and pressing. Hence religious observance must yield to it."[7] The significance of such an analysis appears from the fact that "we always find ourselves in this situation whenever we have to act."[8] We must always choose between competing values. In every instance at least this is true, that by performing some other action than the one we elect we might achieve some other value than the one to which we give precedence.

That Jesus invoked a human value is clear; that he saw a conflict with some other value is not. For healing on the Sabbath conflicted, not with the Sabbath as prescribed in the Decalog, but with one of the myriad regulations with which Scribes had spelled out the simple command "That day you shall not do any work" (Ex. 20:10; Deut. 5:13). By New Testament times they forbade carrying a bed on the Sabbath (Jn. 5:10), tending a sick person (Mk. 3:2; Lk. 13:14), plucking a few grains of wheat (Mt. 12:2), or walking more than two thousand paces (Acts 1:12).[9] A code of twenty-two works forbidden on the Sabbath is known to have existed in the second century before Christ, and a catalog of thirty-nine is recorded by the later Pharisaic teachers.[10]

"It was over the validity of this growing oral law that the Pharisees and Sadducees [the two chief parties of Jesus' day] were divided. Josephus has expressed the matter thus: 'What I would now explain is this, that the Pharisees have delivered to the people a great many observances by succession from their fathers, which are not written in the law of Moses; and for that reason it is that the Sadducees reject them, and say that we are to esteem those observances to be obligatory which are in the written word, but are not to observe what are derived from the tradition of our forefathers; and concerning these things it is that great disputes and differences have arisen among them' (Antiqu. XIII. x. 6)."[11]

Similar debates flare again today. This is not surprising, for as Jews felt the Law held the answer to all problems, so Christians have considered the Gospel adequate to their moral needs. Yet neither the Old Testament nor the New provides detailed guidance on most moral issues. So now as then, "exegesis resolves the difficulty: ingenious reasoning deduces the new precepts from the divine letter. . . . This exegesis does not invent, but only justifies, a law which derives all its value from tradition."[12] Thus it has happened in Christian times, too, that despite the gap between subsequent precepts and the initial record, and the fallible human reasoning which bridged the gap, and "although the oral law came to be presented in isolation from the text of scripture, nevertheless, it was regarded as of equal obligation as the written law."[13] Consider, for example, the detailed prohibitions of artificial contraception or of artificial insemination; their distance from Scripture; and the manner of their presentation. These examples remind us that in Christendom as in Judaism those in authority have sometimes backed such derivations and urged them as the sure will of God, admitting no exceptions, while others have contested the claims.

From this point-by-point comparison alone no verdict can be drawn. But the parallel appears close enough to warrant concern. And it suggests the possible relevance of Jesus' treatment of the Sabbath. We may not infer, it is true, that he opposed precise precepts in general or their rigorous application in all cases; that question we shall consider later, in the second series of examples. It does seem evident, though, that he opposed any conception or interpretation of the divine will which takes no account of human welfare.[14] The Law, like the Sabbath, is for man, not man for the Law.

Thus, to characterize Jesus' healing word as "work" was to stretch the term unreasonably, and to forbid the healing as contrary to the divine command was to forget the sense and finality of the command. The Sabbath was to be a day of rest (Ex. 23:12), a sign of liberation (Deut. 5:15), and here, without any exertion beyond the moving of his lips, Jesus freed a man from his long affliction (cp. Lk. 13:16).

Opposition to such an act may appear perverse. But let us not be too hard on the Pharisaic interpreters of the Law. They were asking only a day's delay. And on matters of far greater moment many a Christian moralist has felt similarly constrained to disregard human gain or human suffering, for basically similar reasons, in all good faith. Hence the relevance of this first sample in our series.

B. Saint Paul on Celibacy

Saint Paul advanced more cautiously from the message received when he wrote:

On the question of celibacy [or: virginity], I have no instructions from the Lord, but I give my judgement as one who by God's mercy is fit to be trusted.

It is my opinion, then, that in a time of stress like the present this is the best way for a man to live — it is best for a man to be as he is. Are you bound in marriage? Do not seek a dissolution. Has your marriage been dissolved? Do not seek a wife. If, however, you do marry, there is nothing wrong in it; and if a virgin marries, she has done no wrong. But those who marry will have pain and grief in this bodily life, and my aim is to spare you.

What I mean, my friends, is this. The time we live in will not last long. While it lasts, married men should be as if they had no wives; mourners should be as if they had nothing to grieve them, the joyful as if they did not rejoice; buyers must not count on keeping what they buy, nor those who use the world's wealth on using it to the full. For the whole frame of this world is passing away.

I want you to be free from anxious care. The unmarried man cares for the Lord's business; his aim is to please the Lord. But the married man cares for worldly things; his aim is to please his wife; and he has a divided mind. The unmarried or celibate woman cares for the Lord's business; her aim is to be dedicated to him in body as in spirit; but the married woman cares for worldly things; her aim is to please her husband.

In saying this I have no wish to keep you on a tight rein. I am thinking simply of your own good, of what is seemly, and of your freedom to wait upon the Lord without distraction. (1 Cor. 7: 25–35)

Though the apostle's argument may seem problematic to many, especially in our day, this much is obvious: like Jesus in the synagogue, he weighs values in arriving at his verdict. A chief difference, though, is that whereas Jesus concluded to what *should* be done, on that occasion and (by implication) on others like it, Paul speaks only of what "is best" and "what is seemly," without wishing to hold his readers "on a tight rein."

A possible explanation is the counsel-precept distinction, as traditionally understood: "A *counsel* is an exhortation without binding force to do or say some specific thing for a particular purpose. Among deliberate actions or omissions that can be directed to God as to their ultimate end, some are a matter of duty (precepts), others are proposed only as a matter of free choice (counsels). The latter are helpful toward an easier and more secure attainment of one's ultimate end."[15] To make good sense, such statements about classes of acts must apply to individual instances. If celibacy, for example, can be described as free in general, then it is free case by case. Save for a special command from God, no one is obliged to stay single. Within this common perspective it is evident why Paul issued no precept. If no one has the obligation, he could hardly say that all do.

An alternative explanation, however, is ready at hand: perhaps some are obliged, some not; or some are bound to marry and others to remain single, according to their circumstances. In this supposition, too, a universal norm would not hold. Awareness of such personal variations does in fact appear earlier in the chapter, when Paul writes: "Because there is so much immorality, let each man have his own wife and each woman her own husband. . . . All this I say by way of concession, not command. I should like you all to be as I am myself; but everyone has the gift God has granted him, one this gift and another that" (1 Cor. 7:2–3, 6–7).

Such reasoning (so translated) suggests that by adding a suitable qualifying clause, Paul might have formed a precept: "If anyone feels himself able to do so, he *should* forgo marriage." This teaching would have the same force as that concerning the eating of meat offered to idols: a person *might* eat it if no weak brother was scandalized, but were such a person present, *then* to eat it would be *wrong* (1 Cor. 8:12). Here Paul does in fact give a personal command. If he formulates no comparable precept with respect to celibacy, it is perhaps because the variable in this case (capacity for continence) is more difficult to determine than in the other (the presence of a weak brother); or because other circumstances and other reasons besides personal weakness might make marriage advisable; or because in the case of marriage a notable good is forgone whereas in the other a notable harm is done; or for a combination of these reasons. However, Paul's words do not permit us to determine with precision just how he performed his value-balancing.

This is a significant fact. For the present sample was not chosen solely to illustrate value-reasoning in apostolic times, or the rudimentary level at which such reasoning often remains, at least in its expression; it was also meant to prepare discussion of a fundamental issue in Christian ethics: the distinction between precepts and counsels. Near the beginning of the next chapter I shall consider the traditional Catholic view (now widely questioned) that counsels remain counsels even in the individual case — that the choice of a celibate life, for instance, is never obligatory, even in specific circumstances for a specific person. In support of this position our present passage (1 Corinthians 7) is frequently cited. It is, in fact, the favorite text for that purpose. Jesus may have said, "Let those accept it who can" (Mt. 19:12), but Paul declared unequivocally, "I have no instructions from the Lord" and "If, however, you do marry there is nothing wrong in it." So it is important to note, first, that even without a command from the Lord Paul might conceivably have formulated as firm a directive concerning celibacy as he did concerning food offered to idols and, second, that if he did not do so, various explanations are possible. I have cited three or four plausible ones, none of which implies the traditional view. The issue remains open.

C. Ignatius' First Method

As the body, writes Saint Paul, has many members, but all have not the same office, so also is Christ. Some of his people are called to celibacy, some to marriage; some to one service, some to another. There is a task for each in life. But which? A key section of Saint Ignatius Loyola's *Spiritual Exercises* offers guidelines for just such decisions as these.

The passage merits special attention, here and hereafter, for three major reasons. First, the qualifications of the author, the wide use of the text, and the vast body of commentary it has elicited make it the classic treatment of individual decision-making in Catholic spiritual literature. Second, recent developments heighten the importance of such decision-making for ethics generally and not just for "spirituality" (see IV, E, G; V, A, B). Third, the text and the commentary on it integrate two types of thought too often separated in ethical discussion: the one more analytic, stressing the balance of values, and developed most fully in philosophical writings; the other more intuitive and religiously oriented, stressing the theological dimension so often ignored in more analytic literature.

Ignatius distinguished three "times" in which an election may be made. The third time, which alone interests us for the moment, he described as "one of tranquillity: when one considers, first, for what man is born, viz., to praise God our Lord, and to save his soul; and when, desiring this, he chooses as the means to this end a kind or state of life within the bounds of the Church [for example an office or benefice to be accepted or left], in order that he may thereby be helped to serve God our Lord, and to save his soul."[16] Of the two methods Ignatius proposed for use in this time, we shall consider just the first, and specifically its fourth and fifth points:

> The fourth point is to consider the matter, reasoning as to what advantages and profit will accrue to me if I hold the pro-

posed office or benefice solely for the praise of our Lord God and the salvation of my soul; on the other hand, reasoning likewise on the inconveniences and dangers which there are in holding it. And then do the same in the second part, viz., view the advantages and profit in not holding it, and likewise, on the other hand, the inconvenience and dangers in not holding it.

The fifth point is, after I have thus turned over and reasoned on everything with regard to the matter proposed, to see to what side reason inclines; and thus following the weightier motions of reason, and not any sensual ones, I must come to a decision about the matter proposed.[17]

We have here a particularly clear example of what in contemporary writing is termed the weighing or balancing of values. Ignatius' account articulates and expands the approach implicit in the preceding two samples, as in innumerable others where authors, noting the pros and cons of an action, speak of a "double effect." It does so, though, in a manner more appropriate to the majority of cases, for it envisions multiple merits and demerits, not just two.

Thus, to develop the previous example, an individual deciding between marriage and celibate service must consider many factors besides those Paul mentioned. On the one hand he should note, for instance, the high failure rate in marriage (Christian or other) and on the other hand the maturing effect of trials and responsibilities such as married people and especially parents confront. He should also consider such personal matters as his talents and where they would best be used; his parents' needs or those of other dependents; his fiancée, if he has one, and how she would be affected; his debts, vows, health, inclinations, character, present opportunities, and so forth. The pluses and minuses are many.

Ignatius' method possesses this further interest: it extends to the most varied cases. It is quite general, applying as readily to quitting Vietnam as to marrying Jennifer or John. Thus, at the time the American withdrawal was in progress, it inspired the following sample list of pros and cons (where "solution A" can be recognized as withdrawal, and the unnamed countries can be identified accordingly):

SOLUTION A

(Dis)value

More even distribution of wealth in countries X, Y, Z
Mass purge in countries X, Y, Z
End of destruction, demoralization of war in countries X, Y, Z

Elimination of escalation risk
More irenic international climate, with lessened risk of world war
Long-lasting communistic police state in countries X, Y, Z
Greatly increased funds for foreign aid, with probable use of a
     fraction
Greatly decreased unrest in country M
Greater funds, attention for internal problems of country M
Uncertain risk for countries O, P, Q.[18]

This advantage of generality, which is great, is purchased, however, at the price of indefiniteness. The Ignatian technique does not say
what values to watch for in this or that kind of situation but requires us
to start from scratch on each occasion. And perhaps the greatest danger
and most common failure in our moral assessments is that of overlook-
ing important dimensions of value or disvalue. This problem may be
partly resolved by rules of thumb for judging specific types of cases.

D. Saint Thomas on Self-Defense

If, with Webster, we define a rule of thumb as "a rough measurement or calculation," then ethical norms may earn the label in three
ways: (1) They may state a general norm quite generally, not mentioning yet recognizing the possibility of exceptions. "Tell the truth," as usually understood, is an example. (2) They may designate indefinitely the
behavior forbidden or enjoined, thereby leaving unclear the possibility
of exceptions. "Honor your father and mother" exemplifies the manner.
(3) They may describe the behavior more definitely but slip in a veiled
request for calculation. "Tell no more untruths than necessary" illustrates the move. It always applies, you should never act otherwise, but
it leaves you on your own to determine whether you have or have not;
the mere meaning of the words does not tell you, as it does in (1). Thus
this norm too, in its different way, is only a "rough measure."

This third type of rule—half description and half recipe—comes
closer to Ignatius' formula, especially when the recipe enjoins balancing values. The affinity is evident, for instance, in Saint Thomas' treatment of self-defense:

A double effect may follow from the act of self-defense: first, saving one's life; second, killing one's attacker. Such an act, then,
since it is done to save one's life, is not illicit; for it is natural to do
everything to preserve its existence, so far as it can. Yet it may hap-

pen that an act performed with a good intention becomes illicit if it is not proportioned to its purpose. Thus if to protect himself a person uses more violence than is necessary, his action will be wrong, whereas if he resists his attacker in moderation, his defense will be licit.[19]

The more transparent part of this reasoning clearly resembles Ignatius' weighing of values. Life is first balanced against life, then life against mere injury, as the price of saving one's life. The result is a rule of the third kind; it says: "You may defend yourself against an attacker, provided you employ no more violence than necessary"—then leaves each defender to determine how much that is.

With its description and its proviso such a rule moves some distance from Ignatius' general method not only toward greater definiteness but also toward narrower applicability and utility. Hence many such rules are required in place of the single method. And numerous kindred rules, based on similar reasoning, do in fact occur in Thomas' writings. For instance, "if . . . one's need is so urgent and evident that it is clear it must be met by means of things at hand . . . a person may then licitly use another's goods to satisfy his need."[20] One man's life outweighs another man's enjoyment of his property, but a solution which respects the property, if feasible, is preferable to one which does not. The correct balance between the gravity and urgency of the need, on the one hand, and the drawbacks of the means, on the other, is left for the individual to determine in his own case. The same rule, if broadened and adapted to cover the needs of whole social classes (thus providing a point of contact between traditional social teaching and the thought, say, of Christian Marxists), would entail still more laborious deliberation on the pros and cons: the extent and urgency of the need, the means available, the consequences of each alternative line of action.

However, this rule, like the preceding one, does not say what *should* be done; it considers only what is licit. And one may wonder, especially in the case of self-defense, what verdict Thomas would have given had he been asked to indicate the better, more Christian thing to do. For the observation which tips the scales in favor of the defendant's life is the least perspicuous part of his argument. Are all our natural proclivities—for instance, our proneness to pride and selfishness—a sure indication of value? Or is this particular fact of nature—the strong inclination to preserve one's own life, unmatched by any equally strong concern for others'—somehow a surer guide? To problems of this type in Aquinas' thought we shall return in the following chapter (V, D).

E. Positive and Negative Norms

If asked what a person *should* do if attacked, Thomas might have answered: "In such matters, because of the diversity of individual cases, no universal rule can be given."[21] That is how he did answer in the following much-cited passage, where he considers the right thing to do, and not merely what is licit:[22]

> It is right and true for all to act according to reason, and from this principle it follows, as a proper conclusion, that goods entrusted to another should be restored to their owner. Now this is true for the majority of cases. But it may happen in a particular case that it would be injurious, and therefore unreasonable, to restore goods held in trust; for instance, if they are claimed for the purpose of fighting against one's country. And this principle [i.e., goods entrusted to another should be restored to their owner] will be found to fail the more, according as we descend further towards the particular, *e.g.*, if one were to say that goods held in trust should be restored with such and such a guarantee, or in such and such a way; because the greater the number of conditions added, the greater the number of ways in which the principle may fail, so that it be not right to restore or not to restore.[23]

Clearly, realistically, Thomas here balances values. But it may seem odd, at first glance, for him to say that a principle "will be found to fail the more, according as we descend further towards the particular." Is it not precisely through endless refinements that ethicians strive to assure the validity of their precepts? However, Thomas is quite right, for he is speaking of positive precepts, not negative. So things work out in reverse. When tested by value balance, positive precepts are forced in the direction of ever-greater vagueness and generality, negative precepts in the direction of ever-greater precision and narrowness. Thus consider the following two tables of precepts, the first positive and the second negative:

Positive: Always repay your debts, in full, on time, in the manner stipulated.
            Always repay your debts, in full, on time.
            Always repay your debts, in full.
            Always repay your debts.
Negative: Never kill.
            Never kill your wife.
            Never torture your wife to death.

> Never torture your wife to death while giving her to believe you hate her.[24]

Each list proceeds from more numerous likely exceptions to fewer, the first by becoming more general, the second by becoming more specific. But the first never fully succeeds, whereas the second does. As Aquinas noted, even the most general prescription still admits of exceptions; whereas the most specific prohibition — "Never torture your wife to death while giving her to believe you hate her" — takes care of all likely exceptions this side of the parousia. And this is typical, not a happenstance.

Proscription enjoys a clear logical advantage over prescription. For negative precepts veto *just one* line of action (the one they name and proscribe), whereas positive precepts ban *all but one* (the one they name and prescribe). And each excluded alternative is a rival, which may on some occasion turn out to be preferable and thereby falsify the universal norm. Hence the fewer the exclusions, the better a precept's chances of universal validity. And negative precepts, which at any given level of generality eliminate far fewer alternatives than positive precepts do, therefore have the cards stacked heavily in their favor.

In simple illustration, suppose a father tells his son not to play in the drive. The boy is then free to play in the livingroom, attic, backyard, street, kitchen, or where-have-you. If, however, his father says, "Play in the drive," all those varied options are foreclosed. Despite appearances, prohibition is less severe. A "Don't" is more permissive than a "Do."

It is understandable, therefore, that ethicians in search of exceptionless norms should tend to prefer the negative.[25] Notice, though, how universality is then achieved: (1) by piling dire disvalue on dire disvalue (death, physical agony, mental anguish); (2) by successively restricting the class of forbidden actions (killing, just of one's wife, just of one's wife by torture, just of one's wife by torture while exhibiting hatred). The effect of the first tactic is to make the precept all too obvious: of course we should not treat our wives in that barbaric fashion; we need no rule to instruct us on the matter. The effect of the second tactic is to limit or exclude application: even if a man were contemplating killing his wife (a rare enough occurrence), the rule would tell him only that he should not swear at her as well, or rather that he should not both swear at her and torture her (for as far as the precept specifies, he might do one or the other); it would not tell him whether he should kill his wife. Generally speaking, therefore, the sureness of such norms is inversely related to their helpfulness. Truth and utility seem not to mix.

F. The Utility of Rules

An occasional norm — say the condemnation of rape or of dehumanizing torture — may pass the value-balancing test yet be both universally valid and all too relevant to life as it is actually lived. But such exceptionless norms appear to be rare and are often contested or overlooked. Thus case-by-case consideration, using a method like Ignatius' or a rule of thumb like Thomas', may come to appear the paradigmatic form of moral reasoning; and one can therefore understand why Paul Ramsey should write:

> The crucial question is whether in morality there are only *tactical directives to the players*. Are there not also *rules of the game* itself? . . . Are there any binding moral practices which the individual must adhere to if his is to be the best life he can live? Practices like the rule that prohibits more than eleven players on the field at the same time, or the rule defining "offside." Anyone who said, I think it would be best on the whole, or most fun-fulfilling, if in this instance I was allowed twelve players or a man offside, must be understood not to know the game he is playing or the meaning of a universally binding rule of the game. This is the nature of societal rules and institutions and of moral *practices*. Of course, at the end of the season one can ask whether the game could be improved by changing the rules; and in any society with regard to any moral institution one can ask whether there is a different *rule of practice* that would be more love-embodying and more fulfilling for all persons. But meantime, responsibility calls for individual actions falling within or under the rules of practice governing the society or the moral institution in question.[26]

The rules Ramsey here has in mind are "societal" not only in the sense that they govern social relationships but also in the sense that they are widely acknowledged and followed in society. The acknowledgment may but need not take legal form (as the rules of a game may but need not be codified). "For example," suggests James Gustafson, "in the realm of sexual behavior, there has been a commonly accepted rule, 'Thou shalt not commit adultery.' Reasons can be given for the authority of that rule, but the rule has relative autonomy by virtue of its long usage within the Christian community so that its members do not have to face every human relationship with a man or woman who is not their marriage partner as one that offers the moral possibility of adultery. Indeed, if for various reasons a relationship suggests that adultery might be committed, Christians begin with the rule. The weight of evidence and reflection clearly has to be such as to invalidate the application of the rule in that particular instance. Exceptions to such rules are not made lightly, and the existence of exceptions is hardly evidence for the invalidity of the rule."[27]

When, as in these quotations from Gustafson and Ramsey, rules are viewed as less than absolutely binding yet more than mere summations of individual verdicts, and when their validity is gauged by their furtherance of values, the position is currently labeled "rule-utilitarianism." Distinctions and subdistinctions are then introduced, for instance, between "*actual*-rule-utilitarianism," for which "an action is right if it conforms to the accepted or prevailing moral rules and wrong if it does not, assuming that these rules are those whose acceptance and observance is conducive to the greatest general good or at least a necessary condition of it," and "*ideal*-rule-utilitarianism," "of which there are two main kinds. One holds that an act is right if and only if it conforms to a set of rules general *conformity* to which would maximize utility; the other that an act is right if and only if it conforms to a set of rules general *acceptance* of which would maximize utility, where acceptance of a rule is thought of as falling somewhat short of conformity to it."[28] One might continue and differentiate each of these positions, according as it aims to bring all acts under rules, or only some. However, we shall not penetrate further into this thicket of distinctions and subdistinctions but shall note instead some standard reasons for "beginning with the rule."

(1) In favor of moral rules in general, societal or personal, there is a pragmatic argument which Jonathan Bennett states as follows: "'If every practical problem had to be solved on the spot, on the basis of the fine details of the particular case, the results would be disastrous. Take a situation which falls under some rule which I know to be justified in most situations. There may not be time or means for me to learn much more about the present situation than just that it does fall under the rule; the details of the case, even if I can discover them, may be too complex for me to handle; my handling of them, even if intellectually efficient, may without my knowing it be self-interested or corrupt; by deciding, however uncorruptly, not to follow the rule on this occasion, I may weaken its hold on me in other situations where it clearly ought to be followed; and even if I could be sure that I was in no such danger, I might help others into it by publicly breaking the rule.'"[29]

It will generally be wiser, therefore, to begin — and end — with the rule. But sometimes, as Bennett notes, "these dangers will be far too slight to justify doing what a given general rule enjoins in a particular situation."[30]

(2)   Likewise pragmatic, but in a different way, is a popular brief for rules which Basil Mitchell argues as follows: "It is hard to see how a society of any complexity could survive or be worth preserving if its members approached their obligations in the spirit of Fletcher's official [antinomian] theory. What would become of the institution of marriage if the marriage vow were taken to mean 'I will remain faithful unto you until the situation appears to me to call for adultery'? Or if parental responsibility were interpreted to mean 'We will care for you so long as circumstances seem to justify the policy'? The classical utilitarians with their emphasis upon 'reliability, predictability, certainty' saw clearly enough that this would not do, and would not do precisely because it would be against the interests of all concerned. Hence it is an essential part of our concept of 'duty' or 'obligation' that we are, as we say, 'bound' to act in accordance with them. This does not necessarily imply that there are no circumstances in which we may break our obligations or be freed from them, but it does imply that we are not entitled, insofar as we are bound by such obligations, to do 'what love requires in the situation' if this means acting solely on a simple utilitarian calculus."[31]
(3)   This pragmatic case for rules easily merges with another, nonpragmatic rationale, suggested already by Ramsey's allusion to games. The moral rules operative in a society do not merely serve ulterior ends, any more than do the rules of games; they establish forms of life. Thus, without the rules of chess, chess would not exist; without the rules of monogamous marriage, monogamous marriage would not exist. And these patterns of life possess their own inherent interest and appeal, much as do speech, art, dance, music, worship. Their value cannot be equated with that of their results.

"It has sometimes been said," observed Wittgenstein, "that what music conveys to us are feelings of joyfulness, melancholy, triumph, etc, etc. and what repels us in this account is that it seems to say that music is an instrument for producing in us sequences of feelings. And from this one might gather that any other means of producing such feelings would do for us instead of music. —To such an account we are tempted to reply 'Music conveys to us *itself*!'"[32] It would be similarly mistaken to view polygamy and monogamy, in their varied concrete forms, as simply alternative methods, more or less effective, for realizing certain ends. Their appeal (or lack thereof) lies largely *in themselves*.

This perspective elicits corresponding reflections on exceptions. Intentional violations of the rules in a game are of two kinds: those aimed at ending the game and those aimed at winning it. Thus, in basketball a guard may prevent a crucial basket by fouling the shooter, in the hope that he will make only one of his free throws. He has no objection to the game or its rules but takes this exceptional means to win the match. On the other hand, it sometimes happens that a youngster, tiring of a schoolyard game of basketball, starts to run with the ball or otherwise disregard the rules, with the consequence perhaps that the match sputters out.

But it does not generally sputter into a game of football. So, too, violations of societal rules, even when expressive of discontent with the existing institution and of preference for another, do not necessarily establish an alternative institution, or even tend to. Adultery, for example, does not tend to establish polygamy; it simply breaks down the existing institution of monogamous marriage. And a person who prefers polygamy or some other form to the existing institution should therefore consider whether the latter is not at least preferable to no institution at all (as a boy might consider whether the basketball match under way is not preferable to no game at all, though he perhaps prefers football).

(4)   Still, a person might work for changes in the existing institution (as he might for changes in the rules of a game) or for the adoption of a different one, and even if he prefers the existing institution and approves its present rules, he may occasionally decide to break them, without any inconsistency. But once we shift to a fourth perspective, these options become questionable. The prohibition of adultery, says Gustafson, has relative autonomy "by virtue of its long usage within the Christian community." And it is doubtful whether he would attach equal weight to the Moslem practice of polygamy, even within Moslem society. For a Christian, Christian marriage and its rules are something more than a convenience, something more than a form of life he or she prefers over others; they bear the stamp of divine approval. Questions may arise, however, concerning just how far the approval reaches (does it descend to details or does it cover just the institution as a whole?) and how exclusively (does it commend only this institution and disapprove all alternatives?). More simply, does it preclude any change in or of the institution?

Christians have traditionally assumed that in *pre*scribing the Christian form of monogamous marriage, Christ *pro*scribed not only alternative forms of that institution but also alternative forms of sexual union. They have frequently supposed, furthermore, that his prescriptions were quite precise or at least could be rendered precise by suitable interpretation. Thus sealed with divine authority, the norms have been thought to exclude all exceptions: regardless of the consequences or of the particular circumstances, adultery is always wrong, premarital intercourse is always wrong, divorce and remarriage after a sacramental, consummated marriage is always wrong.

G. Exceptionless Precepts

As we have seen, within a value perspective such assertions are problematic. How can rules of right and wrong ignore the configuration of values in individual cases if "right" and "wrong" subserve value? Does not charity come first? Are not rules for people, not people for rules?

A typical expedient in Scholastic ethics (though not only there) in support of exceptionless precepts has been the kind of argument Cathrein employed to establish the following thesis: "The marital bond is so indissoluble in virtue of the natural law, that it can be dissolved only by divine authority."[33] Though it sounds somewhat like a theory of chemistry or physics, Cathrein's thesis, of course, refers, not to a physical or psychological or merely social bond, but to a moral tie; nor to a physical or psychological power, but to a moral possibility. It would be wrong for a couple to separate and remarry. His defense goes as follows, first stating the general advantages of permanence and then adding an argument by which exceptions are excluded:

> *The primary end* of matrimony is the proper rearing of offspring, and for this end both certainty concerning the father's identity and collaboration by both spouses are required. *But* such certitude and such cooperation would be hindered if matrimony were humanly soluble. For the partners could be separated and the wife could be joined with another man (S. Thom., C. gent., 1. c). Nor should it be suggested that this difficulty is avoided if divorce is granted only for the gravest reasons, say adultery or sterility. For if even occasionally and by way of exception, for most serious reasons, divorce were granted, human inconstancy and the desires and difficulties often associated with marriage are such that there would frequently be danger of dissolution, without any sufficient and efficacious natural remedy, so that the giver of natural law himself would be at fault.[34]

Here empirical consequences are invoked to establish an absolute norm, not to challenge it (the more common procedure). "A wise lawgiver," the argument seems to say, "who foresaw the consequences of permitting exceptions would surely exclude them. Hence the divine lawgiver, being omniscient, has doubtless so decreed." Not that he has publicly proclaimed his will; Cathrein does not appeal to revelation. The law he alleges is a "natural law," written in men's consciences. But how does the transcription occur? How might the law be there inscribed, so categorically?

A wife, let us suppose, is contemplating divorce and remarriage.

She recognizes contrary reasons, such as Cathrein cites at the start, and agrees that dissolution is generally unfortunate. But viewing her own situation and its special reasons, she concludes that the step is warranted. At this point Cathrein might wish to put this further thought in her mind, so as to give effect to his closing, clinching observations: "I, like the rest of mankind, am so inconstant, and my marriage has been so troubled, that I may not have decided with perfect objectivity." This is a salutary reflection, here and on other occasions when passion and self-interest threaten to cloud one's judgment. But the proper conclusion, it would seem, and the one we would naturally draw, is not "I mustn't do it," but rather "Let me examine my motives still more carefully; let me be thoroughly objective."

Some other consideration, therefore, will have to be introduced if exceptions are to be excluded categorically, in this or similar arguments. As it stands, Cathrein's brief is incomplete, indeed not fully intelligible. To complement it and others like it, we might turn to the fuller reasoning Paul Ramsey deploys with regard to the patient's informed consent prior to experimentation on humans. On behalf of this requirement and in opposition to any relaxation, he develops the following version of the "opening-wedge," "toe-in-the-door" type of argument:

> Precisely because there are unknown future benefits and precisely because the results of the experimentation may be believed to be so important as to be overriding, this rule governing medical experimentation upon human beings is needed to ensure that for the sake of those consequences no man shall be degraded and treated as a thing or as an animal in order that good may come of it. In this age of research medicine it is not only that medical benefits are attained by research but also that a man rises to the top in medicine by the success and significance of his research. The likelihood that a researcher would make a mistake in departing from a generally valuable rule of medical practice because he is biased toward the research benefits of permitting an "exception" is exceedingly great. In such a seriously important moral matter, this should be enough to rebut a policy of being open to future possible exceptions to this canon of medical ethics. . . . A *physician or experimenter is more liable to make an error in moral judgment if he adopts a policy of holding himself open to the possibility that there may be significant, future permissions to ignore the principle of consent than he is if he holds this requirement of an informed consent always relevant and applicable.*[35]

Assessing only the research, we might countenance rare exceptions; appraising the researcher, we advise him or her to forget that possibility. Yet who, precisely, do we thus judge and thus admonish? Typical researchers, typically placed and typically motivated? Then the ban does not apply universally: others may be better motivated and better placed. So is our warning addressed to all researchers, regardless of persons and circumstances? Then the thesis of unreliability may be as difficult to sustain as the universal norm it is intended to support. After all, in the crucible of decision it is the researcher and not the cool ethician who will have to bar exceptions, in view of the researcher's own likely bias. And that calls already for considerable objectivity. Thus the very condition required to make the norm operative appears to conflict with its basic premise. Ramsey's argument proves as difficult as Cathrein's to transpose from the printed page to the individual conscience.

H. Obedience

Once we envisage legislation — church legislation, say, concerning marriage or civil legislation concerning informed consent — these particular problems tend to disappear. (The individual need no longer seek the exceptionless norm within his private conscience or attempt to censor his own judgment.) But analogous problems then arise. The legislation is aimed at excluding exceptions, in view of the common good. So are exceptions never permissible? Must obedience be blind, absolute, once the law is recognized as a good one? Or may the recipient set himself up as judge of the law and set it aside in the individual case?

Clerical obedience or religious obedience in fulfillment of one's vows poses similar problems when viewed pragmatically as by Karl Rahner. While recognizing a "religious dimension" of such obedience, he accords primacy to the "functional dimension," which "rests on the simple and sober persuasion that in any society there must, if it is to exist and act, be order, interdependence, authority, and accordingly a prompt and effective will to obey and to exercise the common will of this society, which cannot exist unless it is determined by someone, who (notwithstanding a sincere democratic mentality for the formation of this common will) ultimately determines what in the concrete is to be done."[36] Obedience serves the common good. However:

> Everyone will agree that a superior, even with the best intentions, can issue an order which is objectively wrong. If one does not consider as sins only those things which are expressly labeled as such

in confessional manuals, then it will be hard to deny that what is materially false can also very often be objectively immoral. What is more, it is not easy to explain why this is not generally so. Let us invent an example. A higher superior tells the principal of a boarding school that he must under all circumstances make the boys go to confession once a week. Suppose that the subordinate, in this case the principal of the boarding school, clearly realizes what the superior in his idealistic remoteness from life cannot comprehend — namely, that such a demand will eventually prove very harmful to the spiritual life of his charges. Question: have we here merely a case of ill-conceived pedagogical instructions which must be carried out because this is an order, or have we in fact a demand which, however innocently made, is unjustified; an order which, since it actually poses a serious threat to the genuine spiritual development of these youths, should not be carried out by the subordinate? . . . The just "presumption" that the command of a superior will be morally unobjectionable not only subjectively but also objectively does not constitute a simple dispensation from the essential obligation of every man to attain moral certitude as to whether a free action is morally licit before it is undertaken.[37]

So we must balance values, in the way these quotations suggest: on one side the advantages of obedience in general and case by case, on the other the drawbacks of obedience on this or that occasion. The drawbacks alone do not decide, for the advantages are lost if obedience comes merely to this, that we obey when we agree, otherwise not, and so end up doing simply whatever we think best. As Mitchell observed above, "it is hard to see how a society of any complexity could survive or be worth preserving if its members approached their obligations in the spirit of Fletcher's official theory . . . acting solely on a simple utilitarian calculus."

Here is one possible answer to the question Rahner raised above, as to why obedience to a command believed or known to be mistaken is not always immoral. It preserves the institution, the way of life. A second answer is of equally general interest. Exceptions may be made, it is sometimes said, so as to avoid doing harm (as in the case Rahner imagines), but not (or at least not as readily) to assure greater good. If, for instance, the principal of the school judged he would achieve more on the missions or working in a ghetto, and his superior disagreed, in that case he should obey. We shall examine this distinction, more generally, in VIII, B.

I. Church Teaching

For a member of a hierarchical church the question of authority assumes special importance. It interests the individual as a moral agent not only on those occasions when it concerns any member of a society in which authority is exercised but also on any occasion and in any area where the church provides moral guidance in an authoritative manner. The issue of obedience may arise even in one's private life; for instance, with regard to abortion or artificial contraception. Consequently, it is important that the person be clear concerning the role of church teaching in moral reasoning. At what moment of the process and in what precise way should it make its influence felt?

On this topic J. P. Mackey offers the following advice, analogous to Rahner's in the preceding section and to Bennett's and Mitchell's three sections back:

> Authority can only be based ultimately on what is true and what is right. We automatically follow and respect men whom we know to habitually speak the truth and to preach and practice what is right. On the contrary, we insist that all authority ceases when a man, in whatever position, teaches what is in fact untrue or immoral. Obviously, however, we cannot all of us check, nor can any one of us check in every instance, the truth or rightness of all the rules and beliefs by which we live and act. . . . Though checking is in principle and in varying degrees possible, it is simply not practical for most of us, for most of the time and in most cases. The result is that some people are specially commissioned, by men or by God, to teach a true philosophy of life and to see it implemented. . . . The need for such leaders and the presumption in their favour is the connecting link between the two types of authority — the basic authority of obvious truth and righteousness and the authority of legal office in society — so that one can be seen to flow from the other. We do, then, recognize that when, but only when, there is considerable evidence, after the most careful checking, that a stand taken by leaders is not, or not completely, true or right, we may question the legal type and exercise of authority in favour of the more basic authority of the truth itself.[38]

To complete the picture, Mackey might have spoken more fully about the intrinsic values realized in the Christian community "by thinking and feeling alike, with the same love for one another, the same turn of mind" (Phil. 2:2) and concerning the disvalue of conflict, especially when it is open. Even then some readers might be surprised that a

Catholic author, in a Catholic journal, left the matter there, without mentioning infallibility. However, it needs to be recalled that no action (in the sense of chapter 2, which concerns us here) has been declared *ex cathedra* (that is, with the church's full teaching authority) to be always right or always wrong. And if the value-balancing perspective is basically correct, the guidance of the Holy Spirit may take the form, not of assuring the truth of any such future teaching, but of ensuring that the teaching does not occur.

We shall have to say more on this topic in chapter 9. Here, though, the sample already serves its purpose. It illustrates value-balancing such as many a Christian would find natural, with regard to church teaching as with regard to church legislation. There may be value in personal verification, but greater values would be sacrificed were that alone relied on. Truth itself would suffer, and "order, stability and progress in community."

J. The Case for Democracy

So far we have seen value-reasoning applied to an individual act (the Sabbath cure), to individual acts in general (Saint Ignatius' method), to classes or types of acts (self-defense; the possibility of exceptionless norms), to societal rules and practices (for instance, marital fidelity), to ways of life (celibacy), to obedience within a society (its legislation, its teaching). And during the course of these discussions reference has been made to the value of this or that society, say of the church or of a religious order. The individual act, practice, or vocation is assessed largely within this broader setting. But the question naturally arises whether the society itself is desirable, at least in its present form. And it arises most acutely for civil society, since political power, being greatest, most threatens individual liberty.

A variety of arguments — some negative and pessimistic, others positive and optimistic — are advanced to justify political society in general. And still more varied arguments support this or that form of government. As a further illustration of value-reasoning, consider, for instance, Reinhold Niebuhr's summary of the case for democracy:

> Modern democracy requires a more realistic philosophical and religious basis, not only in order to anticipate and understand the perils to which it is exposed; but also to give it a more persuasive justification. Man's capacity for justice makes democracy possible; but man's inclination to injustice makes democracy necessary.

In all non-democratic political theories the state or the ruler is invested with uncontrolled power for the sake of achieving order and unity in the community. But the pessimism which prompts and justifies this policy is not consistent; for it is not applied, as it should be, to the ruler. If men are inclined to deal unjustly with their fellows, the possession of power aggravates this inclination. That is why irresponsible and uncontrolled power is the greatest source of injustice.[39]

Jacques Maritain proposes a more positive rationale: "This political philosophy would admit on the one hand that civil society has as its essential purpose not the freedom of choice of each individual, but the temporal common good which is the right terrestrial life of the multitude; and on the other hand it would admit that this temporal common good (which is not only material but also moral) embraces in itself as a principal element — not certainly the office of conducting the human person to his spiritual perfection and to his full freedom of autonomy, which proceeds from something higher than the State — but certainly the development of conditions of the environment which will positively help the multitude attain a degree of intellectual and moral life making possible for every person the conquest of autonomous freedom."[40] Like others, Maritain would argue that this development is best achieved in a system which gives fuller scope to the exercise of the individual's powers of judgment and decision, and in particular where he is actively engaged in the political process itself.

Here I have been illustrating not only the basic similarity between these arguments and the preceding, where advantages and disadvantages were weighed in the balance, but also the wide diversity of argumentation possible within the same value-balancing approach. It is not as though, having opted for Euclidean geometry rather than some other, we all reach identical conclusions by identical routes. Facts may be seen differently, values variously rated, and both may be diversely organized and emphasized. Thus Maritain stresses the benefits of democracy, whereas Niebuhr cites the dangers of authoritarian regimes. And utilizing materials from Chesterton, we might argue in a manner quite different from either, that "the things common to all men are more important than the things peculiar to any men"[41] and that, once given control of policy, the mass of men will effectively assure these basic needs — nourishment, health, work, marriage, the rearing and education of children, free speech, worship, and so on — in which all take an interest. Majority rule will mean majority satisfaction, and majority satisfaction will mean the common good.

Such arguments reveal a further similarity with rules, and specifically with positive rules: as long as the arguments remain general, they are more readily accepted but less readily applied, whereas more detailed versions would afford more guidance but admit of more exceptions. Even as they stand, their universality may be challenged. For while perhaps preferring democracy in general and as an ideal, we might still question whether it is invariably best in the concrete, for a given people at this or that stage of economic or political development, torn perhaps by deep antagonisms or beset by massive, intractable economic problems. So here, too, as with regard to rules of action, authors sensitive to values, who proffer rationales like Niebuhr's or Maritain's, are slow to dogmatize. There may be exceptions.

K. Teilhard's "Grand Option"

If, however, we advance to a still higher plane, the situation alters. Most Christians take for granted the desirability of political, social, and economic organization and activity. This assumption is the unquestioned framework within which they devise individual solutions. But Pierre Teilhard de Chardin, familiar with other mentalities and cultures, discerned here a fundamental *"problem of values*, deeper than any technical question of terrestrial organisation, which we must all face today if we are to confront in full awareness our destiny as living beings, that is to say, our responsibilities towards 'evolution.'"[42]

"*A priori* (by 'dichotomic' analysis of the various outlets theoretically offered to our freedom of action) as well as *a posteriori* (by classification of the various human attitudes in fact observable around us), three alternatives, together forming a logically connected sequence, seem to express and exhaust all the possibilities open to our assessment and choice as we contemplate the future of Mankind: a) pessimism or optimism; b) the optimism of withdrawal or the optimism of evolution; c) evolution in terms of the many or of the unit."[43] This classification "is more than a flight of fancy. The four roads are not a fiction. They exist in reality and all of us know people embarked upon one or other of them. There are both pessimists and optimists around us; and among the latter there are 'buddhists,' 'pluralists' and 'monists.'"[44]

The third option determines one's specific political bent, but the second decides one's orientation generically, toward or away from politics in any form. So let us focus on that more basic choice and note how Teilhard states and argues the case for "optimism of evolution" over "optimism of withdrawal":

The second alternative seems to pose a more delicate problem. "Withdrawal—or evolution proceeding ever further?" In which direction does a higher state of consciousness await us? Here, at first sight, the answer is less clear. There is nothing contradictory in itself in the idea of human ecstasy sundered from material things. Indeed, as we shall see, this fits in very well with the *final* demands of a world of evolutionary structure. But with one proviso: that the world in question shall have reached a stage of development so advanced that its 'soul' can be detached without losing any of its completeness, as something wholly formed. But have we any reason to suppose that human consciousness *today* has achieved so high a degree of richness and perfection that it can derive nothing more from the sap of the earth? Again we may turn to history for an answer. Let us suppose, for example, that the strivings and the progress of civilisation had come to an end at the time of Buddha, or in the first centuries of the Christian era. Can we believe that nothing essential, of vision and action and love, would have been lost to the Spirit of Earth? Clearly we cannot. And this simple observation alone suffices to guide our decision. So long as a fruit continues to grow and ripen we refrain from picking it. In the same way, so long as the world around us continues, even in suffering and disorder, to yield a harvest of problems, ideas and new forces, it is a sign that we must continue to press forward in the conquest of matter. Any immediate withdrawal from a world of which the burden grows heavier every day is denied to us, because it would certainly be premature.[45]

This is value-reasoning on the grand scale—too grand, some might say. Others might question whether the "optimism of evolution" is a Christian option. I shall touch on both these issues later on. In the present chapter it suffices to have suggested, through divers samplings, the typical way in which the most varied Christian thinkers—Protestant and Catholic, past and present, conservative and progressive—have approached at all levels the most varied options.

Talk of levels, and of ever-more basic options, suggests that within the perspective of value-balancing one perhaps arrives at a position comparable to Hegelians' "Truth is the whole." The actions of an individual must be assessed within the context of his society, but his society must be judged in the setting of history: history of salvation, history of damnation, or meaningless happenstance. Thus, the most general options of all, though also the most indefinite, are perhaps the most decisive nonetheless. And as Hegel's logic opens with being and nonbeing, so the logic of decision might perhaps be seen as starting with "To be or not to be," then moving on, through the next two options on Teilhard's list, to a form of government or a form of religion, then to ever more determinate frameworks, with each prior determination a necessary but not sufficient condition for the next. This theme — moral choice within Christian horizons — is one to which we shall return in chapter 10.

L. Review

"The idea is basically simple," I said at the start concerning the rationale common to all these samples. But the samples are not simple, and amid their complexities that guiding notion may have slipped from view. So here it is again: "One judges the right thing to do by considering the values and disvalues entailed in each alternative line of action, then comparing the alternatives to see which is preferable." The alternative "lines of action" may be particular (e.g., performing the cure today versus delaying it) or general (e.g., self-defense versus nonresistance), and so may be the object of pinpoint deliberation (e.g., Ignatian value lists) or of general calculations (e.g., rule-utilitarian estimates in favor of rules). They may be actions (e.g., restoring borrowed goods, divorcing and remarrying, obeying an order); ways of life (e.g., celibacy, vowed obedience); institutions (e.g., democratic government); or overall orientations (e.g., Teilhard's "grand option"). Yet in each instance the mode of appraisal was similar: (A) Jesus looked to the good of the handicapped man, recognized no comparable value in delay, and so argued the rightness of healing him on the Sabbath. (B) Similar weighing of advantages prompted Paul to recommend celibacy over marriage and to proscribe eating meat when a brother would be harmed. (C) Ignatius generalized the approach in his method of tabulations pro and con. (D) Thomas applied it to self-defense, comparing more- and less-violent modes of self-preservation and pronouncing against the former. (E) He recognized that similar balancing might sometimes tell against the general norm of restitution and saw this as typical. (F) Believers in precepts, like Ramsey and Mitchell, adduce the advantages of rules over no rules or of this rule over that. (G) They have sometimes pressed their reasons more strongly, not only in favor of specific rules but also against all exceptions. Value is best served by their exclusion. (H) Rahner countered similar rigidity in the practice of obedience by citing possible countervalues and insisting that they be taken seriously in assessing right action. (I) Similarly, Mackey noted the usual advantages and occasional disadvantages of conformity to church teaching and advised that these contrasting values guide decision. (J) With respect to political structures, Niebuhr advanced negative arguments, Maritain positive ones, in behalf of democracy. The right regime is the one that best promotes human welfare. (K) At a loftier level Teilhard's apologia evinced the same thrust. It would be wrong to pluck the cosmic fruit before it is mature. Value should be maximized.

Such a survey is helpful, to start with, even descriptively. It opens our eyes to basic similarities where perhaps we saw only disparate thoughts on the most varied topics. It brings to view an overall gestalt or family resemblance, veiled from view in a thousand and one different discussions and deliberations. All appeal to values and disvalues; all weigh and balance them to reach a solution. Equipped with such a chart, we can now find our way more surely over the bewildering landscape of Christian moral reasoning, past and present.

This descriptive, clarifying purpose explains already the limitations imposed on our discussion. Why, for example, when we considered democracy, did we not decide for or against it, but simply present various reasonings (Niebuhr's, Maritain's, Chesterton's)? Why, despite our difficulties with the logic of Cathrein's case against divorce and of Ramsey's plea for informed consent, did we take no stand on either issue? Because our interest centered on reasoning rather than on results. Because we wished to chart, not the "kind of decisions which are said to be right," but "the reasons given and the arguments used."

And those interest us not solely or principally for historical or descriptive reasons. The varied samples we have gathered, being typical of so many, provide not only materials for mapping but also evidence on which to base a final verdict. If a Christian wishes to be faithful to his heritage, we asked, what criterion of right and wrong should he adopt? Going by the evidence just surveyed in this chapter, he would seek to maximize value and minimize disvalue. That would be his rule. However, other evidence remains to be considered. And once it too has been reviewed, the question will become: What criterion should a Christian adopt if he wishes to be *both* true to his Christian past *and* consistent in his (or her) moral reasoning? Where does the *main current* flow?

5

Alternative Approaches

THE FOREGOING EXAMPLES illustrate what I have called value-balancing and what contemporary ethicians often term the teleological approach to moral questions. In this recent usage "teleological" has a broader sense than in Thomistic ethics, say, where it means that right and wrong are defined, subjectively or objectively, in relation to man's final end (*telos*). In one influential author the term now signifies, for instance, "that the basic or ultimate criterion or standard of what is morally right, wrong, obligatory, etc., is the nonmoral value that is brought into being. The final appeal, directly or indirectly, must be to the comparative amount of good produced, or rather to the comparative balance of good over evil produced."[1] Though a version of value-balancing, this is not the precise form we shall adopt, nor the one represented by the samples just considered. For one thing, a forward-looking focus requires that "good over evil produced" be replaced by "prospective good over prospective evil." For another thing, the reference to "nonmoral value" is too narrow, for reasons we shall note (VII, A, 6). And the present chapter will add further refinements. The need will be seen, for example, to consider a wider range of values than teleologists often have (V, I) and to include the contemplated act itself, and not just its consequences, in calculating values (V, J). If the aim of Christian ethics is "that they may have life and have it more abundantly," then doubtless the period of action must count as well as subsequent periods, and no type of value may be disregarded. These developments will lead us closer to the position of "deontologists," who likewise insist that morality cannot be judged solely by consequences or by nonmoral values, but who do not attempt, as we shall, to integrate their views within a larger teleology.

The chapter's prime purpose, however, is, not to perfect the teleological approach, but to test it and prepare subsequent testing. For our concern is still the one previously announced. Here in part two we wish to examine rather fully how Christians have arrived at their moral judgments so as to determine, in part three, how they should. And our historical survey is only half complete. Christian moral reasoning reveals other trends besides the teleological; other arguments and theories appear, in real or apparent conflict with those of chapter 4. The present chapter lists a series of such countercases and asks of each whether it does in fact diverge from teleological thinking, and if so, how and why. For most of these samples, like the preceding, speak for multitudes, and an analytic account of Christian moral reasoning, attempting an overall assessment, cannot ignore the classes they represent.

When I speak of genuine and not just apparent conflict, I have a contrast like the following in mind. On the one hand, if A bases his prediction of rain on the look of the sky, B on barometric readings, and C on the latest weather report, their criteria do not vary; they are talking about rain in the same sense of "rain" (III, B). Thus, though one uses one clue and another another, their predictions should agree, and their reasoning, though diverse, is not opposed. If, however, A grounds a moral verdict on value-balance (chapter 4), B on natural form (V, D), C on causal sequence (V, F), and D on the arbitrary will of God (VI, B, 2), no common criterion of right and wrong underlies their varied arguments. Conflicting standards are at work, calling for different judgments. This latter sort of divergence, more radical and more decisive (III, B), merits special scrutiny.

In a chapter so focused a reminder seems advisable; like Sidgwick I would underscore that "I have wished to keep the reader's attention throughout directed to the processes rather than the results of ethical thought: and have therefore never stated as my own any positive practical conclusions"[2] (on abortion, contraception, organ transplants, divorce and remarriage, etc.). Nor, for that matter, have I assessed the factual or ethical soundness of the processes themselves, save sometimes from a methodological standpoint, or tried to assure that both sides of an option or all aspects of a practical issue are presented. Nor have I searched out the best, most up-to-date treatments, in the manner of an anthologist of current moral problems. My interest is historical and methodological.

No doubt the reader is accustomed by now to this focus on method and so may not be disconcerted by the heterogeneity of the topics and authors treated in pursuance of the purposes just stated. Here, however, no common thread — not even a shared mode of reasoning — connects the varied members of the series as in the preceding chapter. This fact is significant. It shows that even were the examples all genuinely opposed to the value-balancing approach and even did they represent, collectively, a greater mass of Christian reasoning than that approach does, still they would not constitute a coherent alternative. This point will be considered systematically in chapter 6 after the series is complete. It needed mention here lest the reader be put off by the apparent disorder. The order in what follows is the same as before: the focus is on method, and specifically now on the relation of these samples to those in the first series.

A. Counsel versus Precept

Our investigation of contrary trends, distinct from or opposed to the value-balancing approach, cannot be confined to works of moral theology. The very distinction between moral and ascetical theology, in recent Catholic tradition, merits close scrutiny. Why, for example, in the university where I taught till recently, is there an Institute of Spirituality in addition to the Faculty of Theology, with its numerous courses on Christian morality? The uninformed might suppose that spirituality treats fine points, whereas moral theology lays foundations; or that spirituality centers on states of soul, while moral theology investigates conduct. A more realistic explanation, however, is the age-old distinction between counsel and precept, understood in a way which would seem to conflict with the teleological approach in ethics, so to constitute major evidence against the thesis that that approach represents the mainstream in Christian moral reasoning. The conflict takes shape as follows.

The situationist or value ethician proclaims freedom from unyielding precepts, on behalf of human needs, and so presents his position as liberating. Yet opponents have contended that just the opposite is true: the approach is excessively rigid. For traditional preceptive ethics left large areas of freedom, in which the better thing was merely counseled, not required; whereas the value approach is exigent in every case: it imposes the better thing. Peter Knauer develops the objection as follows:

> To know whether a reason is proportionate or not, one is accustomed to compare it with other values which may be compromised by the bad effects of the act. It will be said that one must attempt to determine which of the different values in question has the highest spiritual dignity. There will be question then of choosing from among several different values the one which is *highest*.

At the very least, this solution runs the risk of rigorism. It recognizes no distinction between the good and the better: for it, if an action is not the best it must be bad. But such an assertion runs counter to the spirit of a morality which takes the good as its starting point. This morality of charity aspires to the most perfect by counsel and not by obligation; it rigorously excludes only sin; in the realm of what is good, it assures full freedom.[3]

Joseph Fletcher accepts the challenge head-on: "The motive and purpose behind law, however hidden it may be, is to *minimize obligation*, to make it clear exactly how much you must do *and no more*. Grace, on the other hand, refuses to put a ceiling or a floor on concern for the neighbor. Love, unlike law, sets no carefully calculated limits on obligation; it seeks the most good possible in every situation. It maximizes or optimizes obligation."[4] Or, as Paul Ramsey succinctly states the case: "'Everything is lawful, everything is permitted which Christian love permits' also means 'everything is demanded which Christian love requires.' The former is Christian liberty, the latter is slavery to Christ. The former, Christian leniency; the latter, Christian self-severity."[5]

"Christian *self*-severity," Ramsey says, for it makes a difference whether one is judging oneself or another. In the latter case one is slower to condemn or to impose an obligation. Reactions also vary according to the magnitude of the divergence among competing alternatives and the clarity with which the disparity is seen. If we fix on cases where the value-gap is great and clearly perceived, we are inclined to assert obligation, especially if we are judging ourselves. If, instead, we consider matters of little consequence, or important choices where the discrepancy is slight or only dimly perceived, we find the terminology of obligation inappropriate, and positively distasteful if we are judging another.[6]

In both instances we experience the subtle influence not only of the facts but also of our accustomed ways of speaking. Words like "duty," "obligation," and "sin" do indeed express value estimates, but they also reflect degree.[7] They are, as it were, heavy artillery, reserved for larger targets and severer criticism. The ethician who notes the similarity of lesser targets and insists on using the same terms for them is guilty, therefore, of *semantic* rigorism; he is right about all the facts— the similarity of the value configuration and the difference in degree (which he too recognizes)—but wrong in the term he applies. For he has failed to note the relevance of degree. His opponent, on the other hand, often commits the same basic error: he overlooks the possibility that the cases form a continuum but that the moral terms cover only part of it.[8]

The moment we reflect on our everyday use of terms, we see how common is this pattern. Consider, for instance, a word like "hot" or "cold": no sharp line, no qualitative discontinuity, marks the transition from hot to warm or from cold to cool. The qualitative continuum continues, but the word does not. And so it is with "sin": no quantum gap separates sin from defect or "positive imperfection."

The semantic roots of the impression come still more fully into view if we consider word pairs like "loud" and "quiet," "good" and "bad," "ugly" and "beautiful," "sharp" and "dull." Many knives are neither sharp nor dull, many paintings neither ugly nor beauiful, many books neither good nor bad, many motors neither loud nor quiet. But no name — no analog of "cool" or "warm" or "tepid" — designates their intermediate condition. Lost in a semantic limbo, they may appear discontinuous, therefore, with items at either end. It is as though they did not belong in the same series. Now, a similar gray zone stretches between what we are obliged to do and what we are obliged not to do. It is the area where we have "no obligation," where morality, accordingly, seems no longer to apply. And verbally it does not: the qualitative continuum continues but words like "duty" and "obliged" leave off.

Given such a semantic situation and theoreticians' leanings, debate about the reach of obligation becomes predictable. We hunger so for unity and coherence and attend so little to words. Accordingly, when we notice the connection between obligation and value imbalance, we are inclined to state an obligation wherever an imbalance occurs, no matter how slight. We feel constrained to do so for consistency's sake.[9] Our "theory" requires it, regardless of usage. Others, sensing exaggeration, feel obliged to reject our account, even where it applies. For they too must be consistent.[10] Whether the terms we use require such "consistency" we may easily fail to consider. (It is as though we felt constrained to call a jaywalker a criminal or a naughty child a sinner.)

Section B of the last chapter cited some reasons why a teleologist, too, might distinguish between matters of precept and matters of mere counsel. The present section has now added another: the question of degree. If, for instance, a person is offered the choice between delicious pizza and digestible stew, few would insist that if the value balance tips to digestion over taste, or vice versa, the person is obliged. Obligations come in larger sizes. Once again, therefore, we cannot conclude that the counsel-precept distinction indicates a nonteleological criterion at work in Christian thinking. Closer scrutiny might, of course, reveal some such criterion behind the distinction, at least on certain occasions;

but I have not detected any, nor do the nonteleological criteria soon to be considered appear likely sources of the distinction.

B. "Second Time" versus "Third Time"

From the discussion of exceptionless norms in the preceding chapter and of counsels in the preceding section, the reader may now surmise what developments I had in mind when I spoke of the new importance attaching to situational decision-making and therefore to Saint Ignatius' classic treatment of the topic (IV, C). According to a long-dominant view absolute precepts govern large tracts of life, whereas other areas, being merely of counsel, lie outside the precincts of morality altogether. In the former areas deliberation on an individual case was excluded; in the latter it was not recognized as ethical. Now both limitations are increasingly questioned. Catholics as well as Protestants more readily acknowledge that even the best of precepts may require occasional testing and that no vital issues are "merely of counsel." Within this double movement Ignatius' discussion assumes unrestricted moral relevance: it applies to all areas, including those "of precept," and all areas are of ethical concern.

We have seen his description of the third time "when a correct and good choice of a way of life may be made." The other two "times," less evidently teleological in inspiration, must now be considered:

> The first time is when God our Lord so moves and attracts the will, that, without doubt or the power of doubting, such a devoted soul follows what has been pointed out to it, as St. Paul and St. Matthew did when they followed Christ our Lord.
>
> The second time is when much light and knowledge is obtained by experiencing consolations and desolations, and by experience of the discernment of various spirits.[11]

The Spirit blows where it wills (Jn. 3:8) — sometimes strongly, so that there is no mistaking the direction ("first time"); sometimes gently and intermittently, so that one must attend more carefully to detect its direction ("second time"). Ignatius believed that we can both know its sound — that is, recognize the movement as coming from God — and discern its direction. He provides detailed instructions on how to do so. Yet there is no "method" of divine inspiration, as there is a method of calculating reasons for and against ("third time"). The Spirit breathes where and when *it* will, for reasons we do not comprehend.

The modern man — perhaps even a Christian — who does not believe in a personal God who deals personally with his creatures will naturally prefer the third time and dismiss or reinterpret the first and second times. The person who, on the contrary, not only believes in God's action in history and in the human soul but has had some experience of that action, as Ignatius had, will consider such guidance a definite possibility and may prefer that means (first and second times) to his own poor (though not unaided) efforts (third time). The problem will be how to discern the divine action and its direction.

From God, says Ignatius, come "consolations" — "interior peace, spiritual joy, hope, faith, love, tears and elevation of mind" — while from the enemy come just the contrary: disquiet, sadness, dryness, propensity to low thoughts and base desires.[12] So the retreatant, "proceeding in his meditations on Christ our Lord, should note, when he finds himself in consolation, in what direction God moves him, and likewise for desolation."[13] (When he is full of faith, hope, and charity, what does he wish to do? How, on the contrary, is he inclined when disturbed, vain, angry, fearful?) Or, "when he feels consolation, he puts before God first one then the other of the alternatives to be chosen and notes to which side the consolation inclines him, in which he finds more peace, more joy, more spiritual relish, in a word, on what side he feels more the effects of consolation in mind, heart, and will."[14]

"If our preference during consolation," writes Piet Penning de Vries, "agrees with our aversion during desolation, then God's will becomes clearer."[15] Likewise, if our discernment of the spirits moving us agrees with the advantages and disadvantages we note and weigh, we are reassured. Third time agrees with second.[16] But suppose the two conflict. What then? Which verdict should we follow?[17]

José Calveras replies: "That which shows greater signs of sureness, after we have reviewed the reasons of the third time and examined the psychological data of the second time more attentively. If the latter scrutiny reveals nothing contrary to reason and if the indications of the good and evil spirits are more decisive than the pros and cons of the third time, we should decide once for all in favor of the second-time choice. But if the distinctive psychological data prove inadequate, or the indications of the spirits are unclear, on the one hand, and on the other hand the reasons for and against, when well weighed, reveal clearly enough what alternative is more in keeping with the divine service, in that case it will be wiser to follow what the third time indicates. . . . Such is the solution given in the present directory, chapter XXVIII, number 9."[18]

To reach a satisfactory solution, Calveras is obliged to avoid the truly troublesome hypothesis, namely, apparent clarity in both of these different "times," yet opposite verdicts. However, this dilemma may be a false one, and the hypothesis unlikely. For second-time motions are not mere feelings, but "thoughts."[19] And if "hope, faith, and charity" point clearly to one option — if it glows with value when seen by their light — how can it be a clear loser when weighed in the balance of values?

Notice, however, that even did such conflict arise — even did the verdict of discernment diverge from that of value calculation — the disagreement would demonstrate no basic opposition. It might then be as in weather prediction, where different methods on occasion give different results (as do even identical methods applied by different people) without the methods conflicting. Human error is possible whatever the method used — barometers or bird signs, value tables or discernment of spirits. Only if both methods were infallibly applied would the divergent answers reveal divergent criteria.

C. Jesus on Divorce and Remarriage

Ignatius offered his advice for those cases where, as Saint Paul put it, he had "no instructions from the Lord." There were others where he did. And there value calculations would seem to be ruled out. Of course we might still suppose that such considerations underlay the commands. But in the prime instance in the Gospels of an apparently absolute precept, it might seem that Jesus adopted, not the same approach as in the synagogue (IV, A) with regard to Sabbath healing, but quite another, akin to that of the Pharisees.

> The question was put to him: "Is it lawful for a man to divorce his wife?" This was to test him. He asked in return, "What did Moses command you?" They answered, "Moses permitted a man to divorce his wife by note of dismissal." Jesus said to them, "It was because your minds were closed that he made this rule for you; but in the beginning, at the creation, God made them male and female. For this reason a man shall leave his father and mother, and be made one with his wife; and the two shall become one flesh. It follows that they are no longer two individuals: they are one flesh. What God has joined together, man must not separate."
>
> When they were indoors again the disciples questioned him about this matter; he said to them, "Whoever divorces his wife and marries another commits adultery against her: so too, if she divorces her husband and marries another, she commits adultery." (Mk. 10:2-12)

Jesus' citation of Genesis in support of marital permanence recalls earlier connections we have seen (IV, A), linking Sabbath observance with the Exodus (Deut. 5:15) and with the days of creation (Ex. 20:8–11). Analogous thinking occurs elsewhere in the New Testament and especially in the Old but is so unfamiliar to us today that we may automatically assimilate it to moral argumentation of the kinds we know.

In particular, we may take the reference to creation as a premise in a syllogistic argument establishing marital permanence. And observing that the premise does not state a value, we may conclude that the argument is nonteleological. And noting the apparent rigidity of the resulting prohibition, we may surmise that the underlying rationale is not simply nonteleological but antiteleological. "Right" and "wrong" have changed their sense, if indeed they ever possessed a teleological meaning for Jesus.

Yet how might the creation of male and female function as a premise, in what conceivable syllogism, excluding dissolution? Indeed, what such argument has ever been adduced as Jesus' implicit meaning? The attempt would not only look ludicrous but would inevitably conflict with traditional Christian teaching concerning marital permanence. After all, man and woman become one flesh in fornication, prostitution, adultery, nonsacramental marriages, unions subsequently dissolved in virtue of the Pauline and Petrine "privileges." Yet who would declare in all these cases: "What God has thus joined by creating sex, man must not separate"?

A more plausible line of interpretation, therefore, is that suggested by the practice of Jesus' own day. Jewish morality was covenant morality in the form of law. And "when once the law has been fixed as divinely authorized, the simplest way of making it applicable for a later generation with new circumstances is the unwritten law of interpretation, which has been used so widely in Judaism, Islam and Christianity. Strictly speaking, this method is a legal fiction, just as much as is the legal ruling on some fresh set of circumstances given by a judge to-day, which is avowedly based on the precedents of the past, though actually it goes beyond them and so makes new law."[20]

In such a procedure teleological considerations may be decisive yet not rise explicitly to the surface. Thus "the Pharisees went a very long way in their attempts to attach practical and prudential rules by slender threads to Old Testament texts of various kinds, often with dubious relevance and appropriateness. Their starting point was the belief that the actual practices of which they approved must have been valid, and that therefore the divine Law must somehow have authorised them."[21] Jesus did a better job, we may surmise — relating his precept to fundamentals and citing an appropriate text—but basically the same kind of job.[22] His citation confirms, in the currently accepted manner, a conclusion based on other considerations. Accordingly, there is no need to suppose that his motivation shifted here from the concern for human needs evident in the synagogue.

The line of interpretation I have suggested is not coercive, especially in detail. But the only point at issue here is whether the account in Mark 10:2–12 runs counter to that in Mt. 12:9–14 and to teleological reasoning in general. And quite clearly it does not. For there to be conflict, the creation of man and woman, cited by Jesus, would have to figure not merely as a symbol of the divine will for marriage but also as a nonteleological, indeed antiteleological, premise of some kind. Of what kind, though? No plausible answer comes to mind. (See, for instance, the paragraph below or run through the list in VI, B.) Hence nothing but vague surmises weigh in the balance against massive evidence elsewhere that Jesus did indeed desire above all that "they should have life and have it more abundantly." He here urged a rule, to be sure, with impressive finality; but for that, as we have seen, teleological explanations are available (IV, F, G). And as we shall note later on, how final the rule really was (IX, E, 5) and how decisive for future practice (IX, E, 6) is far from self-evident from the text.

D. Arguments from Nature

The outward form of Jesus' argument against divorce and remarriage resembles that of numerous subsequent arguments, which appeal to nature and, implicitly or explicitly, to the will of the Creator revealed therein. Paul, for example, argued: "Does not Nature herself teach you that while flowing locks disgrace a man, they are a woman's glory? For her locks were given for covering" (1 Cor. 11:14–15). Likewise, "some hold that the very nature and purpose of speech, the manifestation of one's thoughts, suffices to prove the intrinsic evil of lying, since the lie by definition violates this nature and purpose."[23] A similar tack has been taken in arguments against artificial contraception:

> What assumptions does the general argument based on nature rest on? Why is it wrong to impede insemination? Why must nature be the ultimate standard? These questions may most fruitfully be explored in the statements of Thomas Aquinas. He articulates what is implicit in earlier writers, and he guides a multitude of his successors.

The basic assumptions of Aquinas are that natural coitus was instituted by God; that the order of nature here is distinguished from the rational order; that natural coitus as instituted by God should not be altered by man. . . . Violation of this natural order is an affront to God, though "no other person is injured."[24]

The difficulties for this position are well known and fairly obvious.[25] I shall not dwell on them. For here, as throughout the chapter, it is not the truth of the solution that interests us, nor even the validity of the argument form, but its relation to teleology as a possible counter-case. Hence our choice of this sample and this particular variant of natural-law reasoning.

"Natural law" means various things.[26] The adjective "natural" may, for instance, indicate that an ethical code or requirement is (a) dictated by nature's given form (as here), or (b) determined by nature's end (e.g., man's ultimate end), or (c) naturally known (not declared verbatim by a divine or human legislator). And within each of these senses further diversity is found. If from these several genera I have selected but a single species of a single genus, it is because that species alone poses a challenge to consistent value-balancing. The point can be illustrated by sampling other approaches of the three kinds just listed, for instance in Aquinas' writings; then noting their compatibility with teleology; then focusing more closely on the one species where conflict appears. Here, then, are some samplings from Saint Thomas, type by type.

(a) For a start we may note the difference between the present argument, concerning the predetermined form of the act, and Aquinas' frequent citation of natural tendencies, as in the discussion of self-defense (IV, D). "There is in man, first of all, a tendency toward his own natural good which he shares with all substances, namely the desire which every substance has for its own continued existence according to its nature, and in keeping with this inclination whatever preserves man's life and prevents its destruction belongs to natural law."[27] More generally, "whatever man has a natural tendency toward, reason of its nature perceives as good, and therefore to be actively pursued, whereas it apprehends their contraries as bad, and therefore to be shunned."[28]

People are sometimes inclined, however, to "go against nature" — to masturbate, say, or impede conception. So it might seem that the two norms — natural form and natural prompting — may diverge. Thomas deals with the difficulty by distinguishing actual urges from natural and by defining the latter as reasonable, well-ordered inclinations.[29]

(b) In that case, though, reason requires some other guide than sheer inclination. Thomas, like Aristotle, points to man's final end: "In matters of practice the end has the force of a principle, because from it derive the reasons for adopting the means."[30] Consequently the whole of life should be directed by this truth: "There can be no complete and final happiness for us save in the vision of the divine essence."[31] Such is our destiny, such our guiding goal.[32]

(c) Natural law in the sense of what man's destiny requires or in the sense of what his nature inclines him to differs from natural law in a further, related acceptation, which Aquinas called the strictest sense[33]: "Natural law is what nature has taught all animals." All animals, not just man. So man's specific inclinations — for example, his "appetite for the good of his nature as rational"[34] — fall outside this definition. So too do any more detailed matters which, though related to self-preservation or preservation of the species, nature has not taught all animals.[35]

Thomas elsewhere writes, however, that in man "there is a participation of eternal reason, through which he has a natural inclination to the right act and end, and this participation of eternal law in the rational creature is called 'natural law.'"[36] Like any body of law, this one consists of general principles,[37] not of their applications. The latter must be drawn by prudence, considering particular circumstances.[38]

The approaches we have been sampling, all different from the tack Thomas took against contraception, pose no special problem for teleological ethics. The truth all animals know may be teleological. The law reason discerns may have a teleological base. Beneficence may be the criterion of "natural" tendencies. Pursuit of one's final end may follow a similar route.

Faithful, therefore, to this chapter's rationale, we need say no more about natural law in general and may attend to only our initial sample, concerning contraception, and the reasoning it exemplifies. How and why does that argumentation appear to conflict with value-balancing? First because of its absolute verdict, which value-balancing would be hard put to justify, whether in the act-utilitarian manner (IV, E) or the rule-utilitarian (IV, F, G). Second because it exhibits no evident concern for varied circumstances, possible consequences, or contrary values; nature simply imposes its ban without possible appeal. Third because these two reasons make it difficult to suppose hidden teleological meaning beneath the argument's expressions. Since these three reasons apply to numerous demonstrations with similar surface structure (arguments concerning lying, shaving, position in intercourse, cutting one's hair, artificial insemination, *in vitro* fertilization, and so on, as well as contraception), we may recognize here a significant deviation from teleological reasoning.

One might hesitate, though, to speak of an "opposed line of reasoning," for what line is it? What precisely is meant by saying a certain mode of activity (say a certain form of coitus) is "natural" or "instituted by God" and therefore sacrosanct? Was walking with forward progress instituted by God, and is any other way immoral, and should we therefore never jog in place or walk on a treadmill to have our heart checked? What criterion other than the teleological permits us to pass from what the Creator has done to what he would have us do?

Noonan casts some light on these puzzles. It would be incorrect, he suggests, "to suppose that the value placed on insemination in coitus had no reference to its ultimate generative effect. If coitus was taken as sacred, it was because generation was only achievable through this means. . . . Because the sexual act might be generative, and because generation was an important function, the theologian intuited that generation was the normal function. A typical or essential act of coitus, which was generative, was therefore supposed. Other acts of coitus which did not achieve this purpose were regarded as generically generative but accidentally frustrated."[39] To some extent, therefore, what we here find is confused teleology, not opposed deontology.[40]

E. Intrinsically Immoral Means

Of reasoning like that in Saint Thomas' critique of contraception Joseph Arntz observes: "What a difficult dilemma this way of seeing things has occasioned in sexual ethics is well known. But this is not the only sector in which inadequate comprehension of natural law has become manifest in our day. Similar difficulties arise, for example, in discussion concerning the problem of a transplant from a living donor. There is then frequently talk of mutilation, since human integrity is affected. To the query 'What integrity?' the answer is roughly: 'That given by nature!'"[41]

Frequent use is also then made of the saying "A good end does not justify an evil means." And this venerable dictum, so often taken as an unquestionable norm of sound morality, would seem to clash directly with the value-balancing approach. It would appear to deny that we may simply balance values, present or future, and judge an act accordingly. An evil means is not negotiable. So let us observe how the principle is stated and applied in this specific instance, the condemnation of transplants.

Gisbert Sölch summarizes as follows the lengthy argumentation of L. Bender:

An organ transplant consists of two distinct acts (operations), which are related as means and end: The excision of a healthy organ from a healthy person (the means) and its implantation in another person, in whom the corresponding organ is lacking or inoperative as a result of illness.

As Catholic moral teaching agrees, such a double act is illegitimate when the act (the operation) which serves as means to the end is intrinsically immoral (i.e. of its nature). In that case it cannot be justified by even the noblest end (in our case the cure of a sick person).

In the light of this theological teaching, the verdict on organ transplants is clear. For the operation that initiates the transplant and which consists in removing a healthy organ from a healthy person, without doubt falls under the concept 'mutilation'; and by the general agreement of theologians, mutilation—with two exceptions—is to be judged immoral.[42]

The prohibition of evil means here undergoes a crucial qualification: the evil means is *morally* evil and *therefore* not permissible. On this inference all would agree. The most thoroughgoing teleologist would not judge differently. For him, too, if an action is morally evil, then it should not be performed. But in determining whether it is morally evil, he would insist that we take consequences too into account. And this Bender refuses to do. Why?

Not simply because God alone has complete dominion over man's body and life, as moralists have often maintained, for instance, with regard to suicide.[43] For that answer, as Bender notes, elicits an immediate request for proof. Rather "the thesis 'Man does not have dominion over his members' rests on a further thesis, to wit; 'Man may not diminish or mutilate himself.'"[44] So how is that thesis to be established?

Bender's reply sounds momentarily teleological. He recognizes that a blood transfusion, too, consists of two acts—extraction, then infusion—and that the first act serves as means to the desired end. But in this case the means is not "intrinsically evil." "For the difference between cutting off a hand, say, and extracting a small quantity of blood is precisely that the former is a diminishment of the person (he loses his bodily integrity and can no longer do what a whole person can) whereas the latter is not. Without a hand, a person's body is defective, incomplete. A slight loss of blood, on the contrary, causes only a slight, passing weakness."[45] The loss is less notable, Bender would seem to be saying, so more readily justified—teleologically.

However, if the more notable loss is balanced by a still more notable gain, may it not be similarly warranted? Consider the traditional exceptions to the veto on mutilation: "1. A diseased organ which would otherwise threaten the whole body may be removed or rendered useless; 2. a criminal may be punished for his crime through disfigurement or the loss of an organ, provided the severity of the punishment is proportional to the gravity of the crime."[46] If the overall welfare of the person himself, or that of society, thus suffices to legitimate mutilation, why not the welfare of another individual? Why may a mother save her own life through the removal of an organ but not that of her child through a transplant?

"Since man is self-ordained," Bender states at one point, "and not a useful good, ordained to the welfare or utility of another creature, rational or nonrational, it follows that to lessen him for the utility of another creature, even if that other is a *human being,* is an action contrary to man's nature and to the order established by God among creatures. To perform such an act, for example excising an organ so as to insert it in another's body, is to treat a human being (another or oneself) as something useful, as something subordinated to the good or utility of other creatures."[47]

It is not evident that this critique does more than restate the case to be judged, with veiled synonymy, then beg the question. To be sure, the mother's healthy kidney is useful to the child who has none and is "subordinated" to the child's welfare when used to save its life, just as a blood donor's gift is useful to the one who receives it and is subordinated, in an obvious sense, to his well-being. But what is wrong with such subordination? When and why and in what further sense would subordination be illicit? Why discriminate between these two cases, condemning the one and condoning the other? Are the divine intentions altruistic only up to a point, and do they then enjoin the strictest egoism? No coherent response emerges from Bender's discussion; no alternative, nonteleological principle illumines his discriminations.

In their quandary analysts of such arguments have surmised that "the problem seems to reside in a system or theory that attaches exclusive moral importance to the physical structure of an act."[48] Particularly with respect to transplants, traditional reasoning "seems to overemphasize the importance of the *physical* effect in the judgment about the *moral* value of the human action."[49] Some basis exists for this assessment in the present typical reasoning as in that to come. However, the implantation of a kidney or a cornea is as physical as its excision, and the resulting condition of the recipient is as physical as that of the donor. Thus in the broad family of cases represented by our sample (see VI, A) conclusions like Bender's repeatedly result, not from narrowly focusing on the *physical*, but from focusing *narrowly* on the physical — that is, from including just so much and no more, labeling it "intrinsically evil," and understanding this label in a moral sense.[50]

This move has become rarer of late, and practically no one any longer objects to organ transplants. However, our present aim is, not to report the most up-to-date thinking on transplants, but to chronicle major trends, past and present, that apparently run counter to the rule of maximum value. So we have gone back a few decades to Bender and this frequent phenomenon: means recognized by all as unfortunate, but mysteriously metamorphosed into intrinsically immoral means, which are therefore impermissible regardless of circumstances and prospective consequences. In the next section the mystery lifts. An intelligible rule appears, applicable in this and other cases. From a mere countersyndrome we pass to an explicit counterprinciple, eliciting similar arguments in similar cases and leading to similar, nonteleological verdicts.

F. Direct and Indirect

Somewhere, somehow, for some unexplained reason, Bender departs from the teleological perspective and so draws a different conclusion. Just where, how, and why such departures may occur appears in Richard McCormick's account. The tradition he reports (but does not defend) in the following passage poses a major challenge to unrestricted value-balancing:

> The distinction between what is directly voluntary and indirectly voluntary has been a staple of Catholic moral thought for centuries. It has been used to face many practical conflict-situations where an evil can be avoided or a more or less necessary good achieved only when another evil is reluctantly caused. In such situations the evil caused as one goes about doing good has been viewed as justified or tolerable under a fourfold condition. (1) The action is good or indifferent in itself; it is not morally evil. (2) The intention of the agent is upright, that is, the evil effect is sincerely not intended. (3) The evil effect must be equally immediate causally with the good effect, for otherwise it would be a means to the good effect and would be intended. (4) There must be a proportionately grave reason for allowing the evil to occur. If these conditions are fulfilled, the resultant evil was referred to as an "unintended byproduct" of the action, only indirectly voluntary and justified by the presence of a proportionately grave reason.[51]

The practical importance of this distinction, as McCormick then notes, can be gathered from the areas where it has been applied: "killing (self-defense, warfare, abortion, euthanasia, suicide), risk to life (dangerous missions, rescue operations, experimentation), sterilization, contraception, sexual reactions, cooperation in another's evil action, scandal." Doubtless organ transplants may be added to this list. For the immorality of such operations, once widely asserted by ethicians, follows immediately from the third condition cited. The excision of the organ is an evil and is not "equally immediate causally with the good effect," but it is a means to that effect. Thus, failing to pass the third of the four tests, transplants are not permissible.[52]

So interpreted and explained, the negative verdict might seem not to clash with teleology, after all. For the focus has broadened to include a subjective feature. The action is judged subjectively wrong because the intention is wrong, whereas teleological reasoning of the kind we have been considering abstracts from intentionality (see chapter 2). It looks to the act to be performed and lets subjective rightness take care of itself: anyone who does the right thing for the reason that makes it right acts with a right intention.

The conflict, however, is not illusory, but genuine and serious. For the third condition McCormick lists not only yields different verdicts than those reached by value-reasoning within an objective focus; it does so for reasons that challenge that focus itself. "You may not ignore intention," it implicitly warns, "even in prospective moral estimates. For the objective structure of acts determines their subjective figuration; and any structure that entails an evil intention must be rejected for that reason, no matter how acceptable it may appear objectively." Indeed, the teleologist would appear to be hoist with his own petard if this objection holds. For it means that the subjective dimension, which he ignores, decisively affects the overall balance of values, which is his criterion. Among the predictable concomitants of a contemplated action is the intention of the one who performs it, and any act which entails an immoral intention thereby merits exclusion in virtue of a higher calculus of values than the teleologist envisions. The inner evil, being a moral evil, outweighs any nonmoral good we might invoke in the action's favor.

The reply to all this seems fairly obvious. Nonmoral evils adopted as means to proportionate goods do not vitiate intention. The lumberjack who fells redwoods to make houses, the rancher who butchers Herefords to feed humans, the surgeon who makes incisions to remove tumors are not necessarily malevolent. The structure of their actions does not fix their motivation in morally relevant fashion. It does not de-

termine, that is, whether the lumberjack seeks the redwoods' decima-
tion as well as the resultant timbers or paycheck; it does not dictate
whether the rancher intends the cattle's slaughter, for itself, nor
whether the surgeon desires the wounds he inflicts, as an end and not
just as means. And it is only such intending of objective evil for itself
which, by common reckoning, would render their actions subjectively
immoral.

Hence McCormick's examples and their numerous kin, when put
beneath the lens, tend to corroborate the strictly objective viewpoint
proposed in chapter 2 and exemplified throughout chapter 4. Here,
where that restriction of focus is challenged most strongly, we can see
how legitimate and important it is. In every such case it really does suffice, even subjectively, to consider just the act's own structure: the evil
means, the good effect, the balance between the two. If the good outweighs the evil, the act is objectively justified. If the agent performs it
for that reason, his or her deed is subjectively moral.

G. The Order of Charity

The person with two good kidneys shares with him who has none.
This seems perfectly legitimate. Indeed it might even appear obligatory. For the Gospel tells us to do unto others as we would have them do
unto us. So how can we abound while our neighbor is in want? How can
our family, or our country, abound while other families, or other countries, lack the necessities of life? Should not we forego our comforts and
conveniences so that they may live? Is not that what any realistic calculation of values requires? Yet is it what most people, or even most Christians, feel obliged to do?

A. C. Ewing states the conundrum sharply. On the one hand,
"there can hardly be any doubt that, even if we allow for any indirect
evil effects which might accrue, in most cases money given to any even
tolerably well managed charity will do much more good by relieving
the suffering of those in distress than would be done by using the same
money to increase the pleasure of a person who is at all tolerably comfortable by enabling him to have a more pleasant house, better furniture, more tobacco, more holiday travel, etc."[53] On the other hand:

> It still seems plain to me, and I am sure would seem so to almost
> everybody else that, if a man were to deprive his wife and children
> against their will of all comforts and purchasable pleasures, leav-
> ing them only bare necessaries, on the ground that he could use
> the money thus saved to preserve several families from a greater

pain or loss of happiness than he inflicted on his own by giving it to a charitable organization he would be acting wrongly not rightly.[54]

I quote Ewing, not because he is a noted Christian spokesman, but because in stating this position, apparently so opposed to a straight reckoning of values, he speaks for countless Christians. He articulates the inarticulate majority viewpoint, not only in his verdict but also in the way he weights the question. Why, one wonders, does he imagine the man's wife and children to be opposed? For suppose they were willing: Would their self-sacrifice then appear wrong to Ewing and to most people? And suppose the majority of citizens in a prosperous country were equally willing: What would that be but a new creation and resurrection from the dead?

Still, more than sheer self-interest stands behind the common verdict. Discount human selfishness, and a difficulty still remains for single-level, evenhanded charity. Not one, however, that impugns teleological ethics. For the truth which remains in Ewing's claim is teleological: "Once ethical universalism has been accepted," writes Bruno Schüller, "and unreserved assent is given to the obligation of mutual charity, there is no evading the question whether each individual must now concern himself personally about the welfare of every other person, whether, when each cares for each in the long run nobody is really cared for, whether ethical universalism brings about a moral purification and deepening, to be sure, but also a worsening of man's earthly condition. If we consider this an unlikely inference, and one not drawn by Christ himself from his gospel, then we must acknowledge that a distinction and distribution of duties is called for. This in turn requires that priorities be set. Priorities necessitate distinctions such as those between near, nearer, and nearest. Of themselves they set no limit on love as agapé, but they do see to it that this love does in fact lead to a better existence for men on earth."[55]

One is reminded of the Pauline, Teilhardian comparison of a society with a body. In a living organism one for all and all for one is the rule: each cell, tissue, and organ subserves the common good, while the whole organism cares as it alone can for the good of each individual part. However, the relation of part to part is principally indirect, the direct influence of any one cell or tissue being felt within a limited radius. Each serves best the good of each other by fulfilling its own specific role within its own restricted sphere.

Something analogous is obviously true of society. But cell differs from cell, and so does person from person. Some resemble blood cells, traveling to distant parts; there is no telling to what individuals, in what lands, the medical or spiritual missionary may communicate new life. He is mobile by profession. Others resemble stay-at-home muscle cells, pumping the blood, swallowing the food, flexing the muscle, but interacting directly with only a few other cells within a restricted area. Whether in the body or in society, variations are endless. So how each person is to balance the order of charity with the priority of need is a delicate, difficult question which each must face alone.

To this comparison between society and organism, and to the reasoning it illustrates, there may be added a further consideration — teleological yet less utilitarian — briefly evoked by Sidgwick when he cites "duties that arise out of relations where affection normally exists, and where it ought to be cultivated, and where its absence is deplored if not blamed."[56] The networks of special affection which account for preferential treatment are themselves a precious aspect of human existence. "Each counts for one, no one for more than one" may aptly describe the affectivity of beehive or ant heap but fortunately does not reflect the patterns of intimacy and remoteness that characterize human society. The distinction might vanish, though, were human action, at variance with human feeling, to become entirely impartial. For among humans, if not among angels, the inner has need of the outer.

And yet there lingers a disturbing doubt. If, according to classic Christian teaching, a person may rightfully take from another what he needs to survive (see Saint Thomas in IV, D), how is the other not obliged to provide it? Are not right and obligation two sides of the same coin? Are not both determined by the balance of values, and is not the balance the same, no matter which way you look at it? Or is duty annulled by the mere remoteness of the indigent and their consequent inability to lay hands on what they so desperately need? Do not all people without exception have a right to at least minimal sustenance, so to more than hundreds of millions presently possess? We need not resolve this dilemma, such not being the purpose of this section or chapter, but may just observe that if the other, more prosperous millions think otherwise, they may be wrong but do not necessarily repudiate the theoretical norm of value-maximization. Teleological reasons like those we have seen, reinforced by egoism in the way we have noted and therefore by various rationalizations, may tilt the scales decisively in the direction Ewing indicates.

H. Verdict by Definition

Keen awareness of the complex interconnections of society, stressed in the previous section, characterizes John Noonan's comments on abortion:

A balanced moral judgment requires a sense of the limits, interrelations, and priority of values. It is the position of those generally opposed to abortion that a judgment preferring interests less than human life to human life is unbalanced, that a judgment denying a mother's fiduciary responsibility to her child is unbalanced, that a judgment making killing a principal part of the profession of a physician is unbalanced, that a judgment permitting agencies of the state to procure and pay for the destruction of the offspring of the poor or underprivileged is unbalanced. They contend that such judgments expand the right limits of a mother's responsibility for herself, destroy the fiduciary relation which is a central paradigm for the social bond, fail to relate to the physician's service to life and the state's care for its citizens. At stake in the acceptance of abortion is not a single value, life, against which the suffering of the mother or parents may be balanced. The values to be considered are the child's life, the mother's faithfulness to her dependent, the physician's commitment to preserving life; and in the United States today abortion cannot be discussed without awareness that if law does not prohibit it, the state will fund it, so that the value of the state's abstention from the taking of life is also at issue. The judgment which accepts abortion, it is contended, is unbalanced in subordinating these values to the personal autonomy of the mother and the social interest in population control.[57]

In many ways this is admirable. In particular it remedies realistically and effectively the myopic vision which mars so much discussion not only of this issue but of many others. Its horizons are broad. However, it does not avoid a danger which is equally prevalent in moral theology, especially in the discussion of the abortion issue, and which is still more widespread in philosophy and theology as a whole: the confusion of verbal issues with substantive.

"The main, though not the only, reason why abortion is condemned by Catholic moralists," writes J. F. Donceel, "is that it amounts to the killing of an innocent human being. This supposes that from the moment of conception the embryo is a human person. Nowadays the great majority of Catholic thinkers take for granted that it is, that from the start the fertilized ovum possesses a spiritual soul (theory of immediate animation)."[58] Noonan, however, does not simply take for granted the personhood of the fetus."To recognize a person," he argues, "is a moral decision; it depends on objective data but it also depends on the perceptions and inclinations and ends of the decision makers."[59] Thus "if a person could in no way perceive another person to be like himself, he would be incapable of moral response. If a person cannot perceive a cat or a tree as different from himself, he cuts off the possibility of argument. Debate should not end with pointing, but it must begin there."[60] So "the proponent of abortion is invited to consider the organism kicking the mother, swimming peacefully in amniotic fluid, responding to the prick of an instrument, being extracted from the womb, sleeping in death. Is the kicker or swimmer similar to him or to her? Is the response to pain like his or hers? Will his or her own face look much different in death?"[61]

The answer seems clear enough: "Somewhat similar, somewhat dissimilar. And the dissimilarity increases the less developed the fetus." But at no stage do we observe the word "person" or "human being." And in every case we may ask, in the manner of Wittgenstein: "Does it *follow* from the description that the fetus is a human being? How can a *proposition* (e.g. 'The fetus is a person') follow from the observation of the *fetus*?"[62] Were fetuses, or fetuses at this or that stage of development, regularly called human beings, there would be no problem. But they are not. Application of the expression "person," or "human being," like that of most words, has an imprecise border, and that is where these cases fall: on (or in) the border. So Noonan is correct in saying a decision is made when the fetus is judged to be human, but the decision is linguistic, not moral. As he rightly observes, the morally relevant thing is to *see* the *fetus;* the application of the label or refusal to apply it — so decisively important, perhaps, in a court of law[63] — has no moral significance. It follows and expresses one's moral commitment or value appraisal; it does not ground it.

It has been suggested that we do in fact speak of "unborn children" and that usage therefore vindicates Noonan's claim for fetus, embryo, or zygote. However, one might argue with equal validity that "prospective members" are members, "budding scholars" are scholars, "saints in the making" are saints, and so forth, or that when a person "plants radishes," he or she puts radishes (not radish seeds) in the ground. Closer still, the expression "dead men," as common as "unborn children," might be cited as proof that cadavers too have a right to life. The futility of such verbal considerations would then come clearly into view. Corpses have no rights because they are *dead;* our *calling* them men or women is ethically irrelevant. Likewise, if unborn children do have rights, it is because of what they are or will be, and not because, for these or other reasons, we decide with Noonan and others to call them human beings.

A like assessment seems called for when Noonan argues elsewhere: "To make a distinction between the rights of spermatozoa and the rights of the fertilized ovum is to respond to an enormous shift in possibilities.

As life itself is a matter of probabilities, as most moral reasoning is an estimate of probabilities, so it seems in accord with the structure of reality and the nature of moral thought to found a moral judgment on the change in probabilities here. At the point where the conceived being has a better than even chance of developing, he is a man."[64] One might as well conclude that a fertilized chicken egg is a chicken or that a sprouting bulb is already a tulip. The inference is clearly invalid and reflects the same confusion between verbal move and nonverbal. The probabilities Noonan cites really are relevant, for the reasons he states, but the subsequent labeling ("This is a man") is not.

Suppose I plant a pecan seedling, care for it a year or two, and then someone cuts it down. "Why trouble yourself?" he replies to my remonstrances. "It was only a seedling, not a tree, and gave no nuts or shade, nor adorned the landscape the way a fullgrown pecan tree does." I might let him have the word "tree"; it would not be worth arguing for. But I would still regret, as bitterly as ever, the loss of the nuts, the shade, the stately tree-to-be.

I have dwelt on Noonan's type of argumentation, and illustrated it a second time, for several reasons. First there is the fact that a departure here occurs from straight value-reasoning. In the next numbers we shall see arguments which seem to diverge from the teleological approach but do not; here we find reasoning which does not seem to diverge but does. The disputants would probably say that they disagree about the facts and therefore about the values involved, and so reach a different verdict. "And yet," as Milhaven observes, "the pertinent empirical data is limited and undisputed — what is not the case of most questions dividing Americans today, e.g., concerning the Vietnam war, various sexual behavior, law and order, responsibility of whites to blacks, etc. Those who affirm and those who deny that the fetus is a human person accept the same data of the sciences concerning it and use the same data to justify their affirmation or denial. A pretty puzzle, if it were not tragic."[65]

And considerably more than merely abortion is involved. "What determines when a being is human?" asks Noonan. "When is it lawful to kill? These questions are linked in any consideration of the morality of abortion. They are questions central to any morality for man."[66] "It is this question," concurs Fletcher, "how we are to define the *humanum*, which lies at the base of all serious talk about the quality of life. We cannot appraise quality or enumerate human values if we cannot first say what a human being is."[67] "In all these areas," writes Edward Stevens, "two questions call out for moral clarification: (1) What is the meaning of 'human life'? and (2) What are the moral limits of human 'control' over human life? . . . The first question directly relates to your philosophy of man. What criteria do you use to determine whether a truly *human* life is at stake?"[68]

Philosophers and theologians in general, and not just ethicians, tend to lose their way in such questions as these. Time and again the conceptual, the factual, and the evaluative become inextricably entangled, as in the debate on abortion. I have explained this syndrome elsewhere.[69] Here I shall just note briefly that its chief source is our blindness to language. At a first level we fail to recognize our moves for what they are, a revision of language. At a second, slightly more sophisticated level, we realize that explicitly or implicitly we are altering usage, drawing a boundary where none previously existed, but we suppose that the adjustment is required by our findings, or can be justified by other than pragmatic linguistic reasons, or can affect or even decide questions of fact or value. In this way even those who favor a teleological approach may be led to abandon it, unwittingly.[70]

I. "Absolute" Values

Other times the conflict seems evident and is declared insuperable:

Several examples are used by Connery and the critics of utilitarianism to show the impossibility of a teleological theory of norms. One concerns justice, the other fairness. Schüller speaks to both. The justice example is that of a sheriff in a Southern town faced with the alternatives in a rape case of framing a Negro suspect (whom he knows to be innocent) or carrying on a prolonged search for the real culprit. The immediate indictment and conviction of the suspect would save many lives and prevent other harmful consequences. If an action's moral rightness is determined solely by consequences, it is argued, the sheriff ought to frame the one innocent man — a conclusion that shocks our moral sensitivities, but one that a teleologist would be forced to draw.

Schüller argues that a teleologist would not be forced to draw any such conclusion. Overlooked completely is the fact that in the example not only is there question of the life of one versus the lives of many others; the entire institution of criminal law is at stake. The conclusion that the sheriff should frame the one to save others is only justified if this conclusion, raised to a universally acknowledged and practiced rule, would actually promote the common good. Since that is at least highly doubtful, such an exception must be judged contrary to the common good and unjust.[71]

It is not suggested, notice, that this one act would undermine the institution of criminal law, any more than an individual violation would weaken the rules of a game. The point is rather that the rules should prohibit this move. However, as we noted earlier (IV, F, 3), it is sometimes best to violate even a good rule. Rule-utilitarianism must countenance occasional exceptions to its norms. So why not here? Because the sheriff's illegal action, if known, would weaken respect for the law? But "an occasional act of injustice here and there does not undermine the whole beneficial effect of the practice of justice, and, if such actions are performed in secret, they may sometimes not even produce any harmful effects at all."[72] "As the example is set up, only the sheriff, the innocent victim and the guilty man and not the general public, would know there had been a frame-up. Further, even if a few others knew, this would not mean that everyone knew."[73]

Such considerations, though legitimate within a teleological perspective and in an attempt to solve this particular case, bypass the issue which concerns us here, as throughout the chapter. We want to know whether the teleological approach agrees with actual moral reasoning, particularly Christian. And such agreement is not demonstrated by reaching the same conclusion via another route. If teleologists perform complex calculations and the mass of men, Christian and non-Christian, react immediately without noting those larger considerations necessary for teleological agreement, then they would seem to apply different, nonteleological standards. And is it conceivable that their standards — the standards of the majority of moral individuals — are mistaken?

To illustrate the same difficulty from a slightly different angle, let us place ourselves in the imaginary sheriff's situation. We may assume that none of these refined calculations enter his head. He just knows this man is innocent, and he wants to avoid a mass lynching. So he decides to sacrifice him. Now what do we think of that? Are his reasoning and his conclusion acceptable or not, given these (admittedly limited) premises? And if not, does that mean the teleological approach is inadequate in this and similar cases, perhaps in all?

No. For those who spontaneously rule against framing the prisoner do so because the death or suffering of an innocent man carries more weight with them than does the likelihood that others will die. Both aspects of the act are considered and both count as disvalues, as for anyone, but the former disvalue outweighs the latter. Accordingly, for this reason, the act is judged immoral. So we have here a typical weighing of values.[74]

Whence, then, the impression of conflict with the teleological approach? For one thing, in such cases[75] it may appear that the conflicting values are merely the lives at stake — the one life versus the many — and that if our verdict goes in favor of the one, it is clearly not because we value one human life more than many but because we have abandoned value-balancing. "The value of life, each human life, is incalculable, not in any merely poetic sense but simply because it is something not susceptible to calculation, measurement, weighing, and balancing."[76]

Yet if we pick off an armed madman from his tower perch, from which he has already killed a dozen people, but would not shoot him down if he were killing stray dogs, the reason seems evident. We have balanced one human life against many human lives. If we reach a different verdict in the case of the prisoner, some other factor must be present. And from the words of those who condemn his punishment, it is clear what they take that factor to be. The lives or welfare of many are not weighed against just the life or welfare of the individual but against the *injustice* of his punishment. That is sensed as a higher, weightier consideration.

Here we come to a second important source of the impression we are considering. For various reasons and in various ways an aspect such as justice or injustice may appear to be of an entirely different order than other aspects, so that to weigh them in the same scales would be incongruous or incoherent. The appearance may, for instance, derive from the supreme rating accorded the aspect; its conspicuous presence and decisive influence in stating some moral norm; its similar association with a *prima facie*, or presumptive, obligation; the use of the same word (e.g., "justice") in different senses, one of which does negate the parallel with premoral goods and evils; the nonteleological inculcation of a norm in which the value or disvalue appears, causing us to perceive it differently; or some combination of these causes.

Reflection on points like these (stated briefly here, to avoid undue confusion of detail) may reconcile deontologists to the proposed analysis of our paradigm (the sheriff's option) and the class it represents. Justice and lives, for instance, are not as strange bedfellows as they perhaps appeared at first sight; it was just the way they were dressed. So the claim that value-balancing underlies the negative verdict in this and similar cases looks reasonable after all. No forcing is required, no Procrustean bed.

An easier route to the same conclusion is to ask: At what point might we change our minds about the unjust punishment as a means of preventing much violence and bloodshed? If it consisted in ten years' imprisonment? one year? six months? a fine? a reprimand? Surely somewhere down the line. Yet injustice there would still be, only less. And being less, it would no longer *outweigh* the counterconsiderations, as it does before that point is reached. The transition, surely, in this thought-experiment is, not from no balancing to balancing, but from one verdict to another, because the balanced has altered.

J. Values versus Consequences

One of Connery's examples concerns justice, said McCormick; the other concerns fairness. David Lyons states the latter as follows:

> Should one bother to vote when it is inconvenient to do so? One knows, generally, that his single ballot will not be especially significant; therefore, the direct effects of voting and of not voting will hardly be different, if at all. And, regarding indirect effects, while one's absence from the polls will (let us assume) not be noticed by others, and therefore will not influence their behaviour, it would on the other hand be more convenient not to vote.
>
> If we tally up the score, it appears that an Act-Utilitarian must hold that it would be wrong to vote under such circumstances, since the over-all effects of voting are worse than those of abstaining. Thus it seems that mere inconvenience provides a reason overriding whatever good reason we ordinarily have to vote. And this, many would hold, is simply not so.[77]

Abstention might seem still more clearly indicated if the person's candidate were a sure winner.[78] Yet the majority verdict still might be: "Unfair!"

If this judgment is correct, in its reason as well as its verdict, then consequences alone do not determine right and wrong. But according to a common analysis the whole teleological approach is thereby invalidated. Deontological theories as opposed to teleological, writes Frankena, "assert that there are other considerations that may make an action or rule right or obligatory besides the goodness or badness of its consequences — certain features of the act itself other than the *value* it brings into existence, for example, the fact that it keeps a promise, is just, or is commanded by God or by the state. Teleologists believe that there is one and only one basis or ultimate right-making characteristic, namely, the comparative value (nonmoral) of what is, probably will be, or is intended to be brought into being."[79]

This cleavage supposedly emerges into full view only in test cases such as that of the Southern sheriff (in the preceding section) or of the lazy voter (here). And it is true that teleologists do typically attempt to justify the common verdict in such instances through reference to overall consequences. But it is also evident that they often attach great weight to aspects which in their adversaries' analyses belong to the act itself and not to its results. Thus in the previous sample a teleologist naturally does not ignore the innocent prisoner's punishment; for him, too, it is a weighty disvalue, even if not decisive. Yet this same aspect of the act constitutes the "intrinsic evil" on which the deontologist insists. It will not do, therefore, to say that teleologists consider only consequences.

Some may have. But the impression that all have would seem to arise principally from this double source: (1) An act may be narrowly or broadly defined, so that it includes more or less of what would otherwise be termed its "consequences";[80] and these fluctuations may escape notice, as in the example just considered. (2) An act may be contrasted with its consequences or with alternative actions. In this latter perspective the "consequences of acting one way rather than another" often extend to the whole alternative; they are the consequences of the *option* and so incorporate both the act and its results. This more radical fluctuation may also escape notice. Thus Moore, for example, apparently did not note how different were these two statements of his position (the italics are mine): (a) "To assert that a certain line of conduct is, at a given time, absolutely right or obligatory, is obviously to assert that more good or less evil will exist in the world, if it be *adopted*, than if anything else be done instead."[81] (b) "To ask what kind of actions we ought to perform, or what kind of conduct is right, is to ask what kind of *effects* such action and conduct *will produce*. . . . What I wish first to point out is that 'right' does and can mean nothing but 'cause of a good result,' and is thus identical with 'useful.'"[82]

Once the distinction is noted and the option squarely faced, there can be little doubt of the outcome: both consistency and practicality require that a teleologist favor the first of Moore's formulations. Pure consequentialism is untenable.

Consistency, to start with, demands that like values receive like recognition, whether they be prospective or present. If I finance the local orchestra, I bring about future beauty; if I play in the orchestra or conduct it, I realize present beauty. Likewise, if I write a treatise on friendship, I may bring about future friendship; if I assist a friend, stroll with him, engage in amicable conversation, I realize friendship in act. Again, I can dream of apostolic action, wishing like the poet Hopkins "Jessy or Jack there God to aggrandise, God to glorify"; but I may also magnify him myself, here and now.

Come you indoors, come home; your fading fire
Mend first and vital candle in close heart's vault:
You there are master, do your own desire. . . .[83]

In all these instances it would be clearly inconsistent to justify the
forward-looking action by its hoped-for result and to ignore the same
value when present in the act itself. As Dewey might say, our actions are
not mere preparation for living; they are a first installment. The slices
of life we christen "acts" are slices like any others and incorporate similar values.

Practicality too, I said, as well as consistency, requires inclusion of
the act. For the only countermove that might conceivably save consequentialism from the charge of inconsistency would be absurdly im-
practical, even were it theoretically successful. The idea would be to
designate acts with such neutral precision that all values are left over as
consequences (like flesh stripped from bones to which no scrap still
clings). From last night's symphony, say, we might extract the baton
waving, key pounding, bow scraping, and so forth, leaving the beau-
teous sounds and the hearers' pleasure as consequences. From a friendly
stroll or chat we might extricate the leg movements or vocalizations,
leaving the personal experiences they produce as the truly valuable
part. From these consequences, and them alone, we might then assess
the morality of the actions (the baton waving, key pounding, bow
scraping, leg movements, vocalizations, and so forth). However, even
were these combined constituents (active and consequential) fully
equivalent to the dismembered wholes (see VIII, F), and even were the
skeletonized actions really void of value (see VII, B, 2), why go to all
this trouble? Who can talk this way, and why try to?

Thus a "modified teleology," embracing the act in its census of values, is not only possible but necessary. And what Connery's two examples can now be seen to demonstrate is, not the impossibility of any teleological theory of norms, but the need of the adjustments proposed in
this and the previous section. Between them they provide a synthetic solution to the conflict Frankena describes: teleologists invoking only consequences and nonmoral values, deontologists insisting on more. Once
both parties clearly discern the logic of their own positions, through the
mist of words, they may arrive at a common middle position.

On the one hand, the deontologist who condemns an act because
it is unfair or unjust thereby picks out a single aspect of the total act, an
aspect outweighing counterconsiderations which he too recognizes as
values. To bring out the distinction between the criteria operative in
moral reasoning and the verdict which follows from them, he may as

well call fairness or justice a value, along with those other aspects, and even a nonmoral or premoral value, not of course in the sense that it is irrelevant to morality (no values are), but in the sense that it precedes the judgment "right" or "wrong." On the other hand, the teleologist, for his part, should recognize clearly, for the reasons just cited, that the values and disvalues to be considered extend to the act as well as to its consequences. Thereupon the second of the distinctions will disappear which Frankena and others have seen as separating the two factions.[84]

K. "Suppose Everyone Did Likewise"

The case of the lazy voter leads naturally to discussion of a principle which, according to Broad,

> is perhaps more often explicitly used in the reasonings of daily life than any other. This principle or mode of argument I call the *Principle of False Universalization* [PFU].
>
> A man proposes to himself a certain course of action and debates whether it be right or wrong. At a certain stage he will say to himself, or, if he be discussing the matter with a friend, his friend will say: Suppose *everybody* did what you propose to do. The consequences of this hypothesis will then be considered, and, if they be found to be bad, the man will generally consider that this fact tends to prove that his proposed action is wrong. I think the principle is nearly always used negatively, i.e. to condemn a proposed course of action. We do not in general argue that a proposed action must be right because if everybody did likewise the result would be excellent.[85]

"Everybody," says Broad, "is familiar with this kind of reasoning; everybody seems to think that it is valid and important." If his numerical estimate hits close to the mark, then here is a pattern of thought requiring our attention. For "everyone" means Christians too, and it is not evident whether or how the argument in question squares with value-balancing. Indeed, Broad notes a strange paradox: PFU expresses concern for consequences, yet apparently not for real or even likely ones. "We are asked to believe that the rightness or wrongness of many of our actions depends on the probable consequences, not of what we judge to be true, but of what we know to be false. For, in practically every case where we consider what would happen if everybody acted as we propose to act, we know as surely as we can know anything that is not *a priori*, that by no means everybody will act this way."[86] For example, an American or Englishman proposes to falsify his tax returns, whereupon a friend objects: "But suppose everyone did that: services we all count on would not get paid for." Yet both of them are perfectly aware that this hypothesis is false; they know quite well that not everyone will cheat on his or her returns.

This then is evident: the cheater will reap benefits without doing his personal share; he will enjoy services he too desires, thanks to the sacrifices of more honest taxpayers. And this strikes us as unfair. Here, then, is one solution of the paradox. Most reasonable applications of PFU might be explained through an implicit appeal to fairness, based precisely on the realization that the false universalization is false. In these many cases a present or prospective good, to be shared by many, depends on their individual actions and sacrifices. If both the benefits and the sacrifices are fairly evenly distributed, then anyone who seeks to enjoy the former while avoiding the latter is taking advantage of others. The stratagem, quite generally, is not fair.

This interpretation might help to account for PFU's limited range. It might explain, for instance, the restriction Broad cites, the wrongness of actions being inferred from unfortunate consequences but not their rightness from excellent results. Pacifists, for example, do not generally argue that *if* everybody were a pacifist, universal peace would result, *hence* all are obliged to be pacifists. Were they to do so, others would be sure to point out the improbability of the hypothetical situation and to argue that in any likely world protective measures are advisable. Its counterfactuality would now tell against the argument. Why? One plausible answer is that no common good is here in prospect, to be shared equally by unequal contributors, as in the former cases. Hence no unfairness can be imputed to nonparticipants.

An implicit appeal to fairness is not the only explanation, though, either of PFU or of its restricted application. The objection "But what if everyone did it?" might also be taken to signify: "There should be a rule against it."[87] That is, the principle might be given a rule-utilitarian justification, as in IV, F (or in the quote opening section I above). "The rule utilitarian does not consider the consequences of each particular action but considers the consequences of adopting some general rule, such as 'Keep promises.' He adopts the rule if the consequences of its general adoption are better than those of the adoption of some alternative rule."[88] The rules implicitly urged by PFU ("Vote for your candidate," "Pay your taxes," "Don't cheat in exams," etc.) are precisely of this sort.

Within either perspective, fairness or utility, it is understandable that we do not generalize PFU, declaring without restriction or qualification: "If the consequences of everyone's doing *a* would be undesirable, then no one ought to do *a.*" Innumerable actions fit this description: being philosophers, camping at Tahoe, moving to Florida, phoning long-distance at 5 p.m., . . .[89] In each case universalization would be disastrous. Yet no one condemns the actions. Why not? Why don't they invoke PFU here too? One explanation would be that no unfairness is involved; another, that a rule against the action would not make utilitarian sense. (We would have to outlaw not only philosophizing, Tahoe, Florida, and 5 p.m., but every other avocation, camping spot, destination, time, for the universalization of each would prove similarly unfortunate.)

These two lines of thought look at least as respectable as a third, advanced by Marcus Singer in defense of PFU,[90] and they appear more plausible as accounts of the principle's vogue. So they suffice for our purposes. It is clear that the popularity of PFU attests no widespread aversion to value-balancing or its underlying criterion.

L. Conclusion

Here ends our second series. Other samples of ethical reasoning, more or less typically Christian, more or less difficult to harmonize with teleological balancing, might be added to the preceding eleven, and originally were. However, none of those I considered and omitted is so prevalent among Christians, so hostile to teleology, at least in appearance, and so varied in its applications as the thought-patterns just discussed.

Kant's "Categorical Imperative," for example, rates high on the second and third of these three counts but not on the first. "I should never act in such a way," he declares, "that I could not will that my maxim should be a universal law."[91] This norm has a nonteleological ring and applies to countless cases, but its pedigree does not seem particularly Christian. Hence it is not included.

More typically Christian is a nonteleological argument long urged against suicide. Man is not his own property, it has often been said, and accordingly, though a person need not take extraordinary means to prolong his life, he may not actively terminate it.[92] Teleology would emphasize less, if at all, the distinction between procuring and permitting a desirable death and would judge its rightness by its desirability — from a Christian viewpoint.[93] However, no major confrontation arises from this conflict. For the argument from divine ownership has not been extended generally, to nonhuman creation, to human parts and organs, or even, for that matter, to human life itself. When there has been a question of capital punishment or self-defense or legitimate warfare, traditional moralists have fallen strangely silent about the Creator's rights. They have gone ahead and balanced values, as best they might, on the reasonable assumption that he would too.

By contrast, all the syndromes sampled in this chapter surface in widely scattered areas. The counsel-precept distinction (in A) pervades the moral universe. Second-time discernment serves most varied elections (B). Jesus' reasoning on divorce mirrors standard practice of his day, on question after question (C). Arguments from nature like that against contraception generate an assortment of prohibitions, from Paul the apostle to Paul VI (D). Bender's veto prior to value-balancing typifies innumerable arguments on the most diverse topics (E). The direct-indirect distinction, as McCormick noted and we shall see more fully, grounds an impressive range of judgments (F). The "order of charity" determines the duties of individuals, groups, and societies, with regard to the distribution of time, effort, money, and resources, in relation to relatives, clients, members, and dependents (G). Verdict by definition is such a common phenomenon that it appears repeatedly in even the abortion controversy (is the fetus "living," "part of the mother's body," a "child," a "person," a "human being"?) (H). Justice or fairness is a recurring issue, with regard to legislation or test-taking, say, and not just with regard to hypothetical sheriffs (I) or lazy voters (J). Finally, the "Principle of False Universalization" is as broadly applicable — and applied — as rule-utilitarianism (K).

These varied samples all hang on a single, preannounced thread: apparent conflict with the approach of chapter 4. But where and why and how often has the clash been real? And do the genuine countercases perhaps converge or cohere to form some alternative approach? If so, is it preferable to the teleological one? Such are the questions the chapter suggests, and such the ones now to be dealt with in chapter 6. The synoptic view the reader may be longing for will be forthcoming there, straightaway.

PART THREE

Sifting the Evidence

The task will be to determine the methodology of ethics, and to specify the criteria of a moral act, viewed from a Christian standpoint. The topic is important: it concerns the very bases of fundamental moral theology, and has immediate repercussions on human action.
— Pope Paul VI

6

The Christian Criterion
of Right and Wrong

"The field of Christian ethics," wrote James Gustafson in 1965, "has been the location of a debate over the past decades between roughly delineated parties representing an allegiance to the use of formal prescriptive principles on the one hand, and those representing the cause of the more existential response to a particular situation on the other hand. The debate has taken place in Europe and the United States, it has taken place in Catholicism and in Protestantism."[1] And it continues today, almost two decades later. Perhaps, with the proper clarifications, it can be brought to a successful conclusion.

"It is important to notice," observed Gustafson in the same article, "that the debate has located the problem of Christian ethics at a particular point, namely the question, 'how does the Christian community, or any of its conscientious members go about making a particular moral judgment or decision?'"[2] If this question is taken as one of fact, the answer is multiple; for Christians have made and still do make their decisions in widely differing ways. If it is understood normatively, the answer may be simpler. But this will depend on a further basic distinction, that between the process and the logic of Christian moral reasoning.

A. Christian Criteria

By "logic" I mean (here and elsewhere) principally the criteria or ultimate indicators of right and wrong within a given context or universe of discourse; whereas by "process" I mean the various ways in which a person may determine whether a rule, action, program, or institution conforms to these standards. As I shall explain at the start of chapter 9, and as Dan Brock succinctly states, "an ethical theory might provide an account of either or both of these, but there is no reason to believe that the proper account of one must also be the proper account of the other."[3] The prior, decisive question, as we have already seen (III, B), is the logical one. Without clarity concerning the criteria of right and wrong there can be no clarity elsewhere. Specifically, there can be no clarity concerning the validity or utility of universal norms, in general or in particular. For the criteria of right and wrong specify sufficient and necessary conditions for the correctness of any precept, and the correctness of the precept in turn constitutes a necessary though not sufficient condition for the precept's utility. Thus if, for instance, the maximization of value is accepted as the criterion of right and wrong, the familiar observation is forever excluded: "This is right, that wrong, *regardless* of the circumstances and attendant values." It may be that the deed is always right or always wrong, but if so, that is because values are always served or always disserved by so acting. The universality of the corresponding precept is derivative. And as we have seen (IV, E, G), once values are thus made decisive, exceptionless precepts tend to become so particular that they lose their utility.

Hence the crucial question for Christian ethics is whether maximization of value is the criterion to adopt consistently in determining right and wrong. And the interest of the representative series of samples in chapters 4 and 5 is that they provide materials for resolving this issue. What they display, synoptically, is a coherent, widely used approach on the one hand (that of maximization through the balancing of values) and a variety of approaches on the other, most of which do not conflict with the logic of maximization and the rest of which do not individually provide an alternative logic or collectively form a coherent counterposition. To verify this verdict, let us examine each of these latter groupings — first the nonconflicting paradigms, then the genuine but unsuccessful rivals.

In most of the "alternative approaches" of chapter 5 the supposed opposition to teleological thinking was seen to be: procedural rather than logical (as with regard to Ignatius' "times"), or only apparent (as in Mark on remarriage, Ewing on the order of charity, Connery on justice and fairness, Broad on the Principle of False Universalization), or largely a matter of words (as in the debate about counsels), or an unintentional departure from value-balancing by a would-be teleologist (as in Noonan on abortion). Only two items, it would seem, still pose a serious challenge to the criterion of maximum value: (1) the specific type of natural-law reasoning frequently invoked, for example, against artificial contraception; (2) the veto on the use of disvalues as means to valuable ends. Neither of these, to be sure, offers a general approach to ethical problems, as does value-balancing. But each is widely applicable and has in fact been widely applied in traditional ethics. So I shall indicate briefly why neither seems satisfactory nor should be permitted, therefore, to override the verdict of values.

The basic difficulty in assessing the ban on evil means, yet at the same time the clue to understanding it, is the dictum's frequent ambiguity: Are the prohibited means morally evil, in the full, terminal sense that applies to an act as a whole and not to single features, such as fairness (see V, J); or are they evil in the weaker sense that applies to any disvalue weighed in the scales of decision? Is their employment something which, all things considered, must be judged immoral; or is it just one of the things considered that counts against the global action? If the first, then the doctrine is tautological and permits no inference in particular cases. *If* a means is morally evil, then of course it should be forgone; but *that* it is morally evil will have to be established by other criteria than the tautology "Morally evil means are never permissible." If, on the other hand, nonmoral evil is meant, then the exclusion is far from self-evident and requires some explanation. The fact that so often no explanation is attempted strengthens the impression that these two senses are not clearly distinguished by many who invoke the principle. Its vogue is not the fruit of insight, but the legacy of a preanalytic era, when criterial analysis was rudimentary or nonexistent.

This judgment is borne out by the selective application of the norm. Were it the expression of some genuine insight, vetoing nonmoral evil as a means to nonmoral good, it should beget like resistance in all like instances. But, as was previously noted, such is far from the case. Who ever argued, for instance, that corporal punishment is immoral since it seeks a future good by means of a present evil or that bitters on the breast were an immoral form of weaning? Again, were the prohibition born of genuine insight, moral people should not receive such an impression of artificiality from the contrasts drawn between permitted and forbidden procedures in pursuit of identical goods.

In the case of an expectant mother, for example, whose womb is cancerous and for whom the immediate removal of the womb is therapeutically necessary, the doctrine of the manuals allows a hysterectomy, while maintaining its prohibition on any direct abortion, even in cases where the death of both mother and child would certainly ensue. Likewise, it allows the removal of a fallopian tube in a case of ectopic gestation, while condemning as a direct abortion the removal of the fetus from the tube, even if then the tube could be saved. In the permitted procedure the evil consequence is seen as a side effect; in the forbidden procedure it is seen as a means to one's end. And on this causal difference the life of a woman is made to depend in one case and the integrity of her body in the other. Yet it makes no difference to the welfare of the fetus whether there is an induced abortion or a hysterectomy, whether there is removal of the tube or removal of the fetus from the tube.

A similar impression is created when the manuals allow a captured agent to pull the pin on a grenade attached to his belt in order to destroy important documents he has on his person, while forbidding him to pull the pin if the secret information is in his head and he foresees that he will reveal it under torture or drugs; or when they permit a combatant in war to blow up a military installation, even though the explosion will kill a number of civilians as well, but forbid him to kill directly a single civilian who may stand between him and the accompishment of his mission. Here too one is inclined to ask: Does it make any difference to the welfare of the captured agent's country or to his own welfare whether the vital information is in his head or in his pocket, and so whether the destruction of his life is direct or indirect? Does it make any difference to the civilian's welfare whether he is killed by a bullet aimed at him or by a bomb aimed at a factory? May not the former death be preferable?[4]

Once the issue is thus focused, through comparison of concrete cases, I think most people will agree that such causal considerations lack moral significance. "A love ethic that makes the genuine welfare of human persons and human community the fundamental norm certainly demands that all our aims and intentions be oriented to promoting that welfare and excluding everything that militates against it, but it also demands that our moral judgments and decisions take account of all the implications and consequences of what we do, regardless of how they relate physically to the good we are expressly intending. If we really love, it can make no difference ethically that harm is being done to persons as a by-product of our behavior rather than as part of the causal process producing the welfare we strive for."[5]

"If we really love." There lies the nub of the dispute. For the doctrine of directly and indirectly voluntary actions analyzed in V, F maintained, in effect, that one cannot truly love when one intends an evil, albeit as an indispensable means to some greater good. But this contradicts sound common sense. How the idea might arise I can surmise (e.g., from the surface similarity of "intend" in different instances); how it might plausibly be defended I cannot. Countless cases tell against it, unquestioned by even its advocates (see V, F). Love not only permits but repeatedly requires nonmorally evil means: disagreeable medicine, distressing criticism, painful punishment, fatiguing labor, and so forth.

Let us turn, then, to the second item: the traditional appeal to nature in such matters as contraception. Here too one notes unclarity at
the outset, then uncritical fidelity to the tradition thus established. The
authority of Saint Thomas, in particular, has been urged in a manner
that contrasts strangely with his own explicit precept and pioneering
practice. Thus, to many it must have seemed an affront for Noonan to
assess Aquinas' position in the manner we have seen, then to add: "Did
it make sense to postulate one type of coitus as normal, and to treat
every variation from it as accidental, even cases in which it was known
that conception was impossible? Did it make sense to say that old age
was an 'accidental' exception to the ability to generate? Thomas did not
ask these questions."[6]

Nor did he attempt to integrate this one strand of natural-law
thinking with the others we have traced in his thought. In particular he
did not explain how such one-sided emphasis on genetics, at the expense
of other values, might be harmonized with the stronger stress he placed
on charity, or with the Christian expectation of a community of the
blessed where there will be neither marrying nor giving in marriage.
Aquinas, though in advance of his contemporaries, was still a man of
his times. And we would not even be abreast of our own times if we
failed to note these limitations.

Contemporary critics have more frequently stressed the selectivity
and apparent arbitrariness with which this principle too is invoked.[7]
Repeatedly we use our members—our feet, our hands, our vocal cords—
in ways not suggested by nature and see no sin in it. We bypass the organs of nutrition and feed ourselves by injection, again without sin, and
accept the widest variety of chemical and surgical interventions. Why
then this insistence on a single licit use of the genital organs, regardless
of people's needs and circumstances? Why is God offended by just this
deviation from nature and not by all the others? I know no satisfactory
answer to this query.

Nor generally is any intelligible response forthcoming. As Germain Grisez has pointed out,[8] a basic equivocation runs through
natural-law arguments against contraceptive intercourse. The act is unnatural, the explanation goes, and therefore wrong. That it is unnatural is clear enough if "unnatural" is given a purely factual sense such as
"rendered incapable of the result it sometimes achieves." That an unnatural action is immoral is likewise evident if "unnatural" is given a
moral sense. But how and why we may pass from the nonmoral sense to
the moral, and thereby derive a condemnation, the accounts do not explain. And what we cannot discern in this specific condemnation we
shall hardly educe from the disparate cluster of prohibitions previously

cited (concerning position in intercourse, lying, shaving, artificial insemination, etc.). No intelligible criterion emerges, discriminating
"natural" from "unnatural" behavior. Attempting a formulation, one
clutches at a phantasm.

Consequently, if a contemporary ethician like Grisez ventures an
explanation, say of contraception's sinfulness, his account, if successful,
may support a traditional conclusion, but not a traditional principle,
recurring in past condemnations. And if he himself notes, as Grisez
does, that his account is new, it becomes doubly clear that I need not
consider the theory in this sifting of traditional views or explain why I
find it, too, inadequate. My reaction would differ, though, were a modern vindication suggested for the ban on nonmorally evil means; for
that specific, intelligible principle does have some historical backing.

Some, but not much. For it is about as rare for an author to clearly
distinguish between morally and nonmorally evil means, yet insist on
the illegitimacy of the latter, as it is for an author to distinguish factual
"unnaturalness" from moral and still conclude from the first to the second. A further parallel is equally germane to our interests. Were either
of these two nonteleological approaches consistently extended to all
similar situations, the case for its Christian authenticity would be greatly
improved. Quantitatively it would cover a far greater mass of evidence;
qualitatively its claim to genuine insight could not be so readily dismissed. As it is, neither rival can match value-maximization either quantitatively or qualitatively as a Christian standard of right and wrong.

The two approaches here weighed and found wanting do not form
a unified system in opposition to value-balancing, but neither do they
clash with one another. They may, however, conflict with the traditional principle on which Saint Thomas said all other precepts of the
natural law are based: "Do good and avoid evil."[9] If "good" and "evil"
are understood morally—that is, as equivalent to "right" and "wrong"—
then of course there is no conflict; for the principle then specifies no criterion of right and wrong. It just tells us to do what is right, however
that is judged, and avoid what is wrong, whatever that may be. If,
however, we wish to make the maxim truly operative, and thereby validate Aquinas' claim, conflict does arise. For then we must understand
"good" and "evil" in a premoral sense, that is, as designating values and
disvalues to be maximized or minimized through action. Explicitly or
implicitly our reasoning would then run: "Good is to be maximized, evil
minimized; but this line of conduct (general or particular) does maximize good in relation to evil; therefore it should be followed." Here
there is no tautology, no idle repetition, but a supreme norm operates as
a supreme norm should.

The text just cited from Aquinas already points in this direction. And there are others. He writes, for example, that "in all questions of moral virtue, prudence serves as guide"[10] and that "it is the role of prudence to prefer a greater to a lesser good. Hence to leave the greater good is the part of imprudence."[11] "God is not offended by us except insofar as we do something against our own good."[12]

B. Excluded Alternatives

"The benefit of consistency," writes Professor Geach, "is that you cannot be inconsistent without being wrong about something substantive."[13] If values are sometimes consulted and sometimes not, values will suffer. And it should be evident by now that important values may suffer notably if the supreme principle of beneficence, or value-maximization, is not consistently adhered to. Still, it is conceivable that on reflection the position just established should appear vacuous. It might seem that the conclusion follows, not from the evidence adduced, but from the way the question was framed or understood.

My procedure, in other words, may seem comparable to that of a naturalist who maintains that all swans are white. Black ones are then discovered and presented in refutation. "Granted," he replies, "but you can see from their color that they are not genuine swans." He is not to be had. Nothing is permitted to count against his thesis. Now is not that much the way things stand in the foregoing demonstration? For suppose that historical inquiry had revealed that a ban on nonnatural form and another on nonmorally evil means were in fact followed consistently by numerous Christian thinkers. I could not then have complained of arbitrariness and incoherence, nor have dismissed out of hand the claim of immediate insight. So would I have had to admit that here in Christian tradition solid, irreducible evidence had been discovered in opposition to value-maximization? Not at all (the objection might continue): I would simply label conformity to nature a value, and nonmorally evil means a double disvalue, and work them into the value calculus, as I did for justice and fairness. The counterevidence would not be allowed to count as counterevidence. And no matter what weight these items were given, I could always reply as before, that teleology does not dictate value ratings. So the case for value-maximization looks indefeasible, and if indefeasible, then void of interest. Where no alternative is excluded, none is established.

In reply to this objection I shall, as it were, cite a few hypothetical black swans. That is, I shall indicate some alternative approaches which,

if found to be prevalent in Christian practice and reflectively acceptable to Christians, would challenge the rule of value-maximization,
unavoidably. They could not be analyzed away as cryptoteleology. The
samples I shall mention fail, in fact, to satisfy these conditions, as do
others I might add, being either rare among Christians or clearly unac-
ceptable. Since they pose still less of a challenge than do the counter-
criteria just considered, they have been ignored till now. Here their
rapid listing will vindicate the genuineness of the teleological verdict.
Viewed against the background of alternatives like these (especially the
third), it emerges as what William James would call a forced, living,
momentous option.

(1)   Mircea Eliade delineates one such viewpoint in *Myths, Dreams
and Mysteries:* "We are at last beginning to know and understand the
value of the myth, as it has been elaborated in 'primitive' and archaic
societies — that is, among those groups of mankind where the myth happens to be the very foundation of social life and culture. Now, one fact
strikes us immediately: in such societies the myth is thought to express
the *absolute truth*, because it narrates a *sacred history;* that is, a trans-
human revelation which took place at the dawn of the Great Time, in
the holy time of the beginnings (*in illo tempore*). Being *real* and *sacred*,
the myth becomes exemplary, and consequently *repeatable*, for it serves
as a model, and by the same token as a justification, for all human actions. In other words, a myth is a *true history* of what came to pass at
the beginning of Time, and one which provides the pattern for human
behaviour. In *imitating* the exemplary acts of a god or of a mythic hero,
or simply by recounting their adventures, the man of an archaic society
detaches himself from profane time and magically re-enters the Great
Time, the sacred time."[14]

    Such was the attitude of one who insisted on resting the seventh
day because Yahweh did, and such would be the attitude of a Christian
who felt obliged to wash other people's feet because Jesus did so and told
his disciples to follow his example. However, this is not how the imitation of Christ has generally been understood. We intuit the universal
values incarnate in his act — the humility, the concern for others' welfare (even the state of their feet) — and pursue the same values variously,
because our situations differ. The following of Christ, so conceived,
may still fall within Eliade's broad description but does not conflict
with the principle of beneficence. Only literal imitation would. (See
IX, D, and X, B.)

(2)   A kindred view, perhaps more squarely opposed to teleology than
slavish imitation, is voluntarism. For the voluntarist the divine will,
whatever it decides, counts as criterion of right and wrong. Few Chris-

tian ethicians, it is true, have been as frankly voluntaristic as Scotus, Ockham, or Calvin. But a great many who dissent in theory are voluntaristic in practice. "God wills the good," they acknowledge, "because it is good; it is not good because he wills it." But then in their treatment of authoritative texts — in Scripture, Fathers, or magisterium — they proceed to argue in ways little consonant with their profession. "In Christianity," notes Sidgwick, "we early find that the method of moralists determining right conduct is to a great extent analogous to that of jurists interpreting a code."[15]

Even in recent authors, as competent as Gerald Kelly and John Ford, one encounters reasoning like the following: "Among both Catholic and non-Catholic exegetes good arguments can be found for the assertion that Onan was slain for his sin against chastity [Gen 38:4–10]; and this would mean that at least the immorality of *coitus interruptus* [interrupted intercourse] is explicitly revealed; and from this we might draw the conclusion that the immorality of other forms of contraception is implicitly revealed."[16] The authors fail to note that even were Onan condemned for a sexual sin, the condemnation might not extend to all those who, in whatever circumstances and for whatever reasons, perform the same physical act. That is, it might not cover even all cases of *coitus interruptus*, much less all cases of contraception, of whatever (artificial) form.

The possibility, I say, did not occur to these authors that God (if not the biblical narrator) might consider cases individually and the values at stake each time. Yet on other occasions that is the approach they themselves take. So the sample passage just quoted, like many others in the same book, illustrates still more appositely a further alternative to value-balancing. This is the chief real-life rival, pervading most the others.

(3) "A loose combination or confusion of methods," wrote Sidgwick, "is the most common type of actual moral reasoning."[17] Christians, it would seem, are no exception. The main alternative to value-balancing in their deliberations is not some opposed system but lack of system. It is failure to relate and integrate, such as we observed in natural-law theory. It is neglect of criterial questions, such as appeared just now in the quotation from Kelly and Ford. It is confusion like that revealed in Cathrein's discussion of marriage, in Bender's veto on transplants, in Noonan's treatment of abortion. It is circular reasoning such as Sidgwick describes, the natural being defined as the reasonable and the reasonable as the natural. It is all these and countless other vagaries, which it would be tedious and unpleasant to itemize in greater detail.

On this occasion, then, I agree with Karl Barth: "Thanks to the wisdom and patience of God, and the inconsequence of men, it is quite possible in practice that Christian insights and deductions may actually exist where their Christian presuppositions are wholly concealed, or where a closer investigation would reveal all kinds of presuppositions that are only to a small extent Christian. There are many people who live by Christian presuppositions, who even represent and proclaim them, and yet if they were questioned, could only tell us something very far from satisfactory or quite unsatisfactory, something which we might have to dismiss as heathenism or Jewish doctrine. The wise course, then, is to keep to what they actually know and not to what they unfortunately seem not to know or even in their folly to deny. The business of the reader or hearer of this type of ethics is tacitly to supplement and correct its more doubtful — implicit or explicit — presuppositions (as Paul did in Ac. 17), and for the rest to learn from it what it actually has to teach."[18]

C. Value Ethics

What traditional ethics has to teach is allegiance to reason and objective norms. However, it too readily equated objective norms with universal precepts, and rationality with their discovery and application. For such is the culture in which most Christians have long been immersed. In ethics as in Western thought generally — Euclidean geometry, Platonic definitions, Aristotelian logic, Roman law, Newtonian physics — the universal formula has reigned as unquestioned paradigm of worthwhile knowledge. How revealing it is, for example, to see Piaget assert, with hardly a word of justification: "All morality consists in a system of rules, and the essence of all morality is to be sought for in the respect which the individual acquires for these rules. The reflective analysis of Kant, the sociology of Durkheim, or the individualistic psychology of Bovet all meet on this point."[19]

The inevitable reaction that set in some decades back received classic expression in Joseph Fletcher's *Situation Ethics*. To the rule of precepts he opposed the sovereignty of charity. "Only love is absolute."[20] Love must decide whether a precept applies or not according to the circumstances in each concrete situation. Hence the book's title and the doctrine's name: "Situation Ethics."

Strong on loving concern, Christian situation ethics has had relatively little to say about objective norms. It has not replaced one developed rationality with another and so has failed to impress or convert its opponents. In the resulting confrontation between preceptive and antipreceptive ethics a synthesis is called for. Agreement may be reached by harmonizing the truths that war in these extremes within a third position not identical with either.

As a first step toward reconciliation we might forgo the dramatic dictum "Only love is absolute." Many another value is absolute and, unlike love, provides objective guidance. None governs conduct unconditionally, it is true (cf. V, I; VII, C). Each competes with others, and sometimes prevails, sometimes not. However, let us not confuse values with precepts and judge them by inappropriate standards. A precept is absolute if it is to be *followed* unconditionally. A value is absolute if it is to be *consulted* unconditionally (i.e., without fail, regardless of circumstances, whenever it is present). If consulted and weighed in the balance, it is not ignored, even when it is overridden. It is absolute *as a value*.[21]

As a second step toward synthesis and agreement we might drop the label "situation ethics," or "situationism," and adopt, for instance, the title here employed: "value ethics."[22] For, (1) The former designation veils the role of values, which traditional ethics also consulted, and so obscures the basic continuity between the old morality and the new. (2) To veil values is to veil the universality, rationality, and objectivity which remain in the new approach. (3) To emphasize the situation is to stress that which is ephemeral and unique, so at the opposite extreme from eternal, universal norms, whereas recurrent, universal values are not.

With connections and continuities thus clarified, value ethics can be recognized as not less but more rational than precept ethics. If, for instance, an author cites various psychological, economic, or social values for or against private property, monogamy, war, or democracy, then takes the resulting generalization as an absolute rule, so lets it override particular constellations of value which work out differently, that is not rationality but sheer absentmindedness. He has forgotten how he established the norm and where ultimate authority resides in his ethical system. As for the author who now founds his precepts on value, now does not, he has no system.

Value ethics uses reason not only more coherently than preceptive ethics does but also more fully. For it takes greater pains with the individual case. It is relatively easy to declare, "Marriage should be permanent," "Taxes should be apportioned according to people's capacity and the needs of the economy," "Those in authority should seek the common good," and the like. But the task of reason becomes arduous when the continuation of *this* marriage is to be decided, or the fairness and effectiveness of *these* particular taxes, or the advisability of *this* specific program for the common good. It does, that is, when reason does not simply rely on prefabricated precepts but attempts to do for the individual case what moralists do more generally when they establish general norms, teleologically. Just how rational an ethics of value can and should be will appear in subsequent chapters.

As a further step toward reconciliation, I would suggest that value ethics (as opposed to preceptive ethics) is and has long been recognized to be the ethics of God himself. My meaning is this: In answer to the problem of evil, and to objections like those raised by Antony Flew, theologians have traditionally answered that doubtless the evils we perceive are balanced by the good we do not always see. No formula of ours permits us to dictate what God should or should not do on each occasion; thus no individual occurrence disproves his loving providence.

"Were it otherwise," I have noted elsewhere, "the belief would lose its interest. For a providence which was humanly testable and predictable would resemble the kind of exceptionless moral precepts which have come in for so much criticism of late. It would not adapt itself to the endlessly varied contexts and consequences, known to God alone, of actions and events, but would follow instead some fixed law, a law so simple (despite its covering all events!) that we could understand it, and so rigid that we would never need to envisage the possibility of an exception. For the moment an exception was admissible, for unknown reasons which lay outside the law, we would never know concerning any individual case whether it might not be an exception. That is, we would be back in the situation Flew indicates, unable to determine God's love from any single event."[23] This situation, therefore, is one we can gladly accept. We ought not, and indeed do not, hanker for a completely predictable providence.

If Christian charity should resemble the divine, then the knowledge and values which guide Providence should guide our actions too, with like results, so far as we can attain to that ideal. Rules we indeed need, and profit by, given our human limitations (IV, F). But to honor rules above values and thereby make them absolute would entail an inferior ethics. It would mean resembling less our heavenly Father, whose wise dispensations elude our sure prevision.

D. Conclusion

These several steps sketch a synthetic solution to the debate Gustafson mentioned at the chapter's start, "between roughly delineated parties representing an allegiance to the use of formal prescriptive prin-

ciples on the one hand, and those representing the cause of the more existential response to a particular situation on the other hand." The core
of the solution is the way it resolves an underlying tension far older than
this recent altercation.

From earlier remarks (B, 3) the reader will doubtless grasp my
meaning if I observe, paradoxically, that though value-maximization
has been the dominant criterion in Christian moral reasoning, it has not
dominated Christian moral reasoning. (Of the many who climb a
mountain, most may follow no trail, or may follow no single trail; yet
one trail may clearly be the most traveled of all.) And to the extent that
value-maximization has not consistently guided Christian deliberation,
deep tensions have resulted. The most pervasive, perhaps, is that between values and precepts. It can be stated as a conflict between rival
absolutes (understanding "absolute" in the sense of "unconditioned" or
"unconditional," as above, and not of "incomparable" or "incommen-
surable," as in V, I). For universal precepts have frequently been envisaged absolutely: "X is wrong regardless of circumstances, regardless of
consequences, regardless of the values at stake. It is wrong unconditionally." And on the other hand, values too are absolute: "X is good and Y
bad regardless of circumstances, regardless of the verdict, regardless of
whether they tip the scales. X is always a reason for, Y always a reason
against. They are good and bad unconditionally." Now these two sets of
absolutes — absolute precepts, independent of values, and absolute
values, determining what should be done — are incompatible. No man
can serve these two masters.

The opposition can be given paradigmatically Christian form by
asking: Is it conceivable that Jesus came that we might have life and
have it more fully, but that his moral teaching had some other goal, or
none at all, and so was subject to other norms? Is it conceivable that he
himself was morally bound to do things which were not for our good
and to forgo others which our welfare required? If not, then it is clear
which are supreme in Christian ethics — precepts or values.

I imagine that few would contest a verdict for values, provided
the values are broadly conceived. Those who are strong for precepts see
them as safeguards of value, the firmer the more effective. Situationists
view them as threats to value, the firmer the more menacing. This
cleavage may look basic so long as the criterial issue is not broached. Yet
an allegiance to values underlies both positions, waiting to be made explicit and thereby more efficacious. Here, if anywhere — in this mutual
concern that value be maximized, disvalue minimized — lies the Christian criterion of right and wrong.

Even when refined as in the introductions to chapters 4 and 5, this norm may appear so broad and vague as to offer minimal guidance. And in a sense this is true. The option just made, though decisive, does not take us very far. Other, more specific questions wait to be addressed, now that the crucial, criterial query has been answered. *What* values should shape our moral verdicts, and *how?*

7

The Search for
a Guiding Hierarchy of Values

"THE CONCRETE ETHICS of value," writes Nicolai Hartmann, "is the historical reunion of factors which have really been intimately associated from the beginning. Indeed it is, above all, the rediscovery of their inherent connection. It gives back to ethical apriorism its original richness of content, while to the consciousness of value it gives the certainty of a firm foothold in the midst of the relativity of human valuations."[1] This allusion to "ethical apriorism" suggests a possible parallel with traditional ethics which I have not yet mentioned but to which I shall devote the present chapter. The aim of traditional ethics, as widely practiced, was to work out beforehand a catalog of principles and precepts with which to assess individual cases. Now may not value ethics do something comparable? May not it too draw up a list, not of precepts but of values, arrange them hierarchically, and then apply the table methodically to individual cases? May it not be as systematic, in its own way, as traditional ethics? Is not this, perhaps, the principal task—immense but rewarding—which awaits Christian ethicians?

I think not. But the proposal is natural and appealing. And there are signs already that if a "dead end" sign is not posted at this entrance, many may enter it and attempt the impossible.[2] It is necessary to demonstrate, in detail, that the difficulties encountered in this enterprise are terminal and not merely initial obstacles to be faced and overcome. The benefit of the demonstration, however, will not be purely prophylactic. The inquiry will provide a first view of the value landscape and raise issues which are important for any value reasoning, whether systematic or not.

A. Christian Values

Within the overall quest of systematization two projects need to be distinguished: the listing of Christian values and their rating. In the present section and the next I shall consider the first project, leaving the second for the third section. And as a start I shall list values and disvalues already cited in the series of examples in chapters 4 and 5. They furnish rich materials for reflection and analysis, and ample illustration of what is meant by "value" and "disvalue," or "Christian values," within the context of moral decision:

1. "The value of cultic worship" (IV, A).
2. "Restoration of his health" (IV, A).
3. Danger of immorality (IV, B).
4. Freedom "from anxious care, " "care for the Lord's business" (IV, B).
5. "The praise of our Lord God" (IV, C).
6. "The salvation of my soul" (IV, C).
7. "One's life," "his existence" (IV, D).
8. The welfare of one's country (IV, E).
9. "Physical agony" (IV, E).
10. "Mental anguish" (IV, E).
11. "The proper rearing of offspring" (IV, G).
12. "Harm to the spiritual life of his charges" (IV, H).
13. "The genuine spiritual development of these youths" (IV, H).
14. "Order, stability, and progress in community" (IV, I).
15. "Thinking and feeling alike, with the same love for one another, the same turn of mind" (IV, I).
16. "The disvalue of conflict, especially when it is open" (IV, I).
17. "Order and unity in the community" (IV, J).
18. "The temporal common good" (IV, J).
19. "A degree of intellectual and moral life making possible for every person the conquest of autonomous freedom" (IV, J).
20. "So high a degree of richness and perfection," in store for human consciousness, through further evolution (IV, K).
21. "The order of nature" (V, D).
22. "The vision of God" (V, D).
23. "Generation" (V, D).
24. "Mutilation" (V, E).
25. "Relieving the suffering of those in distress" (V, G).
26. "Comforts and purchasable pleasures": "a more pleasant house, better furniture, more tobacco, more holiday travel, etc." (V, G).

27. "The child's life, the mother's faithfulness to her dependent, the physician's commitment to preserving life" (V, H).

28. "The personal autonomy of the mother and the social interest in population control" (V, H).

29. "The entire institution of criminal law" (V, I).

30. "The value of life, each human life" (V, I).

31. "Justice" (V, I).

32. "Fairness" (V, J).

33. "Inconvenience" (V, J).

The list is long. And one has the impression that it could be made much longer. For I obtained these items by attending to only the more fully developed examples and the more explicitly stated values and disvalues. And, of course, countless other issues and examples might be cited, involving values and disvalues not mentioned here. On the other hand, in such collections there is much repetition and overlap. A value like "welfare of one's country" (#8), for example, if further analyzed, might be seen to coincide with other, more specific values on the list (for instance, justice and order) and so perhaps could be dropped. Or, taking the reverse direction, we might group disvalues like physical agony (#9) and mental anguish (#10) under the broader heading "suffering of those in distress" (#25). In these ways, through analysis and grouping, a more systematic, manageable listing might be achieved.

Such listings have often been attempted. Walter Everett, for example, divided human values into eight groups: economic values, bodily values, values of recreation, values of association, character values, aesthetic values, intellectual values, religious values.[3] Bertocci and Millard distinguish existence values, health values, character values, economic values, vocational values, recreational values, affiliative values, sexual values, aesthetic values, intellectual values, and religious values.[4] "The best known of the content groupings is Spranger's (used in the Allport-Vernon test of values): theoretical, economic, aesthetic, social, political, and religious."[5]

I shall not opt for one or the other of these lists, or for some other, or try to construct one of my own. My interest concerns the logic of such compilations and especially the notion that they might perform a function analogous to that of universal precepts. The idea, roughly, is that with a complete table of rated values in hand, we would know what features to look for in assessing an act and how to rank them when discovered. Without a clearer notion of the table's utilization, we cannot tell precisely what form the entries should take. But questions like the following, concerning *what items to include*, would supposedly be germane.

(1)   May *instrumental* values be admitted, side by side with intrinsic, *terminal* ones? Suppose, for instance, that the economic values in Everett's list were so specified that their worth stemmed entirely from their instrumental relation to bodily values, values of recreation, and the rest (cf. VIII, E). In that case, to assess the economic values of an action, then add those others, would be to count the same values twice. So doubtless only intrinsic values should be mentioned.

(2)   Next, should *disvalues* be listed separately? Most evils — hunger, poverty, loneliness, sickness, ignorance — are privations, equivalent to the lack of appropriate goods. But some disvalues are not so related to values. Physical and mental pain, for instance, are not mere privations. They, in themselves, are positive evils and so would seem to require separate mention if the list of relevant considerations is to be complete.

However, if tables like those cited make no separate mention of disvalues, a possible justification even within our present context appears both obvious and valid. Anyone contemplating help to the sick would consider their pain along with other aspects of their illness; both would fall quite naturally beneath the heading "bodily values" (Everett) or "health values" (Bertocci and Millard). No separate listing of the pain seems necessary, either practically or theoretically. For relief of those in distress is and may be treated as a value (#25).

(3)   Other connections between the initial, longer listing and the systematic tables are more problematic. Where, for example, should we locate the value "*order of nature,*" cited in #21? It seems to cut across all the categories in the summary listings and to fall under none. So should we append this item by itself or add a new category to cover it?

The authors of the lists, and I, and perhaps the reader too, would do neither but would drop the alleged value altogether. For even those who cite it in this or that case (contraception, say, or lying) do not universalize it. They do not say, "As pain is always a bad thing, so too is any deviation from nature (in the nonmoral sense here required)." Thus, this item does not belong in a general listing of values. A genuine value is universal. Once a value, always a value, one might say.

(4)   Yet what of gladness or sadness? Surely they belong among the legitimate determinants of action. If an action will make people glad, that is generally a plus; if it will make them sad, that is a minus. However, gladness is not always a good thing, nor sadness a bad thing. Their status depends on their object. Gladness over another's suffering, say, or over success in a crime, is not a good thing, nor is sorrow for sin a bad thing.

The upshot is that gladness and sadness may be listed in a table of values and disvalues, but not in general form. If they appear, their object, too, should be indicated. "Once a value always a value" still holds, but on condition that the value is adequately stated. We must be careful to treat such "*organic unities*" as unities, listing *them* as always good or bad rather than abstract aspects denoted by more general expressions ("gladness," "sadness," "satisfaction," and so on).

(5)   With regard to *happiness*, a kindred value much stressed by ethicians, this further problem appears. As is well known, the way to achieve happiness is to seek the good, not happiness. So should happiness be mentioned among the values sought? The answer would seem to be that whereas our own happiness will largely take care of itself, others' happiness may and should be our concern. So it might seem legitimate, even within the context of decision, to list this item too.

Yet notice that in the tables I have cited, no slot is provided in which happiness might fit. Everett, for instance, cites economic values, bodily values, values of recreation, values of association, aesthetic values, and so on. And happiness belongs in no one of these compartments. For recall the popular form of speech: "Happiness is a bonus at Christmas (economic), a sound night's sleep (bodily), a day on the beach (recreational), a friendly chat (association), a sunset at sea (aesthetic)," and so on. There is truth in this way of speaking: happiness, at least in this life, is no one thing but a variable weave of many things.[6] So to add happiness as a ninth value to Everett's list of eight would be like adding Oxford University to a list of its colleges (to borrow Gilbert Ryle's comparison).

(6)   Perusing further the initial list of thirty-four, we come across items like justice (#31) and fairness (#32), but for them too we find no place in the more systematic listings. If a table mentioned *moral values*, we might accommodate justice and fairness there. However, none of the cited tables does include such a heading.

The omission is understandable. It would be a serious confusion to list the morality of an action among the values to be considered in determining its morality. Its morality follows from the value configuration; it is not one of the determinants. And the same holds for justice, or for charity, in the common sense of an objective, overall assessment of an option. Thus, in our analysis of a case we should hesitate to say, for example: "Other values were also at stake, such as justice, love, preservation of higher personal values."[7] A consistent value viewpoint would probably require us to delete at least one of these.

Yet the justice cited in #31 does belong in the list of relevant considerations for the reasons already mentioned (V, I), and so does the fairness in #32 and the danger of immorality in #3. For the immorality in question is not that of the choice contemplated, for celibacy and

against marriage, but that to which a person might be tempted as a result of that choice. It is seen as one of the consequences of the decision
and so belongs with other consequences, cited for or against.[8] Granted,
either of the first two systematic tables might subsume moral effects under "character values," but objective justice and fairness — of actions,
laws, and institutions — would still need to be accommodated.

(7)   Similar accommodation would have to be made for humility,
friendliness, mildness, forgiveness, piety, and a number of other values.
These, too, are not purely subjective features (not just "dispositions"),
but they characterize action itself. There are forgiving, mild, humble,
friendly, devout *ways of doing the things* we do and of leading our lives
in pursuit of varied values. And these aspects of behavior are themselves
important values: "Love is patient; love is kind and envies no one. Love
is never boastful, nor conceited, nor rude" (1 Cor. 13:4).

Such accommodation is more than an analytic nicety. It means,
for example, that the decision for or against capital punishment cannot
rest uniquely on the calculation of consequences, nor even (supposing
they were shown to be beneficial) on the weighing of these consequences in relation to the criminal's death and prior suffering. If there is
doubt on either score (the second question is often not even raised), a
further consideration is then decisive for the Christian: "Love is kind."
He is disinclined to blindfold the terrified prisoner, to pull the switch, to
wield the axe. Similar reasoning applies to the vexed question of triage
(shall only some nations be helped, while others are left to suffer now
rather than later?).[9] Where calculations are so complex and uncertain,
charity is kind. It prefers this form of life: that of a Mother Teresa to
that of a computer.

(8)   The most problematic listing of all I have saved till last. Whereas
hedonists rate *pleasure* as the supreme value, Christians often omit it
entirely from their list. But to assess the omission accurately (prior to
endorsing or contesting it), a distinction is required. It is one thing to
deny that pleasure is valuable in itself and quite another to reject it as a
motive. For various considerations other than that radical denial might
motivate the rejection (which, once again, I do not endorse but seek to
explain):

(a) Pleasure, like gladness, may have an object,[10] and the object
may be either good or bad (see number 4, above, on organic unities).
Thus a person may take pleasure in the scenery or in another's good for-
tune but also in another's suffering or failure. And in such cases the
pleasure is not a separable aspect with a value of its own. If the object is
evil, the value of the pleasure goes down, not up, as the pleasure increases. The more a person rejoices over evil, the worse is the rejoicing.

(b) The pleasure envisaged by Christian ethicists is usually the agent's. And both altruism and his happiness require that a person focus on others' pleasure rather than on his own. (The focus on first-person pleasure and its consequent rejection as a motive is strikingly illustrated by the number of moralists who in their discussion of contraception have failed to consider the possibility that one marriage partner might seek the other's pleasure and not just his or her own.)

(c) If pleasure is serially related to higher values (any degree of the higher outweighing any degree of the lower), then only the higher values, it might be felt, should be taken into account. Pleasure may belong on an abstract list of values, but not among the determinants of action. Seek first the kingdom of God and his justice, and this too will come your way.

(d) As a matter of mere logic, if a value rates below all other values (as pleasure often does in Christian reckonings), then whether serially related to other values or not, it provides more occasion for abuse. Other things being equal, to prefer it to another value is always wrong, whereas the same cannot be said of any other value on the list. But the more often a value gives rise to abuse, the more likely moralists are to discount it. Fine in theory, in practice it appears dangerous.

(e) As a matter of psychology, pleasure, though rated lowest, attracts strongly, indeed perhaps more powerfully than any higher type of value. It is this disparity between rating and force, I suspect, which accounts above all for the distrust of Christian ethicians and their tendency to remove pleasure from the catalog of legitimate considerations. Pleasure, so analyzed, seems a very Satan among values. Temptation seems inherent in its nature. For the force and the rating appear inseparable: were pleasure either higher or weaker it would not be pleasure. But being so low and at the same time so powerful, it always inclines to deordination.[11]

B. The One and the Many

Every value other than the highest may seem a Satan. For Hartmann can write: "No one does wrong for the sake of the wrong; something positively valuable always hovers before him. This view has not been seriously challenged since Socrates. He who plots injury to another, does not desire the other's harm, but his own advantage; and no one would deny that this is a value."[12]

Hence the problem of pleasure is but a limited instance of a much larger issue encountered at every turn. The good tends to become the

enemy of the better, and the better of the good. And such it must sometimes be. But when it should and how and to what extent — this deserves
careful consideration. For otherwise one value after another may be
stricken from the list of legitimate motives till finally in place of the
many there reigns only one. The following ordered series, moving in
that direction, suggests the dimensions of the problem.

(1)   The "First Principle and Foundation" of Ignatius' *Exercises* begins: "Man was created to praise, reverence, and serve God our Lord,
and by this means to save his soul; and the other things on the face of the
earth were created for man's sake, and in order to aid him in the prose-
cution of the end for which he was created. Whence it follows, that
man must make use of them in so far as they help him to attain his end,
and in the same way he ought to withdraw himself from them in so far
as they hinder him from it."[13] Reading these words within the present
context, one is led to ask whether the Creator's good pleasure is limited
to humankind — whether before, below, and apart from man he did not
look on what he had made and find it good (Gen. 1:9–25). Is beauty, for
instance, purely instrumental? May a Christian be concerned about the
preservation of endangered species only because their disappearance
would impoverish man's habitat? Or is he permitted a more Franciscan
attitude toward "Brother Fox" and "Sister Wren"? If, however, "you admit that any human being ought *ever* to pay *some*, even slight, attention to any non-human value (e.g. the absence of animal suffering in
any single instance), you have abandoned the standpoint of naïve hu-
manism which is . . . that nothing except human welfare is relevant to
any moral action."[14]

(2)   The focus narrows a second time when the humanist further
maintains: "If an evaluatum is not a felt or perceived quality of experience, it cannot have intrinsic value."[15] "Beauty," for instance, "is not a
form of intrinsic value, but only the power in an object of evoking something that has value, the aesthetic experience."[16] "There is indeed nothing which is desirable or undesirable for its own sake and entirely without reference to anything beyond itself except that quality of passages of
experience by which he who experiences them finds them satisfying and
such as he would prolong, or dissatisfying and such as he would terminate or avoid."[17] Thus "by far the most valuable things, which we know
or can imagine, are certain states of consciousness, which may be
roughly described as the pleasures of human intercourse and the enjoyment of beautiful objects."[18] The intercourse and the objects are themselves not precious, but means to the inner end; they drop through the
sieve of intrinsic value, leaving only subjective value-data behind, on a
par with the same author's "sense-data."

(3)   This human, experiential realm of value is narrowed still further by a variety of "puritan"[19] restrictions and not only by the ban on pleasure as a legitimate motive. "The mainspring of the Puritan's mechanism," writes Marshall Knappen, "was his moral consciousness. The beautiful and true were to him only the handmaidens of the good. He could ride to and fro through the Constable country and in his diary record only prophesyings. Psalms might be sung in church, but church music which obscured the sense of the words was an abomination, and little time should be wasted on profane tunes outside the sacred walls. The joys of pure learning, such as the observation of crocodiles, smote the zealous with thoughts of sinful pride."[20] A Christian so intent on higher things is not likely to become a biologist or any kind of scientist; for isotopes, galaxies, and amino acids are likely to appear as irrelevant as crocodiles to the salvation of his and others' souls.[21]

(4)   A twist of the lens, and the focus tightens again: "Theistic morality is concerned with the realization of a certain sort of character and attitude rather than with external observance of moral rules, or even with the obedience to moral rules for their own sake. It is concerned with what a man must become in himself rather than with what specific acts he must do."[22] "The outward acts of worship — the saying or singing of words, the performance of ceremonies, the utterance of prayer or praise, the listening to exhortation or instruction — can only be regarded as valuable because they express and tend to cultivate a right state of the soul, but that right state of the soul is in a sense an end-in-itself."[23] All the queen's beauty dwells within; her deeds are mere clues to something unseen.

(5)   Virtue itself may undergo a like devaluation: "By its very notion," writes Austin Fagothey, "virtue is a means and not an end. Virtue consists of morally good habits, and these habits are called good precisely because they lead man more easily and readily to his last end. Virtue is a straight way, a right direction, a true aiming at the highest good."[24] "Virtue is an indispensable means to happiness, but it is not that happiness itself."[25]

(6)   With goodness, like beauty and truth, made the servant of something higher, an overall focus results: "'Paradise is our native country,' said the Puritan, 'and we in this world be as exiles and strangers: we dwell here as in Meshech and as in the tents of Kedar, and therefore we be glad to be at home.' And again, 'To a mind which misliketh this world, nothing can come so welcome as death, because it takes him out of the world.' Or, 'All is trouble and weariness and vanity to a godly mind: whether he eat, or drink, or sleep, he counteth it a servitude unto the flesh and wisheth with David to be rid from these necessities.'"[26]

Such sentiments find an echo throughout Christian history, in the Latin liturgy as in the writings of Calvin: "If heaven is our country what is the earth but our place of exile? If to depart out of the world is to enter into life, what is the world but a sepulchre? What is a continuance in it but absorption in death? . . . We must learn to hate this terrestrial life, that it make us not prisoners to sin."[27]

(7)   Narrowed from time to eternity, the focus seems to tighten further when Saint Thomas writes: "The last end for man is the contemplation of truth. This alone is distinctive of his nature, and no other [corporeal] being shares it with him. Nor is there any end beyond it, for the contemplation of truth is an end in itself. Hereby man is united in likeness with superior spirits because this alone of human activities is an activity of God and the angels as well. . . . And to this end all other human activities seem to be directed."[28] "Man's final perfection will be to attain to contemplation such as angels enjoy."[29]

(8)   "So it is that the soul approaches its final goal, by successive destructions of all the successive signs which it uses as supports on its forward progress. By making it experience the relativity of all that is not God, the Holy Spirit takes possession of the soul. . . ."[30] But human vision and human bliss are not God. He is our goal, he is the one thing necessary, to be loved with our whole heart and our whole mind and strength. A final contraction, therefore, remains to be made. "Our union with God remains imperfect as long as there endures in us, besides the love which leads us to him, another love which attaches us to persons and things for themselves."[31]

True, the second great commandment suggests the proper interpretation of the first. Love of neighbor goes with love of God. But Christian ardor wishes no limits to its devotion. So it affirms, for example, that the world was created for God alone and for his glory; and: "I love my neighbor as myself — for the love of Thee." This "Act of Charity" does not *say* that obedience to God is the sole motive for loving one's neighbor, just as the "First Principle and Foundation," in (1), does not say that man should treat nonhuman creatures *only* as means to man's end. But neither does it say the contrary. And such silences can be eloquent.

As the mind's thirst for unity leads to repeated reductions in the speculative order (materialism, idealism, determinism, and so on), so the heart's kindred yearning reduces value after value to a servant of the one. Or rather to its slave. For first a value is seen to further some other, and the other is seen to be higher. So the former is subordinated to the latter and made its servant. But a servant is only a servant and cannot be allowed to compete with its master. So the servant loses all rights and becomes a slave. For has not Truth itself declared, "No man can serve two masters"?

Thus Aquinas writes: "Man is placed between the things of this world and the spiritual goods which constitute eternal beatitude, so that the more he clings to the one the more he abandons the other, and vice versa."[32] "There are two things which increase one's charity. First the heart's separation from earthly things. For the heart cannot tend perfectly towards different objects. Hence no one can love both God and the world. And therefore the farther our heart is removed from love of earthly things, the more it is strengthened in love of the divine."[33]

The possible practical implications of such a viewpoint appear when Thomas writes: "On the lover's side we talk of charity being perfect when a person loves to his utmost, which can happen in three ways. First, when his whole heart is always actually intent on God, which is the perfection that charity has in heaven, but cannot have in this life where the weakness of the human condition makes it impossible to be always actually thinking about God and loving him. Second, when he devotes all his zeal to the consideration of God and divine things, leaving aside everything else except what the demands of this present life impose. This perfection is possible for a wayfarer, though not all those who possess charity attain to it."[34]

Jesus' praise of Mary might seem to impart the same basic message. "'Martha, Martha, you are fretting and fussing about so many things; but one thing is necessary. The part that Mary has chosen is best; and it shall not be taken away from her'" (Lk. 10:41–42). However, the tale of the Good Samaritan conveys a different impression. Many things were necessary, it seems: dressing the man's wounds, pouring on oil and wine, hoisting him onto the beast, bringing him to the inn, caring for him, paying the innkeeper, visiting him on the return trip. And it is clear that we live in a world like that road to Jericho.

Jesus himself was a contemplative in action: "My father has never yet ceased his work, and I am working too" (Jn. 5:17). No mere "weakness of the human condition" kept him from constant contemplation, but divine charity, of a kind we are to imitate: "Only so can you be children of your heavenly Father, who makes his sun rise on good and bad alike" (Mt. 5:45) — and in creative, outgoing love brings them and it to existence. His actions reveal his values, and the values reveal his nature. Thus, followers of such a Lord and worshippers of such a God cannot without multiple incoherence esteem him alone. To treasure him but not his works would be like admiring an artist while seeing no merit in his paintings or praising a reformer while deploring his reforms. The heavens cannot proclaim the glory of God if the heavens are trash. Value monism does not square with Christian theism.

Similar incoherence infects all the reductions we have seen. To substantiate this claim, and thereby restore the full range of intrinsic value, let us review the successive restrictions one by one, starting from the last ("Fix your hearts on God alone") and working back to the first ("Of all creation, man alone is an end"). At each step countertexts might be cited from Christian tradition to show that the evidence is far from unanimous in favor of the restriction and, if possible, that it is a minority move. But a shorter, more decisive method is to demonstrate, number by number, that the reduction is incoherent, so untenable, no matter how popular it may be or once have been.

(8) **(God alone)** When related to this chapter's concern for moral guidance, this final limitation reveals a further difficulty besides those just cited: A teleological ethic, bent on furthering value, cannot focus on God alone as aim of action; for God himself is not perfected by human effort. We may educate a child, beautify a park, renovate a ghetto, console a widow, reform a monastery, but God we cannot educate, beautify, renovate, console, reform, or otherwise improve. Hence he is not related to our actions as that which makes them right or wrong, but as motive or final goal (cf. III, B). First in order of value, he does not even belong in a list of competing values such as we are considering. For he competes with no value as a determinant of right action.

(7) **(Vision of God)** The beatific vision, too, drops from the list for a similar reason. It is at most merited, not made. And even if it were a product of our striving, it would not be the only thing desirable. A theologian like Saint Thomas, who stresses the beatific vision as our final end, does not mean thereby to exclude, for example, the communion of saints or to equate these two consummations, the individual and the communal.

(6) **(Heaven)** As for the reductive fixation on heaven alone, occasionally Christian belief in a life to come might influence some moral verdict or at least alter the weighting in the scales of value. Martyrdom, for example, would look different if it ended the martyr's existence ("Better red than dead," the Russellian saying advises). But on the majority of occasions, since heaven is a city we seek but not one we build, it cannot count for or against our actions' morality. Being neither aspect nor consequence, it does not affect the balance of values.

True, without asserting a causal link between the here and the hereafter, we might affirm their continuity: as the present growth of a plant conditions but does not cause its future development (for that sun, air, and nourishment are necessary), so a person's earthly progress in knowledge, love, and community may prepare, though it does not produce, his or her future consummation. This supposition, however, does not restore the futuristic value reduction. If this life anticipates the next and the next is wonderful, then this life too must have some intrinsic worth; if knowledge of God, or knowledge generally, will be valuable then, it is valuable now; if the communion of saints will be desirable then, it is desirable now, so far as it can be realized on earth. Thus we cannot have it both ways. Deny continuity, and the criterial connection is cut; future bliss has minimal relevance for morality. Affirm continuity, and terrestrial values merit recognition. Either way, the otherworldly reduction is untenable.

(5) (**Last end**) For Immanuel Kant a good will is the only thing unqualifiedly good, whereas Fagothey and others treat it as a mere means. So one wonders about the divine will: Is that too mere means? Once again the reduction is not coherent. It results from confusing intrinsic value and final end — criterion and goal — and asserting the unicity of the latter for every virtuous act. The simple truth is that to reach God I must do his will, and to do his will I must know, desire, and pursue what is good. The relation is not linear, one good here and another beyond, in competition for my allegiance and my heart. And though the good I seek in right action be not my own virtue but something else (see note 10 of chapter 2), it does not follow that virtue is then means rather than end. It is neither. Yet it is a good thing for all that — good in itself.

(4) (**Inner virtue**) Personal perfection is not, however, a self-enclosed, self-directed good. A good will is one that desires what is good; a virtuous will is one that hungers and thirsts after justice. So theistic morality cannot esteem inner virtue without prizing virtuous action as well. It is as in the final reduction, at the start of our return series: as we cannot love God without loving what he loves, so we cannot love virtue without valuing what it values. The link between good tree and good fruit is logical as well as causal. All the queen's beauty cannot reside within.

(3) (**Godliness**) The Puritan reduction, too, would "purify" itself out of existence. Focusing on ethical value alone as intrinsically worthwhile — to the exclusion, say, of the intellectual and aesthetic, and a fortiori of the physical and sensual — it leaves no criterion by which to determine the ethical itself. "Handsome is as handsome does," but what makes an action handsome? Its handsomeness?

To avoid incoherence and vacuity, we must recognize other values, served by moral conduct. "Let us recall," notes von Hildebrand, "that our love tends naturally to bestow agreeable things on the beloved, and to avert what is disagreeable from him. It belongs to the display of the [benevolent intention] in every love for a creature that we also want to offer to him a good meal, to make everything comfortable for him, and to protect him from disagreeable things. This clearly shows that legitimately agreeable beings have the character of something beneficent, of a gift for the person. They are objective goods *because* of their being agreeable, and the 'pro' embodied in the agreeable is here the basis of their character of an objective good for the person. Although it occupies the lowest rung in the hierarchy of the objective good for the person, this type nonetheless possesses the dignity that belongs to all members of that hierarchy. We should indeed thank God that there exist agreeable things, such as the fresh breeze or the restorative swim on a very hot day, the warmth in a room when it is very cold, an excellent wine, a delicious meal, a bed or a chair if one is tired. These things have, as such, the character of objective goods for the person."[35]

"But rarely," adds von Hildebrand, "is this importance of agreeable things seen when they are the object of our *own* desire." We are then inclined to treat them as belonging in the category of the merely subjectively satisfying, thus tinged with selfishness and not to be indulged. If, however, we avoid these blinders, the range of value remains unrestricted and is willingly widened. The kingdom we seek and pray for is a many-splendored thing, achieved not only through but also in all manner of values. "Jesus exhibited the wholeness that is the Father's will for His children by the way he acted on behalf of men in his saving acts. He cursed the fig tree because it did not produce figs, and he repudiated the man with the one talent for burying it. Where there was paralysis he released it, where there was withering of limbs he restored them; blindness became seeing; hunger was fed with bread; life returned where it had been lost. All of which is to say that every motion of the Spirit of Christ will be known by the fact that, like Jesus' own acts, it will bring wholeness to the human order, not diminishment."[36]

(2) (**Human experience**)   Without a further step backward along the reductive series, all these varied values would remain mere shadows of themselves: "perceived qualities of experience," "states of consciousness," and the like, within a solipsistic world of inner value. This restrictive analysis, however, contradicts the attitude we do in fact adopt (see the quotation from Wittgenstein in IV, F, 3) and any we could. It is not all one to us, provided the experience stays intact, whether paintings, dances, liturgies, friends, conversations, and God himself go out of existence. Our valuings are ineluctably object-centered.

Thus, the proposed reduction requires a person to split himself in two. As experiencing subject he is to appreciate art and so have aesthetic experiences; be lost in wonder at God and so have a religious experience; value a friend and his company and so experience the joys of friendship; and so on through the list. But then, as moral critic and judge of values, he is to declare the experience alone important; all the rest is mere means to this end.

(1) (Human benefit) Similar incoherence infects the first reduction. If I am to derive any satisfaction from my dog's enjoyment of our romp, I cannot regard his enjoyment as a mere means to my satisfaction. And of course I do not. Nor, quite generally, when I admire a sunset or the magnificence of the Alps, or regret the slaughter of whales or the extinction of the passenger pigeon, are my sentiments compatible with the reductionist thesis. So when I come to catalog values, let me not play make-believe. My human appreciations, like those of the Creator, embrace more largeheartedly all levels of creation.

A lesson of these many restrictions and subsequent restorations is the need to distinguish between the context of sheer evaluation, prior to the constraints of choice, and that of moral decision through the balancing of values. In the latter the watchword is "either-or"; in the former it is "both-and": both human and nonhuman, both higher and lower, both paradise and progress, all this and heaven too.

C. No Feasible Hierarchy

So far the construction of a usable scheme of values may appear an extremely arduous, complex task but still feasible and desirable. Doubtless it would be sanguine to hope, with Locke, that "morality might be placed among the sciences capable of demonstration," but would not even an imperfect system be preferable to none?

Not necessarily. Suppose, to use a homely comparison, that we set out to construct a system of values per pound for oranges, carrots, walnuts, lettuce, spinach, and other produce, with the idea that the list could serve as a guide in commercial transactions. Questions would immediately surface concerning the meaning of the ratings: in rating oranges, for instance, what type of orange are we to consider, of what quality, in what condition, at what time of year, in how good a year, in what region or country, and so on? Even were answers to these queries forthcoming, doubt would remain concerning what purpose such ratings might conceivably serve. If, for instance, the average value of all types of oranges in all regions were calculated for an average year, what guidance would that figure provide a grower negotiating the sale of a specific shipment of oranges, of this or that specific type and quality, in this condition, in this region, at this time of year, with this dealer, by crate and not by pound?

The project of a Christian hierarchy of values, for application to life's transactions, presents analogous difficulties plus others. First of all, how are we to identify the *Christian* hierarchy (as opposed to our personal estimates or preferences)? For example (to take a somewhat concrete instance), how are we to rank knowledge and love respectively? If we turn to Christian thought and its expression, we note, for instance, Aquinas' exaltation of intellectual values and Thomas a Kempis' depreciation of them, and we realize that either preference claims countless Christian advocates. Focusing even on Aquinas himself, we are caught in dialectical puzzlement: On the one hand it was doubtless the Angelic Doctor's love of God which made the beatific vision appear so desirable to him, yet on the other hand how can there be love save of what is known and precisely insofar as it is known? And if love is proportionate to knowledge, is not knowledge more fundamental than love? The pendulum thus swings uncertainly, and we know not where to arrest it. If we therefore decide that closer analysis is needed, we are faced with a typical "paradox of analysis": How can we present as Aquinas' position what results from a fuller analysis than any he undertook? The difficulties begin to look insoluble; yet here we are considering but a single author.

As in the commercial comparison, our problems stem largely from the unclarity of the desideratum. What are we hunting for? What shall count as criterion of "the Christian rating"? Suppose, for example, that we determined precisely the relative importance attached to knowledge and love on the one hand by Aquinas and on the other hand by a Kempis. Which is the Christian rating? One or the other? The mean? And suppose their ratings agreed perfectly: Would they necessarily be "correct"? Might not the valuings of even the holiest Christian deviate from those of God? But if the divine standard alone is sure and absolute, still, how is it to be conceived and defined? And how is it to be ascertained if both Scripture and tradition pose still more intractable problems of analysis than the writings of a single author (scrutinized just for his sense and not the divine)?

None of these conundrums can be illuminated without adequate answers to another set of queries. Let us imagine that we are assigning their respective weights to aesthetic values versus cognitive. Now cognitive values cover, for instance, knowledge of the local bus routes, of nuclear physics, of human nature, and of God; and aesthetic values include symphonies, cartoons, the Parthenon, and sunsets. And the question arises whether the weighting for each such class as a whole should be quantitative or qualitative or somehow both together. If quantitative, shall we consider simply the number of subclassifications (symphonies, cartoons, temples, etc.), or merely the frequency of their instances (the number of symphonies, temples, etc.), or both together? And in the case, say, of symphonies, shall we distinguish between the number of instances (e.g., the number of symphonies written) and the number of realizations (e.g., the frequency with which the symphonies are played or heard)? And should we perhaps go further still and distinguish between the number of realizations and the number of recipients (hearers, viewers, etc.)? And if all these considerations, perhaps, are somehow relevant, how are they to be combined in the overall rating? If, on the other hand, we rate according to quality rather than quantity, shall we follow the average or shall we, instead, read off each rating from the summits of achievement, conceivable or actual? If the first, should we calculate the average from types (symphonies, operas, etc.), or instances (the symphonies of Beethoven, of Mozart, etc.), or realizations (Toscanini's rendering, Bernstein's, etc.), or receptions (Toscanini's appreciation of the result, the players', the janitor's, etc.)? And if we find such analysis intelligible, desirable, even necessary in the case of aesthetic values, will it be equally appropriate for cognitive values? If not, will the ratings for aesthetic and cognitive values be comparable?

Surely the guiding norm throughout, in answering each such question, should be the intended application. One calculation is preferable to another, from the standpoint of this chapter, in proportion as it facilitates decision. But the moment we consider the question of application, we see that none of the proposed formulae is preferable to any other, for they are all equally useless. In a concrete case no abstract rating, whether qualitative or quantitative, whether existential or ideal, would provide any guidance. Suppose, for instance, that I am contemplating a contribution to either the local symphony orchestra or the Smithsonian Institute. Or suppose I have the choice of buying either an atlas or a recording of chamber music. To decide such matters I need to know, in the first option, the competence and preferences of the local conductor, the quality of the performers, the facilities at their disposal, local appreciation of their efforts, and so on. In the second case I need to know the quality of the specific recording, the specific performance, the specific composition. And on none of these points do I receive any light from a rating of aesthetic values in general, or music in general, or chamber music in general, or even Beethoven's music in general. Neither average nor median nor any other such calculation contributes anything to the requisite concrete estimate.

What is said here of aesthetic values applies with equal force in all sectors of value. For in all there is similar heterogeneity, and any global rating would be equally remote from real-life options. No solution can be found short of the particular case. If we descend from aesthetic values in general to music, and from music in general to opera, symphony, jazz, folk, dance music, chamber music, lieder, rock, Negro spirituals, and so on indefinitely, not only does the listing become encyclopedic but the same problems remain. And if we try to descend still further, the prolixity and complexity and pragmatic absurdity become such that we recognize this dream for what it is: a nightmare.

Summarized abstractly, the situation stands as follows. In calculating overall ratings, of whatever kind (serial, ordinal, cardinal), in whatever way (qualitative or quantitative; mean, median, summit, or ideal term), we might conceivably pass from the particular to the general (provided the particular judgments were our own and not derived from humanity at large, or Christendom as a whole, or present-day Christians, or even our own denomination, today). But the reverse route would be closed; we could not infer the particular from the general. Furthermore, even if we could, it would be a waste of time, and worse, to do so. For in assessing concrete cases by means of such value tables, we would be arguing from the derivative to the primitive, from the enormously complex to the relatively simple, from the less known and understood to that which was far surer. It would be as though people estimated the amount of their individual paychecks from the mean for industrial, agricultural, or other categories of workers — after computing the mean from the figures written plainly on their checks.

D. Confirmation

Many ethicians, I imagine, would be unimpressed by this negative verdict. "Like any value-system," they might observe with Norbert Rigali, "the value system of Christian perfection cannot be a collection of unrelated value-units. Rather, it must be an integral unity of interrelated values, which arises out of and expresses a total and unified stance toward the meaning of man's life in this world."[37] Failure to order a mere catalog of value items, it might be urged, permits no conclusion concerning this different ideal.

No doubt such a "total and unified stance" would in turn reflect an overall view of reality, in the manner Frederick Copleston's contrasting illustrations suggest. On the one hand: "A positive evaluation of personality or selfhood will be intensified or reinforced if the ultimate reality, the source of the empirical world, is conceived as being itself personal. Finite personality would then appear, not as something to be negated, but as a limited reflection of divine personality. Further, man is likely to look on himself as having a divine vocation to contribute, by what he makes of himself and by his actions in the world, to the realization of a divinely determined end or goal of human life and history. This is true of all theistic religions, Jewish, Christian or Muslim. We may add, however, that if the divine personality is conceived, not simply in terms of one Person, but in Trinitarian terms, this belief should intensify the ideal of a unified human society, a society of persons, as the goal of history."

Suppose, though, we turn to Eastern thought, and "the empirical world, which for the pluralist is a real world, though not necessarily coterminous with all reality, is believed to be in some sense illusory. That is, suppose that the empirical world is only the appearance of one single reality, the Absolute, and that this appearance is the fruit of ignorance, of the mind's limitations. Individual personality or selfhood will also appear as illusory, as something to be overcome or transcended through the finite spirit's realization of its oneness with the sole reality, the infinite Spirit or Absolute. While ethics will not indeed be abolished or discarded, moral purification will be regarded as a condition for and a step on the way to transcending the finite ego or self. This means that, though ethics will of course include a theory of conduct, of action, the emphasis will be placed not so much on social action as on enlightenment, on progress in realization of the truth about reality."[38]

From each world view there derives a corresponding stance "toward the meaning of man's life in this world" (to use Rigali's phrase). Individual, community, interpersonal relationships, activity in the world — all are emphasized in one, deemphasized in the other. Values shift. Hence we are well on our way, it would seem, to the very thing desired. Spelling out the Christian view more fully and tracing its implications, may we not elucidate an "integral unity of interrelated values"?

No, not of the sort we seek, one to light a path for moral reasoning. This can be seen from the best-known attempt of the kind. Max Scheler did as prescribed. His ascending values — the agreeable, vital, spiritual, holy[39] — form successive rungs in a unified ladder, each value "founded" in the next, in keeping with Rigali's requirement. However, such systematic interrelation makes no difference for our purposes. Shorn as it is of all "inessentials," the listing lacks the concreteness we have seen to be crucial for decision; it says nothing of the degree, the extent, the probability of each value, nor of its specific form with its specific worth. And the same would hold for any such abstract items (e.g., personality, community, purification, and enlightenment, as above), no matter how ordered, weighted, or related.

Rigali himself suggests, by way of illustration, that the values of poverty, chastity, and obedience, which ascetical writers have long related harmoniously in the value system known as "the life of the counsels," be extended to Christian life generally. In the value of virginity, for example, "can be seen a demand for a certain degree of sexual self-renunciation"[40] and, more generally, for "self-renunciation in order to do the will of the Father."[41] So viewed, the value of virginity merges with the "selfless love revealed in Jesus, the man completely for others."[42]

But what is the Father's will, and what does love require? This norm will not tell us. Nor does it indicate a value to weigh with other values.[43] It offers instead a rule for distributing benefits, altruistically and not self-centredly. Whatever the values or disvalues at stake, Rigali's norm would accord the neighbor preference in self-sacrificing service. Thus his suggestion points in a direction our inquiry must now take in part four, which opens with a series of such "preference-rules."

E. Looking Back

Before embarking on this final, positive part of our investigation, it may be helpful to pause momentarily, look back over the sometimes tortuous road we have traveled, and see where it has brought us. The basic option of chapter 6 established an overall principle, distilled from Christian belief and practice: the balance of values should guide Christian decision. But what values and how? Though it focuses chiefly on the second of these questions, the present chapter answers both, in a general way, prior to the detailed discussion of part four.

The chapter's first two sections answer the what-question, the last two the how-question. Thus, section A first culls values and disvalues from part two, then does much sifting and sorting: values like justice and fairness belong in a catalog of values for consultation, and so does pleasure, or modesty, humor, friendliness, and the like in the sense of action-characterizations; but the "order of nature" does not, nor does all-encompassing happiness or a general item like gladness or sadness, with the good or bad object left unspecified. Section B then deals with a series of sweeping limitations on intrinsic value, by which Christians and others have sought to systematize their reflections and their lives. None of the reductions survives scrutiny; all the demoted values do. The full panoply of values that thus emerges midway through the chapter is an important positive result, of general interest for the kind of moral reasoning advocated in this part and spelled out in the next.

Only in the subsequent two sections, however, does a verdict finally appear concerning the nonreductive ideal of ordering values hierarchically and then judging conduct by their means. Section C indicates that such a listing, being general, cannot illumine particular choices, no matter what values it names or how it ranks them. The same difficulty remains, section D then notes, regardless of how systematically one relates the abstract categories. With this negative result we reach the second main option of part three. Chapter 6 pronounced for the rule of values and against that of precepts or of alternate criteria. Chapter 7 now decides against consulting abstract values and for closer scrutiny of particulars. This latter approach will now claim our attention in part four.

Guidelines and Procedures Within the Chosen Perspective

At the level of practical moral reasoning, Catholic moral theology and Protestant ethics share in common a very serious question, namely, how can the Christian community and its members make moral decisions and moral judgments which are both responsive and responsible: responsive to problems emerging in contemporary science and technology, political and social institutions, and interpersonal life; responsible not only for the consequences of actions in new circumstances, but responsible also to the moral values, the moral principles, that are grounded in the faith and life of the Christian community, and to the moral values and principles that are grounded in our common humanity.
— James Gustafson

8
Problems of Analysis

THE PARAMOUNT PROBLEM of analysis is analysis. For analysis as such, it may reasonably be urged, is a solvent of the certitudes men live by. In particular, it has been characteristic of the Hebrew-Christian ethic, writes Professor Anscombe, "to teach that there are certain things forbidden whatever *consequences* threaten, such as: choosing to kill the innocent for any purpose, however good; vicarious punishment; treachery (by which I mean obtaining a man's confidence in a grave matter by promises of trustworthy friendship and then betraying him to his enemies); idolatry; sodomy; adultery; making a false profession of faith. The prohibition of certain things simply in virtue of their description as such-and-such identifiable kinds of action, regardless of any further consequences, is certainly not the whole of the Hebrew-Christian ethic; but it is a noteworthy feature of it."[1] And in important respects it has obviously been a strength. For one thing, a person who excludes all exceptions beforehand is forearmed against rationalization, whereas a person who, when tempted, starts to analyze his particular case is already treading a slippery path. (See IV, F.) For another thing, such unquestioned rules establish firm, fixed points of reference in a familiar moral universe, with all the psychological benefits that entails, whereas thoroughgoing analysis carries with it the threat of anomie. It may erode still further traditional structures of meaning.

An initial response, in answer to the first of these two points, is to admit the danger of treating problematic cases, on which theoreticians focus, as typical of life's options. There are indeed situations in which the individual must agonize over his or her decision despite the general rule; for example, the woman described by Fletcher,[2] for whom pregnancy meant release from a Russian prison camp, must ask herself, doubtless with trepidation, whether she may use extramarital intercourse to gain her freedom and rejoin the family that needs her. Concern for her husband and children may impel her to this stratagem, but her case is hardly typical. In the vast majority of instances a Christian need not and should not think twice about the option of adultery. Were analysis recommended for use on all occasions, it would indeed be a solvent. And not only of morality but also of our humanity. Had Mary, for example, reflected carefully before she broke the flask and done a costs/ benefits analysis in the manner of Judas, she would never have anointed Jesus' head or won his praise. Such an act as hers is not programed; it comes spontaneously from the heart. And though not all life is poetry, such poetry in act has a rightful place amid the prose.

In answer to the second objection, the threat of anomie, it may be conceded at the start that "the pattern of morals is of the essence of social life itself; it is essential to human civilized life, which would be unthinkable without it."[3] However, pattern differs from pattern. And it is instructive to compare Professor Anscombe's samples with an earlier, more authoritative listing. Sifting the essential from the inessential, so as to impose a minimal burden, the church at Jerusalem enjoined: "You are to abstain from meat that has been offered to idols, from blood, from anything that has been strangled, and from fornication" (Acts 15: 28–29). The last of these injunctions is still with us, but what of the other three? If they no longer figure in a sampling of norms like Anscombe's and appear less firmly founded than hers, why is that?

The "pattern of morals" consists of more than precepts. Values and value-reasoning, as chapter 4 attests, boast an equally ancient Christian lineage. Concern for human well-being accounts for Christians' willingness, past and present, to question some previously unquestioned absolutes. Thus, to restrict or reject value analysis is to slight another set of meanings, still more central to Christianity. A "regardless-of-the-consequences" morality, identified as Christian, casts shadows of doubt on the fatherhood of God, the redemptive love of Christ, his having come that we may have life and have it more fully (see VI, A).

Hence the task of the moment, as many see it, is to map a more coherent, and therefore more livable, yet thoroughly Christian, moral universe. Indeed a more truly Christian one. Efforts in this direction will occupy the next three chapters concerning questions of logic, of procedure, and of content. The preceding chapter abandoned the hope of elaborating an overall system, but that does not mean no guidance can be offered, no principles be established.

A. My Good versus Others'

The closest analogues to universal precepts in the realm of value analysis are general rules of preference. Carried to the extreme, they

become serial ratings: any amount of human welfare, it might for instance be alleged, outweighs any amount of nonhuman value; or any
degree of moral improvement, no matter how slight or uncertain, out-
ranks any lower value, no matter how massive and sure; or any benefit
to one's neighbor takes precedence over one's own (provided one's own
is not required for his). The most important of these contrasts is that
between my good and others', for self-interest is strong and is active for
good or ill in most of our decision-making. Appropriately, therefore,
this last rule of preference is the one which has received most consideration in Christian ethics.[4]

The Christian commandment of neighbor-love has been read in
two ways with regard to action: (1) we are to put others on a par with
ourselves; (2) we are to give them precedence. In favor of the first version our equal human nature may be alleged, or the injunction to love
our neighbor "as ourselves." However, that phrase need not be given a
quantitative, distributive sense. It could be taken to mean that we are
to adopt toward others the attitude we assume, unbidden, toward ourselves: forgiving them as we forgive ourselves; recognizing excusing factors for them as for ourselves; concerning ourselves for their welfare as
we naturally do for our own.[5] On the other hand, were the self-
sacrificing death of Christ cited for the alternative reading, that too
would be insufficient evidence. For even within an egalitarian perspective, putting all persons on a par, the good of many prevails over that of
one, and their spiritual good over his physical suffering and death. By
this reckoning, too, "Jesus would die for the nation — would die not for
the nation alone but to gather together the scattered children of God"
(Jn. 11:52).

However, it is clear what interpretation Christian tradition has
preferred. The popular phrase makes Jesus "a man for others," not "a
man for others too," and for this it has scriptural backing. "Among you,
whoever wants to be great must be your servant, and whoever wants to
be first must be the willing slave of all — like the Son of Man; he did not
come to be served, but to serve, and to give up his life as a ransom for
many" (Mt. 20:27–28). "If I, your Lord and Master, have washed your
feet [and not my own], you also ought to wash one another's feet. I have
set you an example" (Jn. 13:14–15). "This is my commandment: love one
another, as I have loved you" (Jn. 15:12).

Texts like these,[6] the overall portrait of Jesus in the gospels, the
constant Christian view of his preferences — all suggest at least a norm
of other-preference, giving the nod to another when that person and I
would benefit equally, reversing the verdict when we would suffer
equally. This is already a powerfully altruistic principle. For it is
stronger than parity, and that norm, as we have noted, would require

that Jesus accept a death he might have escaped if many others would benefit thereby and benefit more than he. It would tell Maximilian Kolbe, too, to step forward from the prison ranks and volunteer to die by starvation in place of a man with wife and children. Yet the perfect imitation of Christ may entail something stronger still than either parity or other-preference. It may, for instance, imply that *any* good of another be preferred to *any* good of mine, or perhaps, more radically still, that a Christian live *solely* for others, not for others too.

These refinements, though important, appear theoretically less certain and practically less decisive than the basic shift from parity to other-preference. For when we envisage those further steps, to serial subservience or total self-forgetfulness, it is generally unclear just how much service of self is required for full service of others (just how much blood the heart itself should receive in order to pump more elsewhere); whereas other-preference, in contrast with parity, repeatedly yields a clear decision. Situations repeatedly arise where equality is not feasible: either he marries her or I do; either he gets the job or I do; either he is promoted or I am; and so on down to the last chop on the plate or the best remaining seat in the theater. In such cases the egalitarian norm is violated however I choose, whereas the more altruistic norm is not. It alone tells a Christian what to do.

True, complications may occasionally arise even in this imperfect world if my rival for the spouse, the job, the promotion, the chop, or the better seat adopts the same altruistic attitude as I do. And these complications are sometimes said to tell against the rule of other-preference. "An ethical norm should be universalizable," the objection goes, "but suppose my fellow theater-goer heads with equal speed for a less desirable seat and we reach it simultaneously. What then? Do we fight for the seat, unaltruistically, or does one of us violate the rule and move off to the better location?"

Such imagined cases and their alleged implications[7] bear a revealing resemblance to the logical and semantic paradoxes that have plagued logicians. Concerning these latter I agree with Wittgenstein:[8] we need not revise the English language because its rules permit the perverse statement "I'm lying" (true if false and false if true?); nor are we obliged to abandon the logic of classes because Russell can tie a similar knot by its means, specifying the class of all classes that are not members of themselves and then asking whether it is a member of itself. A rule is not a bad rule if it does not prevent us from making fools of ourselves or does not tell us on all occasions and in all circumstances precisely what we should do. As Wittgenstein observed, the rules of tennis do not specify how high we should throw the ball when we serve and so do not prevent us from heaving it fifty feet up if we please, but the rule requiring the throw is not thereby invalidated or shown to be a bad rule. Nor is the rule of other-preference disqualified by kindred limitations. After all, the alternative, egalitarian rule, as we have seen, may suffer from more.

B. Good versus Evil

Of equally wide application, so potentially as important as the altruistic norm, is the rule of preference which rates the avoidance or elimination of evil over the promotion or preservation of good. Philosophers have developed the idea more fully than have moral theologians. Frankena, for instance, constructs the following hierarchy:

1. One ought not to inflict evil or harm (what is bad).
2. One ought to prevent evil or harm.
3. One ought to remove evil.
4. One ought to do or promote good.

"One is inclined to say," he writes, "that in some sense (1) takes precedence over (2), (2) over (3), and (3) over (4), other things being equal."[9]

A first major difficulty[10] is that most evils are deprivations of good, so that to do the good is to remove the corresponding evil: one visits the lonely, feeds the hungry, instructs the ignorant, and so forth. A coherent statement of Frankena's position would therefore require that it be restricted to positive evils (principally pains, physical or mental), which cannot be defined reductively as deprivations of good. Even then coherence is not achieved if one asserts with W. D. Ross: "We think the duty of not inflicting pain more stringent than the duty of producing a corresponding amount of pleasure."[11] For what is a "corresponding amount of pleasure" if not one that weighs equally in the scales of value, and so in the determination of action? Is there some separate scale in which they might be weighed, so much pain versus so much pleasure?

The same difficulty arises for Frankena's more general suggestion: "Suppose we have two acts, A and B, and that A produces 99 units of good and no evil, while B produces both good and evil but has a net balance of 100 units of good over evil. In this case, act-utilitarianism requires us to say that B is the right thing to do. But some of us would surely think that act A is the right one."[12] In a coherent act-utilitarian perspective values are defined by their relation to action. "V is one of N's values if, and only if, N is prepared to invoke V favorably — and to acknowledge the legitimacy of its invocation by another — in the rationalization of action."[13] And *V* and *W* are equal values (or disvalues) for *N* if they count equally in the rationalization of action. Within this perspective it does not make sense to suggest that duty might lie on the side of lesser value, or to rate 99 units over 100. For his hypothesis to be intelligible, therefore, Frankena must redefine his terms and so state his disagreement differently. And it may be doubted whether disagreement would survive such clarification, for with their tie to action sundered, value terms would change their sense beyond recognition.

Still, the suggested rule of preference awakes sympathetic echoes in a Christian conscience. According to Matthew 25, as traditionally understood, we shall be judged, not quite generally by our service or disservice of value, but principally by the evil we have or have not sought to alleviate. And Jesus reports his own activity in identical terms: "The blind recover their sight, the lame walk, the lepers are made clean, the deaf hear, the dead are raised to life, the poor are hearing the good news" (Mt. 11:5).

This preference for the needy is readily intelligible from the value-balancing viewpoint. For generally speaking the needy benefit more from the food, time, clothing, instruction, or affection we give them than do those who are not in need. Thus the wounded man on the road to Jericho benefited more from the Samaritan's time, money, and mount than would have other travelers on the road (including the Samaritan). The straying sheep, lost and found, benefits more from the shepherd's search than would the rest of the flock from his staying with them. And sinners, like the physically ill, benefit more from Jesus' attentions than those who have no need of a physician (Mt. 9:12). Thus what the Christian heart dictates, value-reasoning corroborates.

If, in addition, the heart here "has reasons that reason knows not of," that means that help to the suffering and needy, as such, has special value in Christian eyes; it functions as a preference-rule in Christian moral reasoning.

C. Fraternity versus Equality

This Christian residue suggests a partial answer to a problem posed by section A on Christian charity. Self-sacrificing service works well on the individual level, but what of group morality? Justice, not charity, replies John Rawls, "is the first virtue of social institutions, as truth is of systems of thought."[14] For how can laws and institutions be both universal and altruistic? To universalize preferential treatment would be to favor everyone, so no one; the suggestion is incoherent. It might seem, therefore, that specifically Christian principles have little application outside the realm of personal morality. On the broader social scene neutral justice reigns, and the social philosopher, not the theologian or man of faith, is arbiter.

Yet what does the philosopher say? The "General Conception" underlying Professor Rawls's much-discussed theory of justice reads as follows: "All social primary goods — liberty and opportunity, income and wealth, and the bases of self-respect — are to be distributed equally unless an unequal distribution of any or all of these goods is to the advantage of the least favored."[15] This is proposed as a fundamental notion of justice, but to a Christian the concluding clause suggests something more: justice tempered by mercy.

Christian correlations and possible influences come equally to mind when Rawls writes: "Perhaps some will think that the person with greater natural endowments deserves those assets and the superior character that made their development possible. Because he is more worthy in this sense, he deserves the greater advantages that he could achieve with them. This view, however, is surely incorrect. It seems to be one of the fixed points of our considered judgments that no one deserves his place in the distribution of native endowments, any more than one deserves one's initial starting place in society. The assertion that a man deserves the superior character that enables him to make the effort to cultivate his abilities is equally problematic."[16]

Rawls grounds his own claims on "our considered judgments." But who are "we"? "In these considered judgments," replies Kai Nielsen, "we have clearly reflected the values of certain modern Western men — liberal, democratic, individualistic men. But why should only their considered judgments be appealed to in seeking considered judgments against which to test abstract moral principles? There are certainly problems in replying 'Because their considered judgments are the right ones, the most rational ones, the correct ones, the ones reasonable men should accept,' for how do we know that or do we know that? Lukes draws our attention to the fact that there are — just to consider our own present Western societies — 'Ultra-conservatives, clerical authoritarians, Empire Loyalists, fascists, racial separatists, Saint-Simonian technocrats, individualist liberals, anarchists, radical egalitarians' all of whom would in important respects dissent from many of the above typically Rawlsian considered judgments."[17]

The theoretician who would base himself on "reason" alone will find this problem vexing, but not a Christian. He sides with the Son of Man. Jesus' lived and stated preference for the neediest he makes his own. Whereas for a Nietzsche the less-favored are the weak, degenerate herd, for the Christian they are Christ's "least brethren," whose needs alone rate mention at the judgment of the nations (Mt. 25). So in general Rawls rings right.

One may wonder, though, about his "difference principle" and its defense: "The intuitive idea is that the social order is not to establish and secure the more attractive prospects of those better off unless doing so is to the advantage of those less fortunate."[18] Even if the less-favored derive no benefit from the restriction, equality should be preserved. This view, Rawls argues, "does seem to correspond to a natural meaning of fraternity: namely, to the idea of not wanting to have greater advantages unless this is to the benefit of others who are less well off. The family, in its ideal conception and often in practice, is one place where the principle of maximizing the sum of advantages is rejected. Members of a family commonly do not wish to gain unless they can do so in ways that further the interests of the rest."[19]

A familiar slip, it seems to me, falsifies this picture of the ideal family. As the Christian critic of pleasure generally views it from a first-person, self-seeking perspective (see the return treatment of VII, B, 3), so Rawls does here with regard to benefits. He does not consider how the rest of the family does or should react when a single member is offered some advantage. Friends stop by, let us imagine, with place for one more on their trip. Does the family then refuse, on the grounds that either all go or no one goes? Of course not. And though the one chosen may be reluctant, in the way Rawls suggests, the rest urge him on— indeed they practically shove him into the car (in the ideal family we are imagining). "Enjoy the trip," they say, "we'll enjoy it with you!"

It may be that no close analogue is conceivable for society as a whole and that Rawls's restriction is therefore acceptable in practice. We must not assume, he warns, that there is much similarity from the standpoint of justice between the allotment of goods to specific individuals and the appropriate design of society. Our common-sense intuitions for the former may be a poor guide to the latter.[20] Thus in the present connection he might observe that "the expectations of representative persons ["holding the various social positions, or offices, or whatever, established by the basic structure"] depend upon the distribution of rights and duties throughout the basic structure. When this changes, expectations change. I assume, then, that expectations are connected: by raising the prospects of the representative man in one position we presumably increase or decrease the prospects of representative men in other positions."[21]

This supposition appears plausible; therefore, as I say, nothing analogous to that trip for a single member of the family may be conceivable within the social framework. Still, the objection indicates a possible tension between the principles of equality and fraternity, and thus an underlying divergence between the Rawlsian approach and that of the Gospel. For Rawls equality is the first, overriding principle.[22] Equality requires that the less-privileged be favored and rules out any advantage which does not benefit them. But a brother does not insist on his brother's rising no higher, in goods or expectations, than himself. He wishes his welfare without restriction or exception. Thus were there ever the prospect of either some benefiting and thereby creating an inequality or of none benefiting — that is, were there ever the social equivalent of that offer of a ride for one — fraternity would prefer the former. And even where it agrees with the principle of equality in favoring the less-privileged, it does so for different reasons. It helps them, not for the sake of equality, but to improve their lot — that is, because they are brothers and because they are in need. May they have life and have it more abundantly! Such, I would suggest, is the dominant Christian principle — fraternity.

D. Higher versus More Fundamental

Cases of destitution to which Rawlsian principles apply are also prime targets for a further suggested rule, according to which precedence should be given to lower but more fundamental values over higher but less fundamental ones. "Already in his 'Ethics' (chapter 63)," writes Hans Reiner, "Nicolai Hartmann drew attention to the fact that difference of rank is by no means the only norm for prefering one value over another and thereby deciding which has a claim to be actualized. Hartmann showed that in addition to the preference for higher values there is also a preference for what he termed 'stronger' values. These 'stronger' values — I would rather call them 'more urgent,' given the danger of taking the other expression positivistically — are precisely lower, but at the same time more fundamental. Thus a person's *existence*, for example, is a precondition for his realizing higher values such as the artistic or ethical. And accordingly the requirement of assuring a person's 'bare existence' takes precedence over that of realizing the higher values, at least insofar as there is question of the higher ones' being actualized by this particular person."[23] More concretely still, "we must feed a starving man before trying to preach the good news of salvation to him."[24]

This preference-rule differs notably from those we have endorsed, for it does not affect the outcome of straightforward value-balancing, whereas they do. If, for example, one alternative makes me benefit and another confers the same benefit (a choice apartment, a job, a trip abroad . . .) on my neighbor, the verdict remains suspended between these two equal outcomes until altruism tips the scales in favor of my neighbor. The present rule, on the contrary, tips no scales but at most confirms the straightforward value verdict. Thus if, for example, the opposed alternatives are the loss of life and all it permits, on one side, and preservation of life plus all its possibilities, on the other, the latter option wins hands-down in any value reckoning. So one wonders about the utility of the Hartmann-Reiner norm.

"It may alert us to causal dependencies," one answer would go, "which we might otherwise miss. The obviousness of our example may not be typical." However, this vindication fails, for the principle names no dependencies; it remains completely general. It achieves no more than the vague injunction, "Watch out for dependencies!" And that advice, covered already by the evident need to consider causal connections, seems superfluous.

A proponent of the rule might suggest that it invites us to identify fundamental values and that these then provide concrete guidance. The moment, however, we accept this invitation and attempt such a listing, our eyes are opened to the rule's full implications and consequent inexpediency.

"Strength" is a causal notion; being more "fundamental" means being more decisive causally. But in every situation we envision, some values have more influence, some less; so all are more, or less, "fundamental." Thus, if the Hartmann-Reiner rule is carried out fully and consistently, it would seem to entail a massive revision in our standard decision procedure: Instead of calculating consequences once, overall, for a contemplated action, we would also calculate them a second time, piecemeal, for individual values and disvalues; and instead of estimating the pros and cons intrinsically, then balancing, we would also rate them extrinsically, causally, and only then venture to balance. But these are needless complications.

Normally we assess the consequences of an action, weigh the overall values and disvalues it entails, then compare this result with those for alternative lines of action. In the substitute procedure we would assess the action's consequences, identify the values and disvalues it entails, calculate the consequences of each, grade it accordingly as more or less fundamental, combine this rating with the intrinsic rating, balance all these totals so as to apprize the action globally, then compare the result with that for other actions, similarly weighed. Obviously this second procedure is far more complex than the first, and if the simpler one is adequate — as it is — why complicate matters? A preference-rule that lands us in such a morass we had better do without.

E. Overweight through Overlap

Extrinsic value rating such as we have been examining has the further disadvantage that it easily leads to overweight through overlap.

Suppose, for instance, that a national labor union is considering a further reduction in the work week. The extra free time looks attractive for family life and for recreation. Fewer work hours, on the other hand, will mean reduced production. Still, a fresher, happier work force would work more efficiently. And the reduction in hours might make room for more workers and so permit equal production with less unemployment. But then prices would rise, for the workers themselves as for the population generally. And the nation's balance of trade would be adversely affected. The ramifications spread indefinitely in all directions.

Now when we assign each value and disvalue its due weight, we need to be wary of such ramifications. Listing decreased productivity, say, we may be influenced in our rating by the effect it will have on the balance of trade. But then perhaps we list that item, too, and give it full (nonchauvinistic) consideration, with the result that it weighs twice in the scales of decision, once surreptitiously (in its cause) and once openly (by itself). Or perhaps we stress the importance of new jobs, then tabulate separately the foreseen effects which account for this strong rating (a likely boost to the new workers' morale, comfort and support for their families, . . .). Here, again, the consequences count twice, once in themselves and once in their cause.

Similar falsification may result from conceptual overlap rather than causal overlap. Suppose, for instance, that we list the "economic benefits" of some option. Doubtless we intend more than mere goods in the warehouse or money in the bank; we are thinking, for example, of what the money can buy or do. But what it can do is: finance a vacation, stock a library, renovate a chapel, commission a mural, pay for an appendectomy. So the "economic benefits," thus understood, overlap others: recreational, educational, artistic, religious, bodily, and so on. Again, if we insist with Dewey that economic ends are not purely instrumental but are "as intrinsic and final in their place as any others,"[25] conceptual overlap still occurs, though differently. To the money earned we add the earning, and to the steel produced, the producing; and these are not mere means but portions of human life with their own inherent worth, which should be heightened. Work itself must be given emotional, intellectual, social, aesthetic, and religious worth. But now "economic ends" overlap these other values. And where there is overlap, there is likely to be double rating.

These brief remarks are meant to illustrate the reality of the problem. Overweight through overlap is difficult to avoid completely. Yet it may at least be minimized if we are alert to the danger.

F. Knowing Where to Stop

Further basic problems concern the level or extent of analysis. We shall consider three: (1) Values and disvalues might be dissected endlessly, but we cannot go on forever: Where is a reasonable place to halt? (2) If analysis misrepresents, by dissevering seamless wholes, should we perhaps not reverse the process and scrutinize more comprehensive totalities rather than tinier snippets? (3) Our verdicts, being subjectively conditioned, may thereby be falsified every time: Must self-questioning continue indefinitely? More fully now, in the same order, the problems unfold as follows.

(1)   Conceptual overlap is easier to avoid in concrete listings, for or against a given action, than in general, abstract catalogs like those in VII, A, for specific realizations of values can be more precisely identified. Thus, whereas aesthetic values, say, may overlap religious and vice versa, the Pietà of Michelangelo does not overlap the election of Pope John XXIII. However, concrete things, persons, or events, as opposed to pure abstractions, usually incorporate some disvalue along with the value, or value with the disvalue. Even the election of good Pope John was not an unmixed blessing. So if our listing of values stops at such items, the whole purpose of analysis may be jeopardized. After all, we analyze in order to gain a clearer view, permitting more accurate assessment than is possible when values and disvalues are indiscriminately jumbled together. And here, it would seem, at the level of items such as a papal election we meet the same problem all over again unless we carry analysis further.

But how far? An answer appears in the reason for continuing: ideally, we should persevere as long as any item is notably impure. The wheat of value should be pure wheat, the chaff of disvalue pure chaff. Thus, an entry like "communist take-over" should probably be analyzed further, for it would be less helpful than the straight disvalue "purge" or the straight value "more equitable distribution of wealth" (IV, C).

(2)   One reason for saying "probably" is that such thoroughgoing anal-

ysis is not always feasible. There is, in addition, the theoretical difficulty that the resultant values and disvalues, when totaled, may not yield the value of the whole. For the problem of "organic unities," broached in VII, A, 4, remains to be dealt with.

Examining Rembrandt's "The Night Watch" analytically and close up, we may admire the brushwork here, the shading there, the pose of the central figure, and so on; but obviously the perfection of the whole is something more than the sum of its parts' perfections. And might not much the same be said of our actions, indeed of our lives, as wholes, or of human society globally considered? Must not a contemplated divorce, for instance, be seen in its relation to the institution of marriage and so against the background of a pervasive weave in the pattern of our society? And is the worth of such a society or of such an institution equivalent without remainder to any listing of merits and demerits we might draw up?[26]

A negative answer is as impossible as an affirmative. For we have not drawn up the list and do not enjoy the sort of overall view for which it would be a precondition, and thus cannot take the further step of comparing the synthetic whole with the analytic summation. Analytic, piecemeal evaluation is justified not only by the fact that clarity in detail is a prerequisite for intuitive grasp of the whole but more radically still by the fact that such a grasp, of a whole society or institution, is forever beyond us. Our personal affairs we may more readily view synoptically (leaving their remoter ramifications in conjectural penumbra), but a great many economic, social, political, and ecclesial decisions demand consideration of so vast a tableau that the human mind can only peruse it flashlightwise, sector by sector.

We inhabit a macroscopic middle zone, as it were, between the cosmic and the microscopic. Widen the focus too far, and we see confusedly; narrow it too tightly, and value disappears (the ballet becomes a mere series of leg movements, the friendly smile a mere curve of the lips, a creased cheek). The ideal level of analysis is that at which we see individual values and disvalues most clearly yet do not note clearly any difference between their collective worth and that of the whole. This situation is not accurately evoked by the foregoing comparison, at least as presented, for it spoke of the painting's parts rather than of its aspects. It would be more relevant to ask: "Is the overall excellence of the painting distinguishable from the collective excellence of its technique, palette, composition, content, fidelity, feeling, and so on?" If we can give no sure negative answer (and we cannot), then we have no reason to impugn the art critic's analytic approach. And the same holds true in ethics.[27]

(3)   However, in either area—ethics or aesthetics—problems arise with regard to the alleged "seeing." Our moral "intuitions," like our aesthetic "perceptions," are shaped by prior training and experience. And the moral learning process, as Michael Keeling observes, "is one in which an aggressive, anxious, loving and confused being learns from other aggressive, anxious, loving and confused beings, and consequently the moral information which we have is not altogether reliable. A substantial element in our moral 'judgments' is an emotional reaction based on our own past experiences. For this reason we have to be wary of instant moral reactions—both our own and other people's."[28]

Such remarks are more commonly made about moral norms but apply as well to value judgments, our present concern. The connection, of course, is close, it often being difficult to discriminate between a precept and a value judgment it embodies, or between their respective origins. Veto and value verdict coalesce, for instance, in Paul's condemnation of women's short-cropped hair (1 Cor. 11:14) and doubtless rose together from the apostle's milieu. He says that nature teaches so, but a likelier tutor is his experience of contemporary attitudes and mores.[29]

From our vantage point in history we may smile at Paul's assertion. Yet for those immersed in a culture, as we all are, discernment is difficult. And our clairvoyance is specially tested when familiar value features, rightfully invoked till now, are in process of transition. Consider again the example of reducing the work week. We readily cite additional opportunity for rest and recreation on the one hand and decreased productivity on the other (as above). But beyond a certain point both of these reasons need to be reconsidered. When long hours of drudgery were the rule, time to rest and recreate was an obvious blessing; but it is conceivable that with repeated reductions people might finally have more of that blessing than they need or know what to do with. Likewise, when productivity meant providing essentials, any increase was clear gain; but now production increasingly serves merely to fuel the economy and keep it on an even keel, and a crucial question is whether an economy so constructed is not a Frankenstein from which we should be freed.

Shifting doctrinal pressures, subtly and pervasively shaping our value judgments, may be as difficult to trace and appraise. A significant illustration, in view of its wide relevance for questions of innovation and reform, is the contrast between classical and contemporary attitudes toward change. "That must be said to exist most fully, " wrote Augustine long ago, "which always exists in the same way, wholly identical with itself, incorruptible and immutable in every part, not subject to time, unable to differ now from what it was before."[30] Since then Platonism has declined and science arisen: eternal forms (unchanging truth, virtue, beauty, goodness, unity) have been identified with concepts and their fixity with that of logic, not ontology, while history has come alive and, for a Christian like Teilhard, assumed meaning and direction. "What makes and classifies a 'modern' man," he observed, "(and a whole host of our contemporaries is not yet 'modern' in this sense) is having become capable of seeing in terms not of space and time alone, but also of duration, or — and it comes to the same thing — of biological space-time; and above all having become incapable of seeing anything otherwise — anything — *not even himself.*"[31] For Teilhard growth, not eternal sameness, is a value.

Impressed by examples like these, of varied, subtle influences, we may come to distrust our value verdicts. They do not issue from pure intuition but are shaped as well — perhaps misshaped — by early training, subjective experience, cultural conditioning, shifting ideology. So we perhaps envision a solution like the one Bertrand Russell proposed for the problem of empirical knowledge: "In order . . . to arrive at what really is sensation in an occurrence which, at first sight, seems to contain nothing else, we have to pare away all that is due to habit or expectation or interpretation."[32] Thus Frankena recognizes "that we cannot *prove* basic judgments of intrinsic value in any strict sense of proof" but believes we can justify them "by taking what I shall call the evaluative point of view as such, unqualified by any such adjective as 'aesthetic,' 'moral,' or 'prudential,' and then trying to see what judgment we are led to make when we do so, considering the thing in question wholly on the basis of its intrinsic character, not its consequences or conditions. What is it to take the nonmorally evaluative point of view? It is to be free, informed, clear-headed, impartial, willing to universalize; in general, it is to be 'calm' and 'cool,' as Butler would say, in one's consideration of such items as pleasure, knowledge, and love, for the question is simply what it is rational to choose."[33]

A first difficulty, as Alan Donagan notes, "is that the qualifications of ideal observerhood are such that no human being can be shown ever to possess them."[34] Furthermore, comparison with Russell's parallel proposal for reaching pure sensation casts doubt on the ideal itself. If, in our analogous situation, we tried to pare away all that bears the marks of moral instruction (which is debatable), temperament (which is personal), life-experience (which is partial), and culture (which is relative), the residue would not be a collection of pure values but at most pure description. (It would be like weeding out mixed breeds in the local dog pound and ending up with — the dog pound.) Furthermore, the whole selective enterprise, like any purposeful undertaking, would be guided by values, which would not themselves be scrutinized and refined (as the sensations on which Russell relied would not be). We cannot get outside our values to judge our values.

So what is the solution? It is implicit, I would suggest, in the same comparison. Despite important differences, we may treat our value perceptions much as we do our sense perceptions, for instance those of sight: (1) Though all vision is subjectively and objectively conditioned, by factors such as health and lighting which sometimes distort or falsify, we do not on that account scrutinize each and every perception for signs of undue influence. (2) For we are acquainted with the standard forms and sources of illusion or distortion — fatigue, medication, heat, shading, alcohol, lighting, astigmatism, color blindness, and the like — and know when and how they threaten accuracy. We doubt and test when there is specific reason to do so — for instance, when others give a different report or one sense contradicts another. (3) The checking suits the situation and suspected type of distortion; it does not attempt an overall elimination of subjective and objective influences. (4) Hence it does not continue indefinitely. Having resolved the particular doubt, one way or the other, we do not then scrutinize the data employed in the assessment and so on ad infinitum. *Any* item might be tested for distortion, but *all* cannot be nor need be.

Similarly for value perceptions: (1) Though all our value judgments are conditioned by factors which may on occasion falsify, we do not call every judgment in question. (2) For we know the standard forms of deviation and certain warning signs and situations — the aggressiveness, anxiety, and confusion Keeling notes; parochialism of training and mores; massive social shifts; fallible ideology — and are alerted by them, in determinate cases, to proceed more cautiously. (3) If the warning sign is anger, envy, resentment, fear, ambition, or the like, we proceed in one way (IV, C; V, B); if it is ideological conflict, in another; if it is social evolution, in still another. In no case do we attempt to divest ourselves of affectivity, world view, culture, character, and the rest, so as to permit "neutral" assessment. We become more circumspect, in specific ways. (4) These tests having been applied, we cease to test. Not because the beliefs and values employed in the testing are themselves untestable, but because we have no reason to test them. If they in turn show signs of special fallibility, they can be examined closely, and should be. If not, not. We must know where to stop.

My willingness to speak of falsification and distortion, with regard to values as with regard to sight, reflects a belief that our value eyesight, so to speak, differs far less than do our value estimates; variously, pervasively, cognitive factors account for that diversity (see above, and X, E). Still, I do not believe that the human psyche is an invariant, unerring value gauge, provided it is just fed the right facts. No evidence establishes such a thesis (see X, D); nor does the argument that otherwise the objectivity of values is destroyed. After all, we admit defective vision in countless nearsighted, farsighted, astigmatic, and color-blind people without concluding that colors and shapes are purely subjective.

Furthermore, to say that our value judgments differ noncognitively as well as cognitively is not to say that they are irreformable. Even when partly or entirely noncognitive in origin, they may yield nonetheless to argument and analysis. Or they may change because we ourselves change. In our values as well as in our understanding we may become better people, better Christians. We may gradually put on the mind of Christ, first as something admirable, then as something truly shared. Thus what analysis fails to achieve, conversion may. To that process no halt need ever be called.

G. Three Variables

The complexity of moral decisions sets pragmatic limits to analysis. With the full range of values to consult and unlimited alternatives to consider, it cannot be as fine-grained as the deliberations of a businessman, say, balancing costs and revenues, or of a military strategist, with his similarly restricted range of concerns. All that seems feasible and necessary is that in assessing each reason for or against an option, we take account of the following three variables (three dimensions, as it were, in the overall volume of the concrete value or disvalue): (1) the relative excellence of that particular type of value (cp. VII, C) or relative gravity of that particular species of evil; (2) the extent to which it would be affected (produced, increased, preserved, diminished, destroyed); (3) the likelihood of this outcome.

This prescription is important, because it applies so generally. All conduct, we said, should be judged by its values and disvalues; all values and disvalues, we now add, should be assessed in this threefold way to arrive at a final verdict on the contemplated conduct.

Moral values and disvalues are no exception. They too must be reckoned in the same triple manner: kind, extent, probability. I mention them because of the widespread impression that they are somehow special and so cannot be treated as other values and disvalues are. This impression stems in part from the confusion already discussed, between the overall rightness or wrongness of an action on the one hand and constitutive moral values or disvalues on the other, such as justice or injustice or the action's likely effect on one's own or others' subsequent morality (cf. V, I; VII, A). The final, overall verdict cannot figure in its own calculation, whereas all constitutive values or disvalues, of whatever kind, can and must be counted in. Thus the wrongness of framing a prisoner, say, does not show it to be wrong, but the injustice of the resulting punishment may (V, I).

However, even when this confusion is cleared up and the need is recognized to consider moral aspects along with others, it may still be felt that they enjoy a special primacy that sets them apart. Did not Jesus say to seek God's kingdom and his justice before everything else? Did he not judge it preferable that a man be cast into the sea than that he cause a little one to stumble, morally (Mk. 9:42, Lk. 17:2)?

Yes, the words might be read that way. But moral lapses, like other evils, are more or less serious in kind, more or less extensive, more or less probable. And it may be doubted whether, for example, Jesus would pass an equally stern sentence on one who invited Tommy Isakson to raid the neighbor's kumquat tree and won his ready assent. A millstone round the neck of Dick Brown, his successful eight-year-old seducer, might not be a preferable alternative.

For one thing, Tommy's misdeed is not the unforgivable sin; he has not sinned against the Holy Spirit. Nor is his failing of the kind for which moralists long denied any "paucity of matter," labeling every instance "mortal." Nor is it, we may suppose, as knowing and deliberate a lapse as many others. Indeed, if Tommy is young enough — if he has not reached the "age of reason" — then many would say there is no sin at all save in the sense of an objective injustice. But that, of course, is also a moral disvalue of a sort, and it too may vary in gravity. If the owners of the tree have no need of it, Tommy's offense is slighter than if they rely on it for food.

Quantitatively, too, the moral evil brought about by the invitation may be less than that induced in some other manner. For it is one thing to pilfer ten kumquats, quite another to embezzle ten million dollars. It is one thing to invite just Tommy, another to make the rounds of the neighborhood and organize a raid en masse. It is one thing to invite him once, another to invite him many times. For theft as for any moral evil the question of *extent* is important.

So too is probability, and the sureness with which moral good or evil is effected. It is one thing to shout in passing, "I'm off to raid the Johnsons' kumquat tree," another to suggest "Why don't you come along?", another to add "please," another to twist his arm. The likelihood of acquiescence mounts. More seriously, it is one thing to adopt a policy—say school prayers or corporal punishment—that *may* work long-term moral benefit or harm, and quite another to frame an innocent prisoner and thereby virtually ensure the injustice that follows (V, I). A surer result, as such, weighs more heavily in the balance than does a problematic one, even though both are moral.

What I have done here, in a simple instance, is to run through the three considerations mentioned at the start and, while illustrating them, show that they apply as well to moral values and disvalues, such as often count for or against some line of conduct. Moral pros and cons, like any others, must individually be assessed for their kind, extent, and likelihood to reach a proper weighting and thereby a proper solution. Their presence in the value ledger, on one side or the other, does not yield an automatic verdict for or against the action being considered. The fact, for example, that Dick leads Tommy into sin does not signify automatically that Dick had better be thrown into the sea and drowned —or even be imprisoned or removed from the neighborhood.

H. The Use of Numbers

The overall rating of each value or disvalue is a function of the three variables just mentioned. Double the qualitative rating, or the quantity, or the likelihood, and the overall rating doubles. Or so we would naturally judge. However, the numerical statement of value relations raises serious problems.

As a comparatively simple illustration, let us examine Henry Sidgwick's deliberations when, as a young man of twenty-three, he envisioned his future. "The only choice with me," he wrote to a friend, "is between the Bar in London and Study in Cambridge. For the Bar there are: (1) The prospect, very problematical, of attaining the position of a practical politician (for which I doubt my fitness). (2) The certainty of the precious (to me) stimulus of intellectual society. (3) The conviction that the work of that profession, if vastly more absorbing, is vastly more improving than Tuition. Against it is: (1) The chance of failure, involving the renunciation of domesticity and the adoption, wearied and baffled, of the career (of literary action) which I now renounce. (2) The certainty of neglecting in professional and political engagements the deeper problems which now interest me, especially the great one of reconciling my religious instinct with my growing conviction that both individual and social morality ought to be placed on an inductive basis. This is my present personal subject of meditation; if you will give me any advice it will be received with interest. [(3)] I ought to have mentioned a repugnance, perhaps unreasonable, to advocacy as practised in England."[35]

From this listing no verdict emerges. For numerically the advantages and disadvantages balance evenly, at three each. And even if they did not, that would not decide the issue. For some of the items are more important than others. And their weights depend on the complex correlation of rank, extent, and likelihood just described. So the overall situation, even in this thumbnail sketch for a friend, is still far from perspicuous.

So perhaps young Sidgwick, versed in mathematics as well as in the classics, adopts the following solution. Attending to each item in turn, and assessing its composite weight, he assigns it a number (plus or minus) on a scale from one to five. When finished, he checks back to make sure that in each case roughly equivalent values have received the same number, and greater values a proportionately higher number. The resulting row of digits, parallel to the verbal listing of advantages and drawbacks, now reads 2, 3, 3, -3, -5, -1. Simple addition yields the negative number 1, and thus a verdict against the bar and for a life of study at Cambridge. A notable career is on its way.

Such use of numbers, to measure and not merely to order, is a natural stratagem and sometimes appears indispensable. But theoretical objections have been urged against it. And the humanistic, religious mind readily labels it "rationalistic." Even people familiar with analogous procedures in sociology or psychology sense an aberration when numbers are thus applied (cardinally and not merely ordinally) to values. The chief source of difficulty, it seems, is that this measuring is compared with other varieties, which are taken as paradigmatic, and is found to differ from them. They, for instance, are often quite precise, so precision is required and found wanting: "We may on a particular occasion *prefer* reading a book to taking a walk: the former, then, we say, would give us (on this occasion) the greater pleasure. But is there any conceivable sense in which we could say that the intensity of the pleasure to be got from reading is twice rather than three times or one and a half times, the intensity of the pleasure to be got from walking? Would we not, by trying to make our comparison of intensities mathematically exact, reduce it to meaninglessness?"[36]

The answer is that numbers mean what they are used to mean. A pollster who requests that the president's performance be rated on a scale from one to five does not suppose that people are applying a precise measure. And so it is in a value table like the one I have cited. Nothing exact was intended. In place of the numbers Sidgwick might have written: "Assessment of the reasons for: (1) The goal is worthy, in view of the common good, but is rendered doubly problematic by my limitations; so low rating. (2) The value is certain, but personal; so considerable importance but not great. (3) The same appraisal; so similar weighting. Assessment of the reasons against: (1) The possibility is real and the prospect dreadful; so considerable weight here too, on the other side of the balance. (2) The likelihood of the result and its importance for myself and for others seem sure; so top rating. (3) Uncertain, yet deserves listing; minimal weight."

These jottings, to be sure, are imprecise. But they are perfectly legitimate and the best he can do (a more detailed account would be still less manageable). And the numbers replacing them say the same things: "low rating," "considerable importance," "top rating," and so on. So they too are unobjectionable.

And they are useful, indeed sometimes indispensable (in more complex matters or in fuller reflection on even personal problems like Sidgwick's). For the verbal analysis is no more surveyable than the verbal listing. Without further calculation it does not indicate where the preference should fall. And further calculation would consist in comparisons of a kind the numbers alone express manageably and perspicuously: this equivalent to that, a third equivalent to both combined, and so forth.

Implicit in this process of comparison is the answer to another, commoner objection. "It has been suggested that there are not amounts, but only degrees, of goodness, and that in consequence all that we are entitled to assign to different goods is not cardinal numbers, implying that each good contains a certain number of units of goodness, but only ordinal numbers, implying that the two goods occupy different places on a scale of goodness, or are unequally far removed from the zero-point of indifference."[37]

"Now such a state of affairs," the same author continues, "would be all that is needed if we had, in choosing which of two actions we should do, to compare a single good which will be produced by one with a single good which will be produced by the other. But this is not usually the case."[38] "In principle, if we ever are justified in thinking that a certain combination of lesser goods is more worth (or that it is less worth) producing than a single greater good, we must know more about the goods than that they fall in a certain order on the scale of goods."[39]

The "assumption of homogeneous unitary elements"[40] as required by cardinal measurement stems from prominent paradigms like rulers and tapes. Even scales, however, such as those that symbolize justice, differ from a ruler in this respect. They are not marked off into units. And other forms of balancing depart still further from the simplistic norm.[41] Suppose, for example, that I am browsing through a bookstore to see what I can purchase with my ten-dollar gift certificate. Several five-dollar buys — a collection of prayers, a storybook for the children, a mystery, a book of verse — attract me equally, but I am as strongly inclined to a ten-dollar biography as to any two of these. So the decision proves difficult: one book or two, and if two, which two? We might express this situation, of single and additive equivalences, by saying that I find the more expensive volume twice as valuable, or twice as desirable, as each of the others. So speaking, we would use a number, and use it cardinally, in a clear enough sense related directly to action (the purchase); yet the books in question, and their respective merits, are by no means homogeneous.[42]

Now this account may be extended to value ratings generally. If two items are of roughly equal importance, we assign them the same number. If another is roughly equivalent in importance to both of these combined, we double the number. And so on. All numbers on the scale can be generated in this way. We must make such comparisons in any case, so why not express them, in difficult decisions, by means of numbers, permitting ready grasp and calculation?

"It is true," writes Kurt Baier, "that the introduction of numbers does not produce complete scientific objectivity. However, it has one justification: to make an overall judgment possible, where there would otherwise be no way of computing the partial merits due under each heading. The procedure is similar to that of introducing the concept of volume *as the product of* length, width, and height. This concept could not have been introduced if the 'dimensions' of which it is made up had not already had numerical values. If I said that the house was as long as the fence, as wide as the river, and as high as the gum tree, then there would be no way of working out *the volume* as the product of these three dimensions. Similarly, if I say that the merit of the car as a whole is made up of the attractiveness of the body styling, the good finish of the bodywork, the neatness of the interior, and so on, no over-all rank can emerge. But if I allocate numbers to each item and add them up, I can arrive at an over-all result."[43]

The same technique can be used for group decisions, but it then requires adaptation. A chief issue is the following. If several people rather than one, addressing a common problem, work out a value table like the preceding and then fill in the ratings individually, a group verdict may be reached in either of two ways: (1) by totaling their final yea's and nay's; (2) by totaling the ratings for each item and then adding up the totals. It is conceivable that answers reached in these ways would differ, much as in an American presidential election the verdict of the electoral college might differ from that of the popular vote (on the one hand, the winning majority might be slim; on the other, the minority's totals might be more one-sided than the majority's). However, this eventuality seems unlikely. And special problems arise concerning the logic and legitimacy of collective number ratings. Thus the first method seems preferable.

Whether for group or individual decisions the legitimacy of personal number ratings is important. Without them calculation is unreliable in any comparison of complex, fairly evenly matched alternatives. And without calculation the lists are worthless.

I. The "Moral Systems" Revisited

No ethical system equips its adherents to decide all cases with certainty. Thus any ethic must face the issue: If we have done our best and still cannot see our way clearly, what then? May we act with a doubtful conscience? If we may not, yet must act nonetheless, what exit is there from our impasse? To such queries as these, preceptive ethics responded in characteristic fashion: it provided further, reflex principles, in addition to those for acts, with which to resolve subjective doubt and assure a moral decision in all cases.[44] Second-order rules of preference we might call these norms (thus explaining their present position at the end of this chapter). Our question will be whether such guidelines are valid or even applicable within a value ethic, and if not, what may replace them.

Within a morality of law the issue emerges as follows. If a moral law clearly applies to a particular case, a person is bound. If it does not, he is free to act as he pleases. But suppose he is uncertain, even after diligent inquiry. Then the question becomes: How probable should the case for freedom appear before he may act on it? To that query a wide range of answers has been given, including these principal three: probabilism replied "Probable," equiprobabilism "Equally probable," probabiliorism "More probable."

Within a value ethic the issue undergoes a metamorphosis. Probability appears there in the manner just discussed under G, that is, together with rank and degree in the assessment of each value. And only if the totals for opposed, optimal alternatives turn out to be even, does a situation arise analogous to that debated by the traditional systems. A person might then feel uncertain what to do and desire further guidance than that provided by the general rule of beneficence or its refinements in this chapter. He still might wish to know *the* right course of action.

One reflex rule, modeled on the traditional ones, might ordain:

"If and only if the tallies are exactly equal may you do as you please." Another might say: "Given the inexactness of the individual ratings, you may act either way whenever the totals are close." This laxer norm would be analogous to probabilism and the other to equiprobabilism. But there would be no analogue for probabiliorism. For without some further specification, neither option would stand in the place of law and so deserve special consideration.

Now which of these two guidelines — the stricter or the laxer — should we adopt? The correct answer, I believe, is "Neither." For if we attend to the intended function of such norms, we note another major difference between the viewpoint here favored and that which begot reflex principles for doubtful consciences. A fairly sharp distinction was supposed, even in particular cases, between counsel and precept. And the reflex principle was to specify when that border was crossed. On one side lay duty; on the other, complete freedom. Now, however, this conception of obligation versus mere counsel is challenged by Catholic and Protestant alike (V, A). And with the denial of the sharp border, the precise reflex pointer loses its purpose. It is as needless and meaningless as an instrument to mark the moment when night turns to day.

Consider this closer comparison. As two objects placed in a fine balance make the balance quiver this way or that, so two options weighed in a Christian conscience tilt this way or that — or perhaps remain in perfect equilibrium. In that case there is no shadow of obligation; otherwise there is at least a shadow. And the human instrument feels it, feels its strength, and thereby learns all there is to learn and all it needs to know.

A reflex principle would supposedly indicate, in addition, which tilts of the balance pass the marker "obligation" and which do not. But there is no such marker (V, A). At no point along the continuum from negligible to enormous imbalance has any authority, human or divine, inscribed the indication "Beyond this precise point lies duty." Hence a conscience that feels the tilt, and feels its strength, knows all. No rule could give fuller guidance.

We can now see, in retrospect, that the rules considered and approved in this chapter all affect the tilt of the balance, not the reading of the tilt. They are not reflex principles. Rather, some are rules of preference: in favor of the neighbor (A), of the needy (B, C) . Others are norms of analysis: concerning its form (E), its terminus (F), its components (G), its legitimate tools (H). And over them all reigns the general maxim, previously established, that value be maximized. This supreme directive they both clarify and refine.

9
Questions of Procedure

IT MIGHT EASILY BE assumed that if the balance of values makes an action right or wrong, then balancing values is the only acceptable way to determine right and wrong. Since this conclusion is objectionable, the premise too may appear suspect. However, the fault lies in the inference, not the premise. We may not pass so facilely from meaning to method.

One might as validly suppose that since rain consists, by definition, of watery drops descending from clouds, such drops are the only evidence one should consult in predicting rain. The guiding concept narrows the range of suitable methods, it is true (III, B); we do not base our rain predictions on Dow Jones standings, batting averages, the orbits of Venus, or the *Congressional Record*. We are free, however, according to our abilities or circumstances, to consult a barometer, the sky, bird behavior, satellite photos, aching joints, or the latest weather bulletin. The single definition does not dictate a single method. Quite varied clues and calculations may signal the selfsame future phenomenon: drops of water falling from clouds.

Similarly, in the area of ethics Dan Brock notes, with Bales, that a distinction between act-utilitarianism "as an account of the right-making characteristics of actions and as an account of the proper moral decision-making procedure is useful. An ethical theory might provide an account of either or both of these, but there is no reason to believe that the proper account of one must also be the proper account of the other. Many of the usual criticisms of [act-utilitarianism] are justified when it is interpreted as a decision-making procedure but not when interpreted as an account of right-making characteristics of actions."[1] Sidgwick drew a like distinction with regard to a different doctrine: "The adoption of the fundamental *principle* of Egoism, as just explained, by no means necessarily implies the ordinary empirical method

171

of seeking one's own pleasure or happiness. A man may aim at the greatest happiness within his reach, and yet not attempt to ascertain empirically what amount of pleasure and pain is likely to attend any given course of action; believing that he has some surer, deductive method for determining the conduct which will make him most happy in the long-run."[2]

The point can be illustrated, through Ignatius' three "times," apropos of the stance favored here (IV, C; V, B). Only in the third does typical value-balancing appear; yet all three obey the same logic: in all three "right" and "wrong" retain the same sense. It is evident then that though the Christian criterion of right and wrong, like the criterion of rain, excludes certain procedural options (a hedonistic calculus, say, or legal positivism), it specifies no single method as alone legitimate. At the point we have reached, therefore, the question of procedure remains wide open.

In treating this broad topic the present chapter will not attempt to touch all bases. They are too many, and my competence too limited. My purpose will be rather, first, to indicate some important ways in which decision-through-value-tables is inadequate as a comprehensive, universal model of procedure; second, to draw some positive conclusions for procedure from the preceding analyses.

A. Creative Spontaneity

When the psychologist Karl Stern, his wife, and their one-year-old son arrived in Montreal from Europe, some forty years ago, the heat and humidity were such as they had never experienced before. "It was as if the ceiling were closing imperceptibly down towards the floor, with us in between."[3] The air in front of their hotel window vibrated. Then a call came from a woman who had heard of their arrival. "It must be ghastly in a hotel room," she said, "with a baby, on a day like this. Listen, my husband and I are leaving Montreal for a few days. Why don't you stay at our place? We are going to leave the key to the house under the doormat. There is food in the Frigidaire." Stern's wife told her that she was taking a great risk, since she had never even seen them. She replied that she was ready to take it. So for a few days the Sterns found themselves "the inhabitants of a beautiful house. There were wood-carvings on the walls, and pewter and silver in glass cupboards, old French-Canadian and English handicraft. Everything was laid out with taste. There was a cool lawn around the house." It was indeed a welcome change — and a welcome.

One senses that when Christianity buds in deeds like this, it is not programed. There is something more here than mere value calculations; namely:

(1)   Alertness to others' needs, so readiness to ask, "What can I (we) do?" Others might not have thought of the baby, the unaccustomed heat, the scene from the hotel window ("an endless forest of roofs, signboards and fire-escapes"). Not having placed themselves imaginatively in the others' situation, they would not sense the problem sharply or consider possible action.

This is a general point. Value tables help in finding an answer. But if no question is asked, no answer is given. And people can live surrounded by grave problems without asking themselves squarely, urgently: "What can I, should I, do about it?"

(2)   Besides, the question put to value tables is not that general one "What should I do?" but more specifically "Should I (we) do X or Y?" For instance, "Should we hand these strangers the keys to our beautiful home?" Many a person might think of the need but never think of that question, whereas for this Canadian couple there may have seemed little need of value calculation once the possibility was conceived. Their reaction was perhaps, "Of course!"

(3)   Both these observations show how much depends on the subject of the decision, how relatively little on techniques.[4] In a book like this one, where the perspective is objective (see chapter 2) and the concern is with moral reasoning, so with procedures and their underlying logic, little has been said about the subjective dispositions of those who do the reasoning (or do not). But this silence, due to a restricted focus, should not be misconstrued. There can be little doubt that an uninstructed person who is yet profoundly Christian will both do and judge the good far more readily and effectively than a person who, though fully informed on the matters here discussed, is less concerned, generous, disinterested, and receptive to grace. Charity will find a way where egoism does not even ask or seek.

B. Love's Labor

From such cases, however, it cannot be inferred that reasoning is in general useless or unnecessary. On the contrary. Paul's hymn to charity (1 Cor. 13:4–7) might be revised to say: "Love is patient, persistent, because it is kind; it cares enough to take pains. Love is never boastful, nor conceited, sure it is right and others wrong when opinions differ; it does not equate its will with God's. There is nothing love cannot face in an effort to determine the better solution, the surer way; it is ready to inquire, reflect, weigh, probe, seek fuller data and guidance, from God or man."

Thus the relationship between charity and reason, as between heart and head, is one, not of estrangement or conflict, but of interaction and mutual dependence: "The nature of the motive will, in large part, determine the way in which the agent analyzes the situation of choice, what kind of empirical knowledge he will look for in the course of deliberation, to what extent and in which respects he will consider the feelings and values of others who will be affected by the act, to what extent he will be concerned for future consequences, how much time he takes for deliberation prior to choice, and so on."[5] Let us consider these points one by one.

(1) Analysis of the Situation: Problems and Alternatives

"It is misleading," notes Stuart Hampshire, "to speak of 'the facts of a situation' in such a way as to suggest that there must be a closed set of propositions which, once established, precisely determine the situation. The situations in which we must act or abstain from acting, are 'open' in the sense that they cannot be uniquely described and finally circumscribed. Situations do not present themselves with their labels attached to them."[6] Nor do problems. One senses that something is wrong, and perhaps one can give it a name, say "population explosion." But that does not specify where population is exploding or why. It does not say, for instance, "The very people who individually want the most children are those who collectively can least afford them," nor does it explain, "And they want them because in a rural economy children are an asset and in a primitive polity they are a promise of support in old age." Such specifications must generally precede any search for solutions. To the helpless query "What can I do about it?" the reply may be "About precisely what?"

Previous discussions in this book do not reveal, but perhaps obscure, the significance of such an inquiry. For in all the cases of value calculation in chapter 4 the alternatives lay before us: to cure the man or not, to marry or not, to defend oneself or not, and so on. And once the values were reckoned on both sides, we saw what to do. But repeatedly alternatives are not thrust upon us (as when a man comes at us with a knife) but are freely specified by us (as when a person is concerned about the population problem and searches for a solution). From innumerable lines of possible action we hit on one or two and put them to the test. Value-balancing follows this step; it does not prepare it.

Indeed it could not. Suppose that, in order to spot the very best thing to do, we attempt to list exhaustively all those particular actions (or series of actions) which have the same agent, occur in the same time span, are performable, and are mutually incompatible in pairs,[7] and we then seek to determine, through comparison, which of these acts is the best. We shall never succeed. For the set is not numerable.[8] And it is always conceivable that some unexamined member of the set would be preferable to any we have so far considered.

Someone familiar with recent developments in the philosophy of science may have noted by now a close and revealing parallel. For long it was thought that Bacon, then Mill, had disclosed the real and ideal order of scientific inquiry. To discover the cause of a given phenomenon, one varies all the relevant circumstances in such a way as to detect which feature or features are constantly associated with the phenomenon. From this calculation one concludes to a causal connection. Now some cases do conform more or less to this model. If we think, for instance, that mosquitoes may be causing malaria, we protect some people from mosquito bites and see if they too succumb. We vary the circumstances and establish a causal connection. But notice that the difficult, decisive step precedes the checking. For we do not know all relevant circumstances in advance, nor do the corresponding possibilities form a denumerable set. So we generally work *from* and not *to* a theory. Once we have hit on a likely hypothesis from among many, we try to falsify it (for instance, by seeing whether people protected from mosquitoes also contract malaria). But we do not reason to the hypothesis (by process of elimination, say, from an infinite set). That comes suddenly. The more intelligent the scientist and the better versed in the problem, the likelier is the inspiration. And, other things being equal, the like holds true in practical, moral matters. Love must do its homework.

(2) Analysis of the Situation: Possibilities

The alternatives a person envisages or takes seriously depend in large measure on his conception of possibilities, and this estimate in turn depends largely, for instance, on his faith, hope, and charity. Both points are attractively illustrated (if not with sure historicity) by a tale from the "Little Flowers of Saint Francis." In the saint's absence three famous robbers come to his hermitage and ask Brother Angelo for food, but he upbraids them roundly and sends them away empty-handed. When Francis returns, he orders the brother after them, with bread and wine and a promise of support if they change their ways. And, sure enough, they do. Thus, where a "reasonable" man may glimpse no possibility, there a saint may venture and succeed.

Sometimes it is charity that revises estimates, sometimes personal experience. "For example, in a group of very heavy smokers undergoing treatment at the Yale antismoking clinic, one man showed a sudden transformation after seven weekly meetings at which he had consistently described himself as hopelessly addicted to cigarette smoking. At the eighth meeting, he reported a dramatic 'conversion' experience. He told the group that a few days earlier he had visited a close friend in the hospital who was dying of lung cancer. After leaving the hospital he had thrown away his cigarettes and hadn't touched one since."[9]

"Our working assumption," comment the authors of this account, "is that many persons who claim that they want to go on a diet, give up smoking, or carry out some other desired form of self-improvement are clinging to excessively bolstered decisions that depend for their continuation upon rather flimsy rationalizations that exaggerate the withdrawal symptoms and other difficulties involved in changing their habits. If these defensive beliefs can somehow be undermined or bypassed, only threadbare support remains for the person's current course of action."[10] Much the same might be said of altruistic intentions. Thus a couple might claim that they desired to help the Sterns, whose plight they had heard about, yet at the suggestion that they offer them their home, they might exaggerate the difficulties and dangers ("After all, they are total strangers, and our house is full of valuables"). Searching about briefly for another solution, they might conclude that nothing could be done. If, however, (in those days before air conditioning) they happened to visit a downtown hotel room — the Sterns' or some other — in the heat of the summer, or to hear a graphic account of someone else's visit, or to recall their own experiences on a similar occasion, the "impossible" and "unthinkable" might suddenly seem quite feasible. Where there is a will there is often a way.

(3) Search for Information

A characteristic first step in the evaluation of alternative options should be brainstorming, stimulated where necessary by wide reading and/or consultation, in search of plausible pros and cons of every conceivable variety, for a characteristic failure in decision-making is to overlook significant dimensions of the situation and to be influenced by just one or two more obvious considerations. And even supposedly evident advantages or disadvantages should then be closely scrutinized, for they too may turn out to be illusory. Such scrutiny and such brainstorming are a test of our sincerity, for the difficulties which impede them lie largely in the will.

"In the day by day decisions of the ordinary citizen," notes John Bennett, "distortion comes from narrow interest, not his private interest alone so much as the interest of the group in which he moves, which usually corresponds with his private interests. In public opinion polls one discovers this to be true constantly except when some great issue is dramatized, as in the case of the issue between famine abroad and rationing at home. In most of these cases the individual citizen is in a better position intellectually to understand the case of the point of view that is closest to his own interests. He gets this point of view from his associates and from the organs of opinion that have prestige in his own circle. There is usually something to be said for it and this something can be stretched far without any conscious dishonesty. In order to correct this natural tendency it is necessary for a Christian to have more than usual suspicion of any conviction that is in harmony with his own interests. He may be helped by reading journals that have their influence in some other circle than his own."[11] Then, "in regard to each report," suggests Yves Simon, "I shall ask myself if it is consistent, if it presents solid proofs, if it contains significant silences. After that, by comparing the documents, I shall arrive at a conclusion sufficiently founded to justify a resolute decision."[12]

More often than one might suppose, there is no need to consult or inquire; the facts stare one in the face. At the risk of alienating some readers (and that risk, be it noted, illustrates clearly the point here being discussed), I shall mention a familiar example. During the Vietnam War a standard objection to American policy was that it presupposed a reality which no longer existed: the communist monolith. American leaders had supposedly overlooked, or were trying to hide, the fact that Russia and China were at odds. But the objection itself ignored the equally obvious fact that despite their differences Russia and China were both supplying massive aid to North Vietnam: China in the form of manpower for repairs, Russia in the form of arms. And either of these colossi alone could have toppled numerous dominoes had it wished. But, of course, the domino theory itself (of countries toppled in series if South Vietnam fell) deserved closer scrutiny than it often received from its advocates. China's genuine intentions needed to be examined, along with counterforces like nationalism.

"According to Hitler's celebrated saying," comments Simon, "the ordinary man, who is accustomed to tell little lies, not big ones, suspects a lie when it is little but does not suspect it when it is enormous. To present a proposition whose falsity anyone can verify is a tactic which often succeeds. The reader tells himself that if the proposition were false it would be too easy to confound the proponents of it; he therefore concludes that it is true. Amongst the rules destined to protect our minds against falsehood, let us give first place to the following: Never admit that a proposition is true simply because it would be easy to expose its erroneousness if it were false."[13]

Sureness and fullness of information have the same significance for moral decision as for the critical assessment of any inductively supported belief, whether market prediction, population estimate, or identification of a cancer-causing agent: the consequence, namely, that no inductive conclusion is well taken and justly credible unless the obligation to muster all available evidence which is relevant to the conclusion has been met. "If we can say, 'This is all the evidence I command which bears upon this matter,' and on this evidence, it is probable that A is the case, then A has just the warranted credibility so determined. But if pertinent evidence is ignored or suppressed, then any probability on the premises specified and utilized does not represent a warranted conclusion or a rationally justified belief."[14] Nor is it the verdict of charity.

(4) Concern for Values

Important values and disvalues, I remarked, are often overlooked. But they are also overridden, needlessly. For the decision procedure frequently takes the following form. The issue is first stated as a dichotomy: either yes or no (e.g., for or against the treaty, for or against the post), or this solution rather than that (e.g., this location versus that, this occupation versus some other). The advantages and disadvantages are then carefully weighed and a decision reached. It may be found that each alternative has much to say for it or against it. But such is life, and a decision must be made. So we regretfully sacrifice the values on one side and incur the disvalues on the other, opting for the lesser evil or the greater overall good.

Thus in discussing important issues, both public and private, people often argue for or against without passing to, or even conceiving, the stage of creative synthesis which is frequently feasible, where one seeks to imagine alternative solutions which will combine a maximum of the advantages and a minimum of the disadvantages discovered in the two opposed solutions. For this failure various reasons can be suggested. It is easy, for instance, to overlook the fact that options stated and then analyzed and evaluated are options stated without the benefit of the analysis and evaluation, and so before the competing values and disvalues, along with their relations to one another and to alternative lines of action, are clearly envisaged. Once this fact is noted, bipolar evaluation may appear in a different light: as preliminary, not terminal, its function being not so much to decide the issue (though it may) as to familiarize us with it in an ordered, feasible fashion. On the one hand we cannot consider all alternatives, and on the other we cannot know prior to consideration which are the most promising. Thus we delimit the debate as best we can in terms of our initial understanding but later seek an optimal solution in the light of fuller understanding, without being bound by the original formulation. Searching more purposefully now amid all the possibilities, we may spot a solution which combines values previously opposed or escapes disvalues that threatened on either side.

Even one who noted all this theory but had not experienced the reality might feel skeptical about the theory's worth. It is a matter of experience, however, that adoption of the method may yield dramatic results. I remember one meeting in which an important issue (the disposition of a valuable library) was decided. After two hours all agreed on one of two diametrically opposed solutions. But then, without impatience about possible "waste of time," the dialectical process was allowed to pursue its course. At the end of the third hour all had agreed once again, but more enthusiastically now, on quite a different plan, which entailed some additional expense but obviated the major objections to both the alternatives previously envisaged. Other times, however, when a decision has been rushed, one can look back some years later and see that the dialectic of pros and cons has indeed run its inevitable course, but experientially and at considerable cost and not harmlessly through deliberation. The disadvantages which were foreseen and accepted finally forced reconsideration when they were incurred and experienced. And then at last it was seen that they were unnecessary. The synthetic solution finally adopted was available from the start, waiting to be detected through an extra hour or two of systematic, probing reflection.

Sometimes, though, no such remedy is possible, the first decision having decided the matter irrevocably. Suppose, for example, that the choice is one of life or death for a terminally-ill person. An old man is miserable and begs for release: Should his plea be heard? We seem faced by a simple alternative: yes or no. However, as Daniel Maguire notes, "perhaps the desire for death is due not so much to the illness as it is to the dehumanized atmosphere others have created for the old man. Perhaps he has never been taught the humanizing and liberating truth that usefulness and meaningfulness do not coincide." Accordingly, "one alternative to his voluntary death might be to create an atmosphere in which he might want to live, an atmosphere in which he may learn that utility is not the measure of man. The 'useless' person can be capable of joy and love, of ecstasy and of humor. In fact the 'useless' person can also, paradoxically, be useful. He can show pragmatic modern man that there are richer forms of living, that to say *homo faber* (man the maker) is not to say enough about man."[15] This third solution might combine values envisaged in the previous two, while avoiding or mitigating the disvalues.

(5) Concern for Consequences

Our experience, no matter how well supplemented by reflection and inquiry, is perforce limited; and what we have experienced (personally or at least vicariously through film or vivid account) carries more weight with us than what we accept as true but do not conceive so vividly. Thus if one person at the time of the Vietnam war read a first-person account of communist tactics in China (prison, torture, brain-washing, interrogation, people's courts) and another person saw films of napalmed children and burning villages, their judgments on the war might differ radically under the influence of these one-sided images. Ideally, then, we should seek to acquire the same concrete awareness of all aspects of a problem requiring decision in order to evaluate them fairly and realistically. But that may be impossible.

More evidently chimerical is a complete survey of consequences. Very soon calculation turns to conjecture in all directions. And though charity, if sincere, will endeavor to see ever farther and more surely, it is perhaps equally important that it realistically acknowledge the limits of its vision. As Peter Berger has convincingly argued, when we take the broader view we must work from a "postulate of ignorance." "If one ticks off some major problems of recent domestic policy (such as poverty, unemployment, education, or racial justice), while there are large bodies of social-science data on each one, it is amazing how much contradiction there is in the literature concerning the alleged basic causes of each — and, therefore, how ambiguous is the usefulness of the available information for the policy maker. If all this is so in the United States (and, by extension, in other Western countries), the point can easily be made *a fortiori* for the countries of the Third World. It is a crucially important point with regard to the formation of any development policy."[16]

Its importance emerges vividly in Berger's comparison of Brazilian and Chinese policies at the time he wrote, entailing massive poverty in one country, massive repression in the other. "It is true that there are harsh realities to the process under way, the legitimators declare, but these are necessary stages as the process moves toward its goal and will disappear when the goal has been reached: No more misery and no more crass polarization when Brazil will have become a 'fully developed society'—no more coercive use of state power when China will have 'attained communism.' But what if these articles of faith are put in question?"[17] The postulate of ignorance then applies. To be justified, this mass of presently inflicted pain would have to be balanced by immense benefits surely foreseen—or rather, clearly foreseen as resulting from these sacrifices alone and not to a comparable extent from any alternative policy. What Berger therefore urges, and charity enjoins, is more careful, realistic comparison of benefits and costs. Dogmatic or wishful thinking has no place where love really cares.

(6) Time for Deliberation

"We cannot deliberate forever," it is frequently said, "we must finally act." This reaction would be especially likely were still another stage of reflection suggested, as in (4), after the more evident alternatives had been fully canvassed and a clear verdict perhaps been reached between them. However, my own experience has been that these words, or the like, were never uttered when a decision was in fact pressing and time had run out. The reason was fatigue and ennui, or satisfaction with the conclusion reached and reluctance to question it, or disbelief in the value of still more exhaustive analysis (especially in contrast with other possible uses of the time), or a combination of these. Yet the amount of time to be saved sometimes seemed incommensurate with the issues at stake: an extra hour for twenty people, say, whereas the lives of hundreds or thousands were to be importantly affected for years to come by the decision.

However that may be, the general rule is clear. This decision like any other should reflect the balance of values; the time expended should match the stakes. "Thus, the criteria will be set rather high when a person chooses a fundamental life plan like marriage with someone, since the interests involved are so fundamental and the costs of deliberation seem, by comparison, slight; and, the criteria will be set rather low when a busy executive has to choose to buy a pair of scissors, for here the price of extended deliberation would be too costly, given the small benefits which result and great costs in terms of forgoing the exercise of deliberation on more difficult and important decision problems."[18]

Time is more of a problem for group decisions. For the issues treated then tend on the whole to be more complex and so to demand longer deliberation. And schedules have to be coordinated, so that limits may have to be set. And the total man-hours lost are now a multiple of the group number as well as of the hours elapsed. So deliberation is especially likely to be cut off prematurely unless the rule just cited is further refined. An obvious corollary, yet one often neglected, is the need to discriminate important matters from less important and to allocate time accordingly. Otherwise much time may be spent on trifles and little be left for essentials. Again, it may be necessary to distinguish between matters which are important but for which a time limit may reasonably be fixed and those which are so weighty that the explicitly adopted norm should be: discussion will continue as long as anyone has anything new and relevant to say. (Neither the leader nor the majority should venture to guess the importance of the points not yet made; even those who wish to make them may not sense their full implications or where they may lead.) Even then, when all have had their say, if circumstances permit and the decision is not merely consultative, it may be well to postpone the verdict and allow more leisurely rumination on the considerations for and against.

The use of value tables may save some time by focusing and ordering discussion, but in general the method is time-consuming. All likely values and disvalues must be identified for each alternative, then be tested, refined, evaluated, and totaled. But we get what we pay for, and (in another sense of the term) pay for what we save. Any shortcut — any failure to list some plausible reason for or against; or to probe the probability, extent, and importance of the items listed; or to total systematically the merits and demerits for each line of action — renders the final verdict that much less reliable. So when the stakes are high, value tables are worth the price. And so is the subsequent search for preferable alternatives, at least when the solutions so far envisaged all entail considerable costs. For the "costs" in question are, of course, some form of suffering or the loss of things we value. So they cannot be taken lightly.

At the end of this section, with its many admonitions, a word of encouragement may be in order. What charity requires is not impossible. Nor is it always difficult. Many a time, when an important decision confronts us and we are tugged this way and that by conflicting considerations, it suffices to put pen to paper: the mere attempt to list reasons for and against, accurately and completely, quickly brings clarity. So the most practical suggestion of this section and this chapter, indeed of the whole book, may be a simple repetition of Ignatius' advice: when in doubt about an important decision, map the Christian values pro and con. Well-trained love, if sincere, will make at least this effort.

C. Alternative Clues

"Pray as though everything depended on God, work as though everything depended on you." So goes the saying with regard to other actions.[19] But does it apply to the activity of making moral decisions?

The first clause is less problematic.[20] We have repeatedly noted the insuperable difficulties that confront us if our morality is to resemble the divine, in fullness of knowledge and sureness of evaluation.[21] Hence to proceed with complete assurance and self-reliance, assessing facts and totaling values without any recourse to a light and goodness higher than our own, would suggest ignorance of our condition, or worse. It would amount to the absence or negation of Christianity in practice, if not in theory. However, we still need to know what form the recourse should take and how extensive our reliance should be. Will it consist only in praying for enlightenment in our rational deliberations, or will the process itself be affected? Shall we consult the same intrinsic evidence, of values and disvalues, listing them as fully and rating them as accurately as possible, so in a sense still working as though everything depended on us, or shall we turn as well — perhaps even primarily — to other, more extrinsic signs of the divine will?

Jesus' example, Scripture, tradition, church teaching might provide such guidance. But let us begin with a source already considered in some detail — the movements of grace described in Ignatius' account of the second time (V, B) — and let us then situate these movements within a broader grouping or "family" of experiences.

As Karl Rahner notes, in the second time "the whole point is to recognize in the very first place from the source of the impulse whether it is good. The recognition of its moral goodness is, therefore, not the criterion of its divine origin (direct or indirect — this is declared to be all one), but what is sought is a criterion of its divine origin that is independent of the moral evaluation of the object to which the impulse prompts, in order that from recognition of its origin the question of its moral worth as being God's will or not, can be settled."[22]

Ignatius states a first clue as follows: "It belongs to God our Lord alone to grant consolation to the soul without any preceding cause for it, because it belongs to the Creator alone to go in and out of the soul, to excite motions in it, attracting it entirely to the love of His Divine Majesty. I say, without cause, that is, without any previous perception or knowledge of any object from which such consolation might come to the soul, by means of its own acts of the understanding and will."[23] If stress falls on the absence of conscious stimulus, we may wonder about a possible unconscious source.[24] If instead the key consideration is the transcendence of the experience, the soul being rapt "entirely to the love of His Divine Majesty," Ignatius' confidence is understandable, but the evidence adduced may be so mystical and rare as to offer no guidance on most occasions to most Christians. Let us turn then to the lowlier, commoner, perhaps more useful testimony of consolations "*with* preceding cause."

"We ought to be very careful," writes Ignatius, "to watch the course of such thoughts; and if the beginning, middle, and end are all good, leading to all that is good, this is a mark of the good angel; but if the thoughts suggested end in something bad or distracting, or less good than that which the soul had determined to follow, or if they weaken, disturb, or disquiet the soul, taking away the peace, the tranquillity, and the quiet she enjoyed before, it is a clear sign that they proceed from the bad spirit, the enemy of our advancement and of our eternal salvation."[25]

When applied to decision-making, this advice does not furnish a criterion which is, in Rahner's words, completely "independent of the moral evaluation of the object to which the impulse prompts." For the object to which the impulse prompts belongs to the evidence by which Ignatius tells us to judge it. Only by prompting us aright can the consolation satisfy fully his prescription for "beginning, middle, and end." But that it guides us well we therefore cannot know for sure, going by just this evidence. Hence Ignatius' further advice would seem to apply, that "various resolves and plans, which are not inspired immediately by God our Lord . . . . be thoroughly examined before they receive entire credit and are carried into effect."[26] Third-time deliberation should complement second-time deliberation.

A pattern such as Ignatius describes may suggest the Spirit's presence. On other occasions events and circumstances may group themselves so providentially that we sense God's guiding hand. Though not an example of discernment, Augustine's well-known conversion illustrates admirably the type of evidence I have in mind. In a moment of interior crisis, spirit warring against flesh, he threw himself down and prayed with desperation. Then it happened: "I heard a voice, as though of some boy or girl from a house not far off, uttering and often repeating in a sing-song manner, 'Take up and read. Take up and read.'" Reflecting that he knew no children's game in which those words occurred, he took up the book which lay nearby, opened it, and read the first words his eye lit on: "No revelling or dunkenness, no debauchery or vice, no quarrels or jealousies! Let Christ Jesus himself be the armour that you wear; give no more thought to satisfying the bodily appetites" (Rom. 13:13–14). "I would read no further," recounts Augustine, "nor was there any reason why I should; for instantly with the end of this sentence, as by a clear and constant light infused into my heart, the darkness of all former doubts was driven away."[27]

Each event in this sequence admits of natural explanation, but a believer is likely to see more than coincidence in their convergence: that untraced utterance of those words, following immediately on that prayer, in the vicinity of that particular book; his eyes then falling on that specific text, so potently appropriate to his problem. And something similar may happen and sometimes does, say in the course of a retreat, as a person meditates and prays over a vital decision. The details may vary greatly. But there may be the same strong impression, from the configuration of events, that God is guiding us in a specific direction. As the example of Augustine shows, evidence may be extrinsic and still clearly favor one line of action rather than another.

His case also suggests a further, separable clue. What before was so appealing to him — "limbs delightful to the embrace of flesh and blood" — now lost its hold, and the continence which before had appeared so difficult drew him strongly, peacefully. This, too, a Christian will see as the work of grace. And even when the rightness of the choice is less evident and the antecedents are less striking, a person may feel similar assurance, for like reasons. Where he had experienced dread and inner resistance, he now finds peace, contentment, even deep joy. What human nature finds abhorrent — obscurity, loss of reputation, deprivation, insecurity, and difficulty — he now accepts, perhaps embraces, for the coming of the Kingdom. In such a situation, especially if the state endures, he may sense the Spirit at work, directing his choice.

Such variations on the second time are largely passive. We cannot give ourselves these graces, nor, when they come, may we need much expertise to recognize their character. A further type of experience, confining more closely with the third time (especially its "second method"[28]), is more within our power to elicit. Here too a comparison may be helpful.

When David took Bathsheba, wife of Uriah, he was blinded by desire. When Nathan told him a parable, rousing him to indignation, his eyes were opened and he recognized his sin (2 Sam. 11). That is, attention to the tale of another's sin revealed the true nature of his own, far more lucidly than the most direct contemplation of the deed itself, before, during, or after. When Nathan said, "You are the man!" David knew it was so.

The kind of experience that enlightened David retrospectively, we too can have, prospectively. Meditating some passage of Scripture or some Christian mystery, and moved to faith, hope, gratitude, or generous charity, we may see our contemplated choice in a new light. It appears more clearly now as an imitation of the Suffering Servant, as an act of faith and not of presumption, or, on the contrary, as untrusting, pusillanimous, self-centered. Such intimations, especially if repeated, always in the same direction, can generate certainty similar to David's: we have no doubt what we should do. The light obtained in this way is once again indirect. Our gaze is turned elsewhere, and we perhaps make no effort to call to mind the option that concerns us, but it emerges to consciousness nonetheless, in resonance or dissonance with the spirit that moves us.

Often, though, when the decision problem is complex, we possess no immediate grasp of the situation in all its essentials, as David did. And no experience truly analogous to his is possible until we reach that level of synoptic understanding. But we seldom do in really complex matters, and even if we did, we could never be sure we had. Hence appears the wisdom, once again, of seeking third-time confirmation — acting, therefore, as though all depended on us, even while we pray as though all depended on God. For "if you, . . . bad as you are, know how to give your children what is good for them, how much more will the heavenly Father give the Holy Spirit to those who ask him!" (Lk. 11: 13). And that he can do in the fashion he pleases — third time, second time, or some other. We should not presume to dictate the way by restricting our own efforts.

D. Jesus' Example

"New Testament writers," notes J. L. Houlden, "enjoin the following of certain lines of conduct or the acquiring of certain qualities, not on the grounds of their intrinsic worth or rightness, but on the grounds that they are characteristics of God or of Jesus and are therefore to be imitated as part of a life of discipleship. I Corinthians xi, 1 is the most general statement of this principle. Paul also applies it to specific qualities: to generosity (II Corinthians viii, 9); and to humility (Philippians ii, 3–11). So does I Peter in the matter of the patient endurance of suffering and persecution (ii, 18–25). So too does the Gospel of John in the matter of sacrificial service (xiii, 15; cf. Luke xxii, 24–7). The portrayal of Jesus throughout the Gospel of Luke shows him as one who displayed exemplary love and sacrificial kindness, and who moved sinners to repentance and drew outcasts to his side (e.g. iv, 18ff.; xv; xix, 1–10). And in the Acts of the Apostles, his followers are shown following his example in their works of power and charity (e.g. iii, 1ff.; ix, 36ff.), and in their bearing in the face of suffering (vi, 8ff.; vi, 54ff.)."[29]

"Where this mode of reasoning operates," Houlden then observes, "and to the degree that it operates, ethics lose their autonomy, and conduct is established on a basis other than those of intrinsic values or social desirability."[30] Were this analysis fully accurate, it would seem to follow that as Kant alleged, "imitation has no place in moral matters, and examples serve only for encouragement. That is, they put beyond question the practicability of what the law commands, and they make visible that which the practical rule expresses more generally. But they can never justify our guiding ourselves by examples and our setting-aside their true original which lies in reason."[31]

Let us start with this Kantian critique and work back to Houlden's. The "true original" validating Jesus' practice and our imitation would be, for instance, the law of charity, or more specifically of favoring others' welfare (VIII, A). Exactly what falls beneath this description, what not, we do not and cannot envisage globally by means of some one essence. The constitutive concepts are, as usual, too varied and indefinite to permit that (III, A). However, for both clarification and validation of the principle we can turn to sure illustrations of its meaning and its truth — for instance, to Jesus' washing of his disciples' feet (VIII, A). There we reach semantic and epistemological bedrock. The "true originals" of reason, in a post-Wittgensteinian perspective, are concrete instances.[32] The tables are reversed.

Thus, what Christian faith surmised, analysis confirms. The rationalist godhead of pure, a priori reason presiding over the moral universe is a myth. One might as well claim that humanity knew a good sonnet when it saw one — before it saw any, or that we are all equipped from birth with character charts, akin to color tables, enabling us to identify which of the people we encounter are genuinely lovable, admirable human beings. Generally speaking (for detail, see chapter 10), Christian morality and Christian values are fallout from that fateful event, the coming of Christ. "We saw his glory, such glory as befits the Father's only son, full of grace and truth" (Jn. 1:14).

This much, however, is true: the imitation of Christ does require discernment on our part. "For example, does the following of Jesus as moral ideal require that one dress as men did in Judea and Galilee at that time? Obviously, no. But does the picture of Jesus require that the follower dress simply, without expensive adornment, without luxury? Is simplicity in manner and style of life the proper inference for those who would follow one who had no place to lay his head, and who told his disciples to take but one tunic with them in their ministry? If it is, the Christian moral ideal in our time would run strongly against the cultural and economic stream which presses more and more consumer goods into life, without regard for simplicity, not to mention self-denial."[33]

Such discernment is something more than immediate intuition and something less than comprehensive calculation. When, for instance, some ethician raises sophisticated objections concerning the coherence or consequences of altruistic charity,[34] a Christian does not wait upon the outcome, decades or centuries hence, before accepting Jesus' preference as basically correct. His attitude is that of a disciple; he believes more firmly in Christ than in fallible theoreticians, especially when they are divided, as they so often are in ethics.

He believes, that is, that Jesus' way is the better way, that it leads to life. Thus no conflict arises between such discipleship and teleological ethics, as Houlden maintained. The reply to that allegation is to stress, once again, the distinction between logic and method, meaning and procedure. The basis on which Christian morality is established (to use Houlden's terms) is its criterion of right and wrong, and that need not shift when extrinsic helps are sought. A teleologist may with perfect consistency consult the example and precepts of One whose wisdom and goodness he knows surpass his own.

E. Scripture

If we distinguish between intrinsic, constitutive evidence (facts and values that make behavior right) and extrinsic, nonconstitutive evidence (clues to behavior's possessing that intrinsic configuration), we may then recognize that second-time movements (V, B; and C, above) and the example of Christ (D) provide both kinds. So does Holy Writ. For it both grounds Christian judgments, by shaping beliefs and values (cf. X, D–G), and offers some ready-made verdicts of its own.

An interesting illustration of the latter, extrinsic type of guidance may have escaped notice at the end of section C, where Luke 11, in harmony with other texts and with Jesus' example, enjoins the important activity of petitionary prayer. This conclusion we do not and could not reach by value calculations. To unaided reason, pleas for divine assistance might appear to impugn God's wisdom or compassion. Scripture, however, stands us surety, testifying from without to the rightness of such behavior. Its witness is more right-attesting than right-making. When it advises, "Thus shall you pray . . . ," it tells us what, for other, intrinsic reasons, is right to do; its declarations do not make the action right.

Such scriptural guidance parallels in other important respects the less-discussed, second-time variety analyzed in section C:[35]

(1)   Much as there (C; see the quotation from Rahner), recognition of the action's rightness (for example, that of petitionary prayer) does not attest the teaching's origin; rather, the teaching's origin attests the action's rightness. The message is Christ's, conveyed by inspired writers. So we trust, accept, and follow it.

(2)   However, this privileged form of assistance is not always available. Biblical evidence, like second-time, may be minimal. Whereas we can always at least attempt a direct value estimate, "the ethical issue at hand may simply not be addressed by the biblical material. Issues such as organ transplants, genetic experimentation, and abortion are all issues which deal with biological data not known or in any way dealt with in the biblical material."[36]

(3)   "Yet even here," the same authors add, "the Bible may play a role in decision-making. An investigation of biblical resources may serve to set the boundaries within which moral inquiry takes place. Surely the biblical stress on the sanctity of human life and on the quality of human existence form boundaries within which these issues must be decided even if the specific issues themselves are not mentioned. This moral framework already begins to limit the decisions that might be taken." Thus we see that biblical guidance, like second-time leads, can take varied forms. "Scripture witnesses to a great variety of moral values, moral norms and principles through many different kinds of biblical literature: moral law, visions of the future, historical events, moral precepts, paraenetic instruction, parables, dialogues, wisdom sayings, allegories."[37]

(4)   In consulting Scripture, as in the second time, discernment is called for to discriminate the human from the divine. For Holy Writ is word of man as well as word of God. Consider, for example, the evident need of discernment in reading Scripture on celibacy (IV, B); divorce and remarriage (V, C); hair styles (VIII, F, 3); altruism (VIII, A); the minimal duties of Christians (start of VIII).[38]

(5)   Scriptural leads, like second-time clues, are cumulative. None is generally conclusive by itself. The prohibition of divorce and remarriage, for example, quoted from Mark in V, C, must be read in the light of Matthew's famous qualification (Mt. 5:32) and of Paul's advice to the Corinthians (1 Cor. 7:12–16) and its subsequent application. More generally, consider "the tremendous pluralism on questions of sexual relationship represented by Genesis 2; the Song of Songs; Proverbs 7; Leviticus 19; 1 Corinthians 7 and 1 Peter 3. No one of these diverse passages could be taken as the final word on the subject."[39]

(6)   Even when the overall thrust seems clear, the link with contemporary options may be far from syllogistic. Thus consider again the pre-

ceding example. A troubled Catholic couple may desire to know with regard to their particular marriage, and a Catholic prelate or theologian may wish to ascertain with regard to such sacramental, consummated unions generally, whether the church's hands are now tied or whether she may continue as before, adapting her legislation to new-felt needs and altered circumstances. But a sacramental marriage as presently delimited is one between baptized partners at least sixteen and fourteen years of age; who are free from specific impediments (e.g., impotency, but not sterility) or have been dispensed in due form from certain of them (e.g., consanguinity in the second degree of the collateral line); who have observed the prescribed juridical form (but not necessarily the liturgical one) — and so on through pages of fine print. And Scripture mentions no such boundary; still less does it specify that on one side marriage is dissoluble and on the other indissoluble, or provide teleological reasons for reaching such a verdict. More germane would be an argument from tradition.[40]

(7)   From the nature and need of such discriminations we are led to infer much as before: logically, that such extrinsic evidence is not fully independent of intrinsic; procedurally, that revelation and reason must complement each other.

(8)   Accordingly, the question of possible conflict can be treated much as in V, B, where we asked: "What if second- and third-time indications point in different directions?" One answer awarded the verdict to the clearer of the two; the other noted the slight likelihood of such a contrast, in view of the two sources' interdependence. So also stands the case for reason and revelation: with revelation guiding reason and reason accrediting revelation, no sharp conflict is likely to develop. An interpretation of Scripture that clashed too squarely with a person's overall convictions would not likely win acceptance as the text's intended message.

F. Tradition

A key test of Scripture's bearing is the subsequent mind and practice of Christendom. Thus, nothing in the New Testament cancels Acts' reported bans on blood and on strangled meat, but tradition does. Other modifications — for instance, regarding slavery and usury — are more recent. Others still, say concerning premarital relations and homosexuality, are the object of current debate.

To deal with such issues, J. Philip Wogaman proposes a procedural principle which he labels "methodological presumption": "It is the method of arriving at a judgment despite uncertainties by making an initial presumption of the superiority of one set of conclusions and then testing that presumption by examining contradictory evidence. If, after examining the contradictory evidence, substantial doubt or uncertainty remains we decide the matter on the basis of the initial presumption. Methodological presumption seems peculiarly useful in approaching moral judgments in the face of continuing uncertainty. If we can establish in advance what is *probably* the best line of decision in the light of our most basic moral traditions, then we have a clear basis for proceeding — even though this method will by no means banish uncertainty altogether."[41]

This approach is widely adopted, Wogaman notes, in the areas of jurisprudence and of executive decision-making. Indeed, he adds, "I believe that we all actually tend to do our thinking on the basis of methodological presumptions, though we often do it quite unconsciously and therefore unclearly. We have instinctive points of reference that constitute our initial presumptions."[42] For the Christian community Christian tradition constitutes one such point of reference.

One must be cautious, as Wogaman rightly observes,[43] in treating this form of authority with too great respect, lest the result be simply conservative or even reactionary. Nonetheless, if we can assume basic identity with the faith and values of previous generations in our religious community, we should give considerable weight to the collective judgment of these forebears on the problems we face today. For example, "a burden of proof should . . . have to be met before Christians abandon the institutions of marriage covenant and family in light of the vast amount of Christian moral experience which previously has confirmed them."[44]

The burden of proof, whether for Protestant, Orthodox, or Catholic, will be especially great when, as in this instance, the tradition is firmly rooted in the scriptural witness of apostolic times. "We know no Christian tradition," all three might agree, "except as formed by the Christian scriptures *and* we know no scriptures as Christian scriptures except as part of Christian tradition."[45] "Between these two a necessary dialogue needs to be maintained. They both have the same sovereign author, the Holy Spirit, and both exist in and for the People of God."[46]

G. Thinking with the Church

In a list of five answers to the question "Who is duped, who Spirit-led?" John Haughey mentions a further extrinsic clue: "There will be a harmony between the one claiming to be moved by God and the wider range of the Spirit's activity in others. . . . What builds the community is of the Spirit; what tears it apart cannot be. Consequently, one's willingness to listen to the believing community and test one's spirit with its wise men and those authorities responsible for the community's order and orthodoxy is [indispensable] for one who would live in the Spirit."[47] As Haughey notes, this criterion, like the other four he cites, is not decisive by itself. One reason, in addition to those he mentions, is that each of the tests is subject to different interpretations in different traditions.

Thus the Catholic bishops of Germany, for example, in a much-quoted pastoral letter of September 22, 1967, develop Haughey's advice in these strong terms: "The Christian who believes he has a right to his private opinion, that he already knows what the Church will only come to grasp later, must ask himself in sober self-criticism before God and his conscience, whether he has the necessary depth and breadth of theological expertise to allow his private theory and practice to depart from the present doctrine of the ecclesiastical authorities. The case is in principle admissible. But conceit and presumption will have to answer for their wilfulness before the judgment-seat of God."[48]

One who views Christ's church as an organic unity, visible as well as invisible, and who conceives obedience to constituted authority as something more than acceptance of those directives with which one agrees (see IV, I) may welcome these words as a salutary warning. I do. But they do not tell the whole story, even from a Catholic point of view. Catholic theologians are readier today than in the past to acknowledge that disagreement with official teaching, in practice as well as in belief, and in public as well as in private, may be not only permissible but obligatory.[49] This side of the question may no longer need to be stressed, for the pendulum of opinion has swung away from authority. Still, within the context of the bishops' statement several points seem worth making.

(1)   First, legitimate disagreement is seen as requiring uncommon "depth and breadth of theological expertise." Doubtless even the general competence of a trained ethician would not suffice; one would have to be thoroughly conversant with the specific topic treated (abortion, nuclear warfare, contraception, organ transplants, or what have you). Now this common supposition seems questionable for several reasons. For one thing, though not an ethician nor an expert on the particular question, the individual Christian might be aware nonetheless of the current much-publicized debate about method, and he might have reason to suppose either that the question of method was not attended to by those who issued the teaching[50] or that they assumed a deontologi-

cal stance. This might suffice to legitimate doubt. For the methodological issue is too basic to be ignored, and the deontological option can hardly be proposed as a datum of revelation. Even an ordinarily instructed Christian may sense that it conflicts with the purpose of Christ's coming, and he may therefore prefer a teleological approach like that sketched in chapter 6. And in that case he might reasonably maintain that he was still "thinking with the church," though he disagreed with a particular verdict of her teaching authority. To consult values and disvalues, concretely and coherently, is to think with the church through the ages and with her founder (chapter 4).

A second possible reason for doubt or disagreement, despite the lack of professional expertise, falls under the heading "subsidiarity." The principle of subsidiarity, familiar in Catholic social doctrine, requires that decisions be made and administered at the lowest level possible, since decisions then stand a better chance of corresponding to people's genuine needs and desires, while the decision-making process develops more fully their powers of deliberation and action. Now something similar holds true within ethics when teleologically conceived. Morality then depends on values, and values on facts, and the persons most conversant with the pertinent values and facts are those directly concerned at the level of action. The individual agent, intimately acquainted with the total, concrete context within which he must act, has this decided advantage over the experts.

Even within traditional, preceptive ethics he was accorded this advantage, but it counted for less. If, for instance, human nature in general dictated the answer and he was weak on anthropology — theological, philosophical, and scientific — he was at a decided disadvantage in any debate concerning what he should do. It was as though he, an ignorant laborer, were to argue with an engineer about stresses and strains in a bridge to be constructed. Precepts being universal, they were to be universally determined, by the whole church, particularly her apostles, fathers, doctors, councils, and popes. The principle of subsidiarity was reversed.

(2) A further observation on the bishops' admonition connects with this last. To disagree with authority is not always to disagree with the church as a whole, for a hiatus may develop between teachers and taught. The value-ethics perspective counters this danger in two ways, one the principle of subsidiarity just noted, another the principle of complementarity. If even at the highest level morality is determined by values and values by facts, then those best acquainted with the relevant facts and values, through experience or training, are as essential to the formulation of Christian moral guidance as are those versed in the his-

tory of each question or in ethical theory. Accordingly, the process should not, as it were, transpire entirely in the church's head, with the brain (theologians and trained ethicians) first excogitating solutions and the mouth (teaching authority) then giving them definitive expression. Instead, here too the Pauline comparison of a many-membered organism should be verified, with each part making its own indispensable contribution. The theologian cannot say to the uninstructed, "Your long and intimate experience does not concern me as an ethician, for I have the answer already from tradition." Nor may he disregard the findings of the psychologist, sociologist, jurist, political scientist, and many others. That would be legitimate only were it possible to say, "Wrong regardless of (and not just despite) the consequences."

Theologians have in fact grown increasingly aware of subsidiarity and complementarity not only as desiderata of a Christendom-to-be but as forces strongly operative in the past. Thus J.-M. Pohier, for instance, observes of earlier changes in Catholic moral doctrine: "The experience of these evolutions, which appeared no less dangerous or impossible, reveals that one of the decisive factors at work has been the 'sense of the faithful.' There is for example the well-known case of the radical shift in Christian ethics with regard to the legitimacy of interest on loans. The magisterium or theologians of the period did not suddenly realize one day that such interest conflicted neither with the natural law nor with the Gospel. Rather it was the ordinary faithful who, amidst economic, social, and political transformations, progressively experienced the compatibility between the concerns of divine life and those of the socio-economic life they had to lead, of which loans at interest were a technically apt instrument. Theologians' reflections and magisterial declarations may have favored the shift through clarification (we know they sometimes blocked the way), but they never did more than follow and confirm an experience which the faithful were often better placed than theologians or magisterial representatives to enjoy. It was the same for other contradictions, which often proved dramatic for the Catholic conscience, as for instance that between Catholic faith and democracy, or socialization, or religious freedom. In each of these instances, it would be easy to show that a radical evolution occurred within less than a century and that theological or magisterial approval of the position previously regarded as inadmissible generally terminates the transition and does not initiate it."[51]

(3)   Finally, the bishops' statement needs to be viewed within a still wider framework. For as the church is not identical with her teachers, so no one communion is coextensive with Christendom. And the principles of complementarity and subsidiarity which apply within a single

communion readily lend themselves to broader application. Indeed
they demand it. For at the local level—parish, town, city, state, nation,
region—those affected, concerned, informed, and capable of contrib-
uting to a wise solution frequently extend beyond the membership of
any one denomination. And at the highest level divergent traditions can
be mutually enriching and enlightening. An ecumenical interpretation
is therefore appropriate when, for instance, Gustafson writes: "Churches
also need to bring into participation persons who represent varieties of
interests, conflicting loyalties and values, so that whatever consensus
emerges is informed by the feelings and judgments of various groups."[52]

True, ecumenism, like decentralization, may threaten unity. But
unity means various things, of varying importance, and its most fundamental forms are those least threatened. Concerning a single communion Charles Curran writes: "How can one attempt a more positive
explanation and reconciliation of the unity of the Church and the possibility of pluralism on specific questions? A good starting point for such
an explanation would be the well accepted axiom—*in necessariis, uni-
tas; in dubiis, libertas; in omnibus caritas* [in essential matters, unity; in
doubtful ones, freedom; in all, charity]. There can and should be unity
in terms of the general values, goals, attitudes, and dispositions that the
gospel and human experience call for. Here attention centers on such
things as the beatitudes of Matthew, the fruits of the Spirit proposed by
Paul, or those basic Christian attitudes such as care, love, hope, forgiveness and compassion which should characterize the life of the Christian."[53] To this listing I would add agreement concerning the principles
of Christian moral reasoning, and I would then transpose the list, unal-
tered, to Christendom as a whole. Such unity can and should be hoped
for among Christians generally.

Within this larger setting two major considerations offset any
danger to other forms of unity than the basic ones just listed. First, a
chief aim, after all, is to discover God's will. And the criterion we are
treating (cited at the start of the section) ran as follows: "There will be
harmony between the one claiming to be moved by God and the wider
range of the Spirit's activity in others." Now the day is past when Protestant or Catholic or Orthodox is inclined to delimit that activity denomi-
nationally. So "thinking with the church" must be rethought. It cannot
mean automatic acceptance of one's own teaching when it differs from
others'. They too have the Spirit. So their views may be the right ones,
or closer to the truth, or right in some way ours are not. Disagreement,
so viewed, becomes an invitation to renewed reflection, inquiry, and
discussion. It contributes dialectically to truth.

Second, an enlarged discursive community has its own intrinsic worth. The process leading to consensus may be as valuable as the consensus, the medium as important as the final message. How effective, for instance, a joint declaration on Vietnam might have been, issued by Protestants and Catholics together. And what a sign it would have been — what an efficacious sign — of unity! Of unity hoped for, sought, and realized. Here is an area wide open for new initiatives at every level. One senses that in ethics now, as in the area of scriptural exegesis somewhat earlier, Catholic and Protestant thought is converging and that the convergence may terminate in equally splendid results. Already the first fruits are appearing.

H. Goals

Whether and how decisively the principle of subsidiarity points upward to the community or downward to the individual depends on the type of action envisaged: whether personal or communal; and if communal, whether local, national, or international. On questions such as contraception, vocation, artificial insemination, and organ transplantation a person is specially competent to judge in his own case; on matters such as the Vietnam War or participation in the World Council of Churches he possesses no comparable competence. The same holds for goals. Though not necessarily the best judge in his own case, the individual obviously enjoys certain advantages in determining his own short-term or long-range goals in life. Concerning nationalized medicine, though, or the desirability of an assured minimal income, a group of experts is more competent to judge than is the typical individual affected by the verdict.

At the highest, most abstract level, it is true, even the broadest goals are often obvious. But descend a step or two, and they become more problematic.[54] Thus, as John Bennett pointed out, there was general agreement among Christians after World War II "that at this stage unity among the great powers was a necessary condition for both peace and justice," and substantial consensus, secondly, with regard to "a concrete reality, the United Nations, about which there could be considerable debate, especially if one belonged to a neutral or enemy nation; and finally support of a particular program [e.g., specific structuring of the U.N.] which was even more ambiguous and about which there was less agreement. Christians must move from one to three or to some equivalent of three, but as they do so the degree of authority that can be claimed in the name of Christian ethics becomes weaker with each step."[55]

A further distinction appears more clearly in a pair of goals proposed by Bennett as "a minimum basis for common action by American Christians:

   a. That the national community acting through government in cooperation with industry, labor and agriculture has responsibility to maintain full employment.
   b. That the national community should prevent all private centers of economic power from becoming stronger than the government."[56]

The first of these objectives specifies a value (employment) such as might appear in a value table; the second does not, but it indicates a strategy (balance of power) deemed advisable in view of unstated values. So the latter more clearly supplements the pattern of decision by direct value-balancing.

However, goals of either variety differ from values as guides to action in that they themselves, like the actions they guide, are subject to value-balancing. For few concrete goals are unmixed blessings, and the heavier is the admixture of disvalue, the less advisable that the goal be set. Tactically, too, a balance needs to be struck. On the one hand, a church or ecumenical body should tackle complex issues, at the appropriate level, for the individual's guidance. Since he or she needs the guidance more the more complex the issues, Christian bodies should not be deterred by past failures and their consequent awareness of fallibility. They should do their best. On the other hand, they should realize that goal-setting, unlike action, is generally not mandatory. Had he been uncertain, Urban II could have refrained from any declaration for or against the liberation of Jerusalem. Had they felt similar qualms, opponents of alcoholic drink might have abstained from either urging or opposing legal prohibition. Goals, when feasible, are handy, as rules are; but they are not always feasible or wise.

I. Summing Up

These discriminations terminate a series in this chapter, all indicating "important ways in which decision-through-value-tables is inadequate as a comprehensive, universal model of procedure." In addition to that schema we have noted: the creative search for alternatives prior or subsequent to balancing; the possibility of complementary, extrinsic evidence from second-time movements, Jesus' example, Scripture, tradition, or church teaching; the relevance, finally, of goals. This procedural diversity, however, reflects no vacillation in values' primacy. It is concern for values that determines the choice of goals (as embodying more value than disvalue); that dictates their precise formulation (refining away demerits while retaining merits); that establishes their respective rankings. It is concern for values, again, that spurs the hunt for synthetic, creative solutions; that turns us toward all available evidence, extrinsic or intrinsic, natural or divine. The children of light, no less than those of darkness, are to be wise in their generation.

The only unity, therefore, in this procedural chapter is criterial, not procedural. This should not surprise us, nor is it a cause for regret. No one would dream of stipulating a single way in which all people on all occasions, regardless of their information, situation, or competence, should estimate the weather, for county or country or continent, for tomorrow or next year. And a like proposal in ethics would make no better sense. It would amount, after all, to the very type of universal norm — positive, specific, exceptionless — that Saint Thomas rightly judged to be unfeasible (IV, E). Here, too, such a norm would disregard the diversity of circumstances and their attendant needs and possibilities and so conflict with the principle of value-maximization. It is no accident, therefore, that the present chapter has produced no single procedure to match the single criterion established in chapter 6. Guidelines are all it had to offer, and all we need.

10

The Distinctiveness
of Christian Moral Reasoning

"The Christian ethic," writes Joseph Fletcher, ". . . is distinct from other moralities only because of its reason *for* righteousness, not by its standards *of* righteousness."[1] Fletcher here speaks for a widespread trend, initiated earlier and continuing strong today. "The result of theological discussion in the seventies has been summarized thus: 'Recent contributions agree in elucidating the material identity between Christian ethics and merely human ethics (faith having *only* the task of conferring salvific sense and intentionality on conduct)'."[2]

This resume might easily mislead the uninformed concerning the "recent contributions" and therefore concerning the issue itself. For the positions thus summarized differ notably from one another. Some, for example, relate to the basis of Christian ethics, alleging "identity of content between the precepts of the Christian moral law and those of the moral law which a rational being can know without recourse to revelation"[3] or arguing negatively that "neither the teaching nor the example of Christ can of itself provide additional answers or arguments for our ethics."[4] Others concern the common applicability, not the common knowability, of Christian moral norms, it being asserted, for instance, that "the criteria for distinguishing between good and bad, honourable and dishonourable, are the same for [non-Christians] as for [Christians]" or that "the principles and commands of moral conduct are the same for a truly human morality as for Christian morality."[5] These theoretical assertions advance no empirical claims; they say nothing about the positions "rational beings" do in fact reach or about non-Christians' readiness to acknowledge the norms that Christian theologians prescribe for them. Thus still another type of thesis, distinct from the preceding, would concern the views people actually hold and where these views would lead if coherently developed and applied.

This last line of interpretation is the one least frequently intended by those who assert "material identity," yet the one on which we shall focus, for the following reasons. (1) Though the least acceptable reading, it is one the noninitiate would readily suppose for assertions like those quoted at the start. Told that Christian ethics coincides fundamentally with other moralities, they would assume that existing systems were meant. (2) So interpreted, the thesis of identity would foster unduly the current trend in which "both institutions and individual lives are increasingly explained as well as justified in terms devoid of transcendent referents."[6] (3) The considerations I shall adduce against this particular rendering provide evidence by which other versions may and should be assessed. (4) At the same time they will complement the preceding treatment of Christian moral reasoning, both descriptively and normatively. We have as yet attended little, for example, to the relevance of Christian doctrine for Christian values and verdicts. Occasion will also be offered within this new setting to develop and illustrate points already considered. (5) More guidance will thereby be furnished the majority of readers than if some other version of the identity thesis were selected for scrutiny. More speculative variants, if they manage to evade the Scylla of tautology ("*truly* reasonable," "*genuinely* human," . . .) and the Charybdis of mythology ("pure reason," "man as man," . . .), may have more practical import than meets the eye.[7] Still, both Christians and non-Christians will be more helpfully enlightened, I believe, by a systematic survey of the way Christians do in fact approach moral issues and how they should (if faithful to their own standards) in comparison with others.

Taken in this down-to-earth sense — part descriptive and part normative (like our study as a whole) — the query "What difference does Christianity make to ethics?" requires a different answer from those cited at the start. To discern how and why they would need to be amended, let us review the chief headings of the preceding analyses — acts, procedures, criteria, values, beliefs, rules — and inquire under each concerning the distinctiveness of Christian moral reasoning. None of these categories, notice, coincides with the "reason *for* righteousness" cited by Fletcher as the sole distinctive feature of Christian ethics. Yet each reveals significant diversity between Christians and non-Christians.

A. Acts

The believer and the nonbeliever may part company even before deliberation commences, for reasons Norbert Rigali explains and illustrates: "The Christian belongs to a community (or communities) to which the non-Christian does not belong. An adult's belonging to any community involves, of course, the decision to belong, which is really an on-going, constantly renewed decision, and responsibilities toward the community. A member of any community is faced with ethical decisions which arise in the context of the community and reflect its specific nature and which do not confront the non-member. Decisions, e.g., to become a Roman Catholic priest, to join the Order of Preachers, to participate in a eucharistic liturgy, to receive the sacrament of penance, to pray with others in the name of Jesus, if they are authentic, are serious ethical decisions which arise within the context of a Christian community's self-understanding but not outside of it. And decisions to proclaim the Gospel in places where it is not yet being preached, to establish a Catholic school or university, to maintain a papal diplomatic service, to create a Vatican Secretariate for Non-Believers, to form any kind of ecumenical group are important ethical decisions which emerge only within the context of a Christian community's understanding of itself in relation to other people.

"Thus, it is true to say that the Christian and the non-Christian can*not* and do *not* arrive at 'the same ethical decisions about particular matters.' But the new statement means here that Christianity creates for the Christian particular ethical matters which have to be decided by him but do not even confront the non-Christian."[8]

Rigali here makes two distinct points, one suggested by the reference to "decisions which arise in the context of the community" and the other by the reference to "decisions which arise within the context of a Christian community's self-understanding." The first point, more evident and familiar, has to do with a person's qualifications (logical, social, political, or other) to perform a specific action: As a man cannot veto congressional legislation unless he is president and a woman cannot obtain a divorce unless she is married, so too a person cannot, for example, pray to God unless he believes in God (whatever he did would not be praying to God), or receive the sacrament of reconciliation unless he is baptized, or become a Catholic priest unless he is a Catholic, or ordain a priest unless he is a bishop, and so forth. The second point has to do with the role of belief in determining the object of deliberation: As a person cannot take under consideration whether to pay a debt by check unless he believes he incurred the debt and has money in the bank, or whether to shoot an enemy soldier unless he believes the gun is loaded and the man is a soldier and an enemy, so too a person cannot consider whether to make vows to God (and not merely utter words) unless he believes in God, or to be ordained (and not merely go through a ceremony) unless he believes in the priesthood, or to celebrate the Eucharist (and not merely perform certain rites) unless he believes in the Lord's Supper, and so on through most of the items in Rigali's list plus a great many others. Sometimes the acts are ones which only a believer is capable of performing, but sometimes they are not; and that brings out the difference between this second point and the first. Thus a Christian may believe that an atheist or agnostic has in fact propagated the Gospel or advanced the Kingdom of God (through persecution, say, or aid to Christian schools); but he could not coherently suppose that the nonbeliever chose to do either or took it under consideration. For him there is neither God, nor Gospel, nor Kingdom of God.

In making these two points I have not indicated an "essential" trait of Christian moral reasoning or a "specific" divergence from non-Christian reasoning. For not all acts are possible just to Christians or just to non-Christians, and not all Christians conceive the Christian acts identically. However, we should not expect to uncover any "essence" of Christian ethics, common to all its forms and present in them alone, nor to be enlightened by it if we did ("logically speaking, this procedure would be rather like defining humanity as the only animal species that laughs, or is subject to leprosy"[9]). The classical essentialist approach which ethicians, too, sometimes adopt would lead, for instance, to the conclusion that the platypus, that oddest of beasts, is not in the least distinctive. After all, ducks too have bills and webbed feet and lay eggs; and muskrats are furry and warm-blooded; and beavers have broad, flat tails. So what is so special about the platypus? The overall configuration, of course. And the same is true of Christian ethics, in fact and in theory.[10]

In the ideal order the internal diversity of the second point would disappear: all Christians would agree in their view of vows, sacraments, church, preaching, and salvation history, and of the related actions. The comparison with a single, relatively invariant species (the platypus) would then be specially apt. But from a descriptive, historical point of view a Wittgensteinian "family resemblance" analysis is more appropriate: "We see a complicated network of similarities overlapping and criss-crossing: sometimes overall similarities, sometimes similarities of detail."[11]

It will be well to keep this distinction and this comparison in mind, for though I shall not repeat them, they apply equally in subsequent sections. When I say that Christian procedures, values, beliefs, and rules are "distinctive" or that Christian moral reasoning is therefore distinctive overall, this is the pattern I shall have in view: a family resemblance and not essential, defining features, common to all Christians and to them alone.

B. Procedures

The biggest difference between Christian and non-Christian moral reasoning is one which philosophers rarely mention and theologians themselves often pass over in silence. They do not sufficiently note, perhaps, the distinction made in chapter 3 and developed in chapter 9, between logic and process, or they fail to notice that the latter does not follow automatically from the former (from value-balance as criterion, for instance, we may not infer value-balancing as prime or sole procedure). In any case, it is clear that no account is complete which overlooks method, and Christian procedures are distinctive.

"To take the moral point of view," writes Paul Taylor, "is not to adopt a specific moral code. It is to be disposed to carry on normative reasoning or normative discourse in a certain way, according to certain rules of relevance and by using a certain normative language."[12] In Saint Thomas' ethics, for instance, the most salient feature is, not a specific catalog of precepts, but the attempt to focus morality on God as man's final end. As we have seen, this focus provides only a motive and a goal, not a criterion of moral action. And a critique like that in chapter 7, on "The One and the Many," which takes account of this fact and decides in favor of the many (i.e., of a full panoply of intrinsic values), may seem to pulverize the lofty Thomistic edifice, leaving only terrestrial rubble in its stead.

This impression of value ethics as a secularized, atomized morality is doubly mistaken. For one thing, as we shall see in E, F, and G below, Christian belief in all its transcendent unity is relevant as never before within a coherent value ethic; it finally operates effectively as criterion of choice and not simply as extrinsic motive. For another thing, as we have already noted to some extent, Christian faith is decisively important for the process of moral judgment as well as for its logic. Granted, God cannot figure intelligibly in our deliberations as a value to be achieved. But he can and should enter them as guide. We turn to our Father for this daily bread, knowledge of his will; we look to his Son as the way to him and as the paradigm human being; we live in openness to the Spirit, sensitive to his motions. This strong, existential focus on Father, Son, and Holy Spirit is missing in preceptive ethics: where a commandment informs us infallibly what to do, in case after case, we need no further guidance.

In value ethics rules remain, some of them strong (see IV, F), but personal assessment of the particular case receives new emphasis. On this a Christian like Ignatius has much to say. He gives prominence, for example, to the discernment of spirits; advises that prayer precede and conclude the tabulation of values; suggests that we view our decision from the vantage point of Judgment Day. Such procedures appear neither in philosophical ethics texts nor in the practice of nonbelievers. They could not. For they express and presuppose the most fundamental Christian beliefs: in human sinfulness and need; in a good, powerful, and provident God; in the active presence of the Holy Spirit in our lives and in our hearts; in a judgment to come and life everlasting. Indeed, it is through their connection with election and action that these beliefs become most operative and real for Christians.

Likewise, acceptance of Jesus as Lord becomes something more than theory through the imitation — or following[13] — of Christ. Here too the difference is one of procedure and not merely of intention or motivation. And it acquires new prominence in contemporary Christian ethics.

The imitation of Christ was long treated as a theme of "spirituality"; it was for ethical calculation to reveal what we *should* do and, if possible, to state it in precepts. But nowadays the rigorous directives of old repeatedly reappear more modestly and circumspectly as rules of thumb. And of vivid Gospel precepts like those in the Sermon on the Mount, C. H. Dodd remarks: "Whatever you make of them, you could not profitably go about applying these precepts directly and literally as they stand. . . . Evidently they were not intended for such use."[14] They encapsulate an attitude, point in a general direction. But, of course, so do the deeds of Christ. And in important respects they do so more effectively than precepts.

This shift resembles one familiar to philosophers. In place of simplistic, forced generalizations the later Wittgenstein recommended the method of concrete models, "set up as *objects of comparison* which are meant to throw light . . . by way not only of similarities, but also of dissimilarities."[15] To be sure, our concrete circumstances generally differ from those of Christ, and our choices cannot be identical with his. Hence "we can avoid ineptness or emptiness in our assertions [our moral judgments] only by presenting the model as what it is, as an object of comparison — as, so to speak, a measuring-rod; not as a preconceived idea to which reality *must* correspond."[16] Yet how enlightening the model repeatedly is, for those who consult it, and how powerful in comparison with a precept. The precept abstractly dictates; the model silently invites. It is precept, goal, and motive all in one.[17]

Scripture and intervening tradition, both decisive influences (IX, E, F), mediate Christ's inspiration. We are assisted too by the example of outstanding Christians, whose lives, like rays from the single sun, radiate the unique example of Christ to distant times and places, including our own. Furthermore, as Haughey pointed out in IX, G, a

Christian should be willing "to listen to the believing community and test [his or her] spirit with its wise men and those authorities responsible for the community's order and orthodoxy." Notice, with these final citations of Scripture and the church and the communion of saints, we have run through most of the Apostles' Creed and have seen how the attitudes and tenets it enshrines do and should exert a decisive procedural influence on Christian moral reasoning.

C. Criteria

The proper logic of such reasoning, argued chapter 6, is that of balanced values and disvalues, with no reductive limitation on either. If Christians see fairness as a value or unfairness as a disvalue, it too should count for or against. If they prize or disprize the act itself and not merely its consequences, that too belongs in the scales of decision. This approach, I further suggested, has not dominated Christian ethics, yet it is the chief single pattern discernible in its deliberations. The same holds true, I would now propose, in moral reasoning generally. "A loose combination or confusion of methods," as Sidgwick observed (VI, B), may characterize moral reasoning as a whole. Yet of the many competing strands, none is stronger or broader than the stress, in various ways, on maximizing benefits and minimizing harm.

The plausibility of this claim can be judged from Geoffrey Warnock's more extreme proposal. "It appears at least enormously plausible to say," he suggests, "that one who professes to be making a moral judgment *must* at least profess that what is in issue is the good or harm, well-being or otherwise, of human beings — that what he regards as morally wrong is somehow damaging, and what he regards as morally right is somehow beneficial. There is no doubt at all that, apart from its high degree of vagueness, this would not be a sufficient characterisation of moral judgment; nevertheless it does appear to me to mention a feature which, in one way or another, any intelligible theory must recognise to be of central importance."[18]

Warnock's thesis looks too strong. Can one really disbar the voluntarist, say, by mere definition? Still, where smoke drifts so thickly, flames are sure to be found; Warnock would have felt no inclination to equate morality with beneficence (so with balanced values and disvalues) had the link not been exceedingly common. The agreement of Christian and non-Christian ethics in this basic respect is indeed massive.

From this fundamental uniformity it follows, however, that Christian moral conclusions will and should diverge somewhat from those of non-Christians. To see why, consider a parallel. If two people agree in their method of addition but add different numbers, their answers may sometimes agree (e.g., when one adds 3 and 3, and the other adds 2 and 4) but will not do so regularly. Likewise, if Christians and non-Christians both balance values to arrive at moral judgments but differ in their beliefs, values, and rules of preference, their verdicts may sometimes coincide but will not do so consistently. For all three factors — beliefs, values, and preference rules — affect the outcome. Now this hypothesis is verified. Christians do in fact differ from non-Christians, and their ethics is therefore distinctive, in each of these three respects.

Values and beliefs I shall leave for later sections and focus briefly here on preference rules. The two basic ones already discussed in chapter 7 tipped the scales, first to the side of the neighbor generally (VII, A) and then in favor of the neediest (VII, B, C). A third, distinctive Christian principle enjoins the universal, impartial application of both rules: "'You have learned that they were told, "Love your neighbour, hate your enemy." But what I tell you is this: Love your enemies and pray for your persecutors; only so can you be children of your heavenly Father, who makes his sun rise on good and bad alike, and sends the rain on the honest and the dishonest'" (Mt. 5:43–45).

Non-Christians, to be sure, may share these Christian sentiments (the muskrat, we acknowledged, is as furry as the platypus, and the beaver as broad-tailed). But one need not look far, even among ethicians influenced by Christian thought, to discover principles different from these two interpreted in this way. The words just quoted from Matthew have quite another ring than the earnest arguments of philosophical ethicians concerning "rights" and "duties" and what can be "shown to be reasonable." And the divergence in other quarters is sometimes dramatic. "At the risk of displeasing innocent ears," wrote Friedrich Nietzsche, "I submit that egoism belongs to the essence of a noble soul, I mean the unalterable belief that to a being such as 'we,' other beings must naturally be in subjection, and have to sacrifice themselves to us."[19] Such a lofty soul did not come to serve. It feels an ingrained aversion to altruism.[20]

D. Values

One understands better Gibbon's anti-Christian animus when the historian states his values: "There are two very natural propensities which we may distinguish in the most virtuous and liberal dispositions, the love of pleasure and the love of action. . . . The character in which both the one and the other should be harmonised would seem to constitute the most perfect idea of human nature."[21] Even a Christian who admitted pleasure as a value in itself (as we did in VII, B) would hardly describe his master as a pleasure-seeker and man of action. "Suffering servant" is a more traditional and more acceptable characterization. For a Christian "the most perfect idea of human nature" is Christ crucified—"yes, Christ nailed to the cross; and though this is a stumbling-block to Jews and folly to Greeks, yet to those who have heard his call, Jews and Greeks alike, he is the power of God and the wisdom of God" (1 Cor. 1:23–24).

Even here, though, the clash of conflicting values is not as sharp as it might be. For the Christian demotes pleasure from this pinnacle, it is true, but he does not generally banish it altogether, especially when he is taking thought for others; nor does he seek suffering in and for itself. And Jesus, though something more than a man of action, was also that: he "went about doing good." So if we limit our consideration to this sampling of Gibbon's thought, his priorities but not his listings differ from a Christian's. Stronger than such a contrast is that between contrary, mutually exclusive listings.

Consider, for example, the experience of Don Richardson, a young Christian missionary to the Sawi of New Guinea. When he had learned their language, he recounted to them the life and ministry of Jesus. "Only once did my presentation win a ringing response from them. I was describing Judas Iscariot's betrayal of the Son of God. About halfway through the description I noticed they were all listening intently. They noticed the details: for three years Judas had kept close company with Jesus, sharing the same food, traveling the same road. . . . At the climax of the story, Maum whistled a birdcall of admiration. Kani and several others touched their fingertips to their chests in awe. Still others chuckled. . . . Nothing I said would erase that gleam of savage enjoyment from their eyes."[22]

One man leaned forward and exclaimed, mysteriously, "That was real *tuwi asonai man!*" The three words expressed one of the deepest undercurrents of Sawi culture—the idealization of treachery. "*Tuwi asonai man*," a Sawi informant later explained, "means to do with a man as Hato is doing with that pig—*to fatten him with friendship for an unsuspected slaughter.*" That is, it means doing what Miss Anscombe in her list of absolutes (at the start of chapter 8) said a Christian might never under any circumstances do—and making a masterpiece of it!

It is not my intention to suggest that all primitive peoples deprived of the Gospel are fiefs of Satan. I have used an extreme example—one which appears such even within the total weave of Sawi thought and life[23] — in order to dissipate the general notion, as old as Socrates, that values are basically invariant from person to person and culture to culture. Let us all be cool and reasonable, the doctrine goes, and gather the requisite facts, then reason them out coherently and accurately, and our moral verdicts will surely agree. But the Sawi were not suffering from ignorance or confusion. There is no indication here or in the rest of Richardson's account that they reasoned to their position or that some implicit rationale underlay it. Quite the contrary. Indeed, what purely factual premises could explain those chuckles, that savage gleam in their eyes, that whistle of admiration? (If a kindhearted person was persuaded that capital punishment is necessary for the common good, would he then take a front seat and chortle at executions?) Heirs of a culture, formed who knows how, these people simply admired treachery.

An equally vivid example of value variance is the practice and acceptance of vendetta among the early Arab tribes: "The moral quality that was demanded for the execution of the vendetta (*th'ár*) was a fearless readiness to accept it as a duty (*ḥaqq*), and to carry it out, with patience and shrewdness, until full revenge had been taken. And so imperative was this sense of 'duty' that not infrequently the second killing would exceed what the injured tribe or family had themselves been made to suffer. . . . As the vendetta is one of the pre-Islamic obligations that has been retained in Islam, though in a modified form, a number of instances may be cited to show how the early poets represented its inter-tribal acceptance as an unquestioned, almost religious obligation, in fact 'comme la plus impérieuse institution de leur organisation traditionnelle' ['as the most peremptory institution of their traditional organization']."[24]

W. R. Rucker questions the significance of such samples: "Behind the specifics which seem at first glance to present gross difference and relativity from culture to culture, are the sometimes heavily camouflaged but nonetheless universal value goals of men. These are *affection, respect, skill, enlightenment, power, wealth, well being,* and *rectitude.*"[25] When, as here, a modern Western thinker, using terms of his own tongue, draws up a table which he declares valid — empirically — for all times and peoples, we may be permitted a certain skepticism — especially if he stresses how heavily the items are sometimes camouflaged. The camouflage may be his words: those labeling the values (e.g., "rectitude" if applied to dutiful vendetta) or those employed in describing their role (e.g., "behind"). That several such values in some sense lie "behind" the Arab and Sawi ideals just described is a safe hypothesis; that the ideals can be reductively equated with them is not. And Rucker's table itself may give Christians pause.

Their misgivings would doubtless stiffen for John Gill's variant list: "A common catalogue of goods includes: *health, wealth, happiness, fame* and *power*. Most desirable objects can be classified under one of these headings."[26] Health and happiness would be acceptable, wealth more questionable, fame and power still more questionable. How sharp the contrast is, for instance, with Saint Ignatius' "third kind of humility," in which one desires and chooses "poverty with Christ poor, rather than riches; insults with Christ loaded with them, rather than honors."[27] The motive, it is true, is "to imitate and be in reality more like Christ our Lord";[28] and his aim was greater service. Even so, it is doubtful, to say the least, whether the Christian ideal, other things being equal, is to be as famous and powerful as possible.

C. S. Lewis nuances and thereby somewhat softens the contrast between Christian and non-Christian when he observes: "There is one vice of which no man in the world is free; which every one in the world simply loathes when he sees it in someone else; and of which hardly any people, except Christians, ever imagine that they are guilty themselves. I have heard people admit that they are bad-tempered, or that they can't keep their heads about girls or drink, or even that they are cowards. I don't think I have ever heard anyone who was not a Christian accuse himself of this vice. And at the same time I have very seldom met anyone, who was not a Christian, who showed the slightest mercy to it in others. There is no fault which makes a man more unpopular, and no fault which we are more unconscious of in ourselves. And the more we have it ourselves, the more we dislike it in others.

"The vice I am talking of is Pride or Self-Conceit: and the virtue opposite to it, in Christian morals, is called Humility."[29]

E. From Beliefs to Values

In Richardson's account of the Sawi ideal no doctrinal roots appear; in Ignatius' account of the third kind of humility they clearly do. Christian faith works this transformation. Believing in Christ, we embrace the values he embraced and put off those of the world. Such a shift cannot then fail to affect our assessments of action. Prospects that formerly pleased now do not, and what argued against now argues in favor. Thus the example leads us to envisage two chief ways in which Christian faith may influence moral judgment. It may shape our expectations, of these or those values realized, to this or that extent, with more or less probability, by a contemplated action; or it may determine the standing of what we foresee, as more or less valuable or as valuable at all, in itself. This second mode will interest us here; the other we shall leave for subsequent sections.

To illustrate the distinction in a preliminary way, suppose two men are bidding on a painting attributed to Winston Churchill. Belief in this ascription leads one of them, a dealer, to conclude that the painting will bring a good price; so, his interest being money, he raises his bid. The other man, an ardent admirer of Churchill ("the greatest prime minister of the century," he is wont to declare), would like to own a painting by his hero, so he likewise ups his bid. In both cases belief in the painting's authenticity is decisive and leads to the same decision, but it does so differently. One bidder values the painting for what it will bring; the other values it in itself.

The distinction between these two modes of influence is not an easy one to draw abstractly or precisely. Even my simple illustration may elicit murmurings. "It's not the painting in itself that the man prizes, any more than the dealer does. The admirer treasures it as a painting-by-Churchill-the-Great; the dealer values it as a painting-sure-to-bring-profits. For both it is surrounded by beliefs of one sort or another and valued accordingly. So where is the alleged difference?" There is no sharp, essential difference between these cases, it is true, as there is not between intrinsic and instrumental value generally. But the distinction is not groundless. One of these men would characteristically hang the painting at home or in his office, look at it with warm interest, be slow to sell it; the other might shelve it in his shop, give it not a glance, and part with it at the first prospect of profit. Of such small details are large distinctions born, like that between intrinsic and extrinsic valuing.

The following varied samples gravitate toward the admirer paradigm. With or without a stated application to action or decision, they illustrate this pattern: intrinsic valuings affected by Christian beliefs prior to verdicts on conduct.

(1)   Some years ago, as a priest friend of mine was distributing the Eucharist, a man vaulted the communion rail and attacked him with a penknife. While his assailant stabbed him repeatedly — twenty-one times, as I recall — the priest made no resistance, his only concern being to protect the sacrament. Doubtless some Christians would judge his heroism admirable but misguided. But it is not my purpose to justify or to chide. The point is that we have here a case of moral decision dictated by a value based on a belief. The man's faith, rooted in the words "This is my body," as interpreted from the time of Paul, made him take toward the sacrament in his hands the same attitude he would toward the person of his Lord.

(2)   Generally similar, yet more clearly akin to our initial paradigm, is the phenomenon of pilgrimage, whether motivated by the veneration of saints' remains (as at Canterbury or Compostello) or by associations with the person of Christ (as in the case of Loretto and Palestine). The very expression "Holy Land" bespeaks the type of attraction that draws the pilgrim. "The spirit in which the more devout pilgrims drew near to the Holy Land is touchingly conveyed by Friar Felix who lost his appetite and his sleep through eagerness for a first glimpse of the shore, the hills, the mountains where God had pitched His tent among men. 'My only pleasure,' he writes, 'was to sit at the prow of the galley up on the horns thereof, and from thence to look out ceaselessly across the wide sea.' He used to be at his post before dawn, hoping that the first rays of the still invisible sun would reveal some silhouette to his aching eyes."[30]
(3)   Unmistakable kinship links this example with a familiar type of theological reasoning: "Just as by becoming a particular man God has raised every human being to a unique value and dignity, so by choosing a particular people God has raised every people to a unique value and dignity. The heritage of a people, then, is something sacred."[31] This is not yet a judgment on any act or policy, but it provides the stuff from which such judgments are fashioned. It takes us halfway from a Christian "is" to a Christian "ought."

Multiple misgivings assail the reader of such statements. One thinks, for example, of a comparable case in which a young German science teacher had his rent reduced by the grateful proprietor of his apartment: in Germany, where the teaching profession stands so high, his presence honored the establishment. Surely, one inclines to say, the genuine value of the apartments was unaffected: that aura of respectability was a purely subjective phenomenon. The very frequency of such cases, though, should make us think twice. An American reader perhaps chuckles knowingly and shakes his head — then pays extra for some dilapidated house George Washington reputedly slept in. Heirlooms, hometowns, keepsakes, and the like reinforce the lesson. "Sentiment" so pervades our valuations that the attempt to eliminate it may be as illusory as the attempt to distinguish sensation from perception and isolate "what one really sees" (VIII, F, 3).
(4)   One may also wonder: "Where will this stop? Did Jesus ennoble bread by breaking it and wine by drinking it? Did he enhance the value of bathing by washing his face and the value of sunsets by watching them?" Sometimes, however, the influence of belief or of its lack is indeed clearly universal in scope. Thus Paolo Valori writes: "Meditation on the 'triumph of death' comes to seal this primordial mysteriousness of the human condition: the possibility of the annihilation of my own be-

ing and therefore of any reality-for-me seems to annihilate as well my every project, effort, explanation, aspiration, passion, generosity, heroism, etc. As Ionesco writes: 'I have always been obsessed by the idea of death. From the age of four, ever since I knew that I would one day have to die, anguish has not left me. It was as though all at once I had grasped that there was no way of escaping death and that therefore there was nothing to do in life.'"[32] From the absence of Christian belief there followed the devaluation of all values. For to the Christian query "Quid ad aeternitatem?" — "What for eternity?" — the answer came back: "Nothing!"[33]

(5)   Applied to man himself, this reply devalues the valuer. "Western civilization," writes J. Philip Wogaman, "has a habit of speaking rather casually about the 'sacred' or 'infinite' worth of the individual. It has become a cliché, even among people whose economic or political practices betray anything but concern for the worth of individual human beings. Christian faith is not opposed to this habit; indeed, it is to a considerable degree the source of it. However, we should remember that personal or individual life is not self-validating. The dignity and worth of individual life cannot be derived from analysis of individual life itself. Man is not 'the measure of all things.' Whatever value human beings have is strictly transitory unless it is in our relationship to some ultimate source of value outside ourselves."[34] Within that transcendent setting,

> This Jack, joke, poor potsherd, patch, matchwood, immortal
>   diamond,
> Is immortal diamond.[35]

The contrasting "majority report" of this century, Wogaman suggests, may well have been expressed in Bertrand Russell's arresting words: "Brief and powerless is man's life; on him and all his race the slow, sure doom falls pitiless and dark." "But if so Christian judgment must reverse this majority report and insist rather that each individual life is of infinite value. It must insist that no life can be disregarded as unimportant. Whenever it is apparently necessary to treat persons as objects to be used or to be removed, the burden of proof must be met that such an exceptional action is clearly necessary for the sake of God's whole human enterprise."[36]

In these closing words Wogaman takes the step from value to moral judgment, as he did previously from belief to value. Both times the transition is natural and typical, and not specifically Christian in mode; the starting, intermediate, and terminal positions, however — the belief, the value, and the moral application — are characteristically Christian.

F. From "Is" to "Ought"

The popularity of views like that of Fletcher quoted earlier — "faith having *only* the task of conferring salvific sense and intentionality on conduct" — is a puzzling phenomenon. For beliefs, whether religious or nonreligious, obviously do make a difference in our moral evaluations. And their role is emphasized in contemporary teleological ethics. And religious beliefs, including Christian beliefs, differ from others. So how is it possible for a teleologist like Stephen Toulmin to declare: "Ethics provides the *reasons* for choosing the 'right' course: religion helps us to put our *hearts* into it. There is no more need for religion to compete with ethics on its own ground than with science on its: all three have their hands full doing their own jobs without poaching"?[37]

Doubtless one explanation of the phenomenon is a tendency to equate factual beliefs with "empirical" beliefs, with the result that the most decisive religious tenets drop out of consideration. For the same reason the practical divergence between Marxists and Catholics, say, may be attributed to differing moral principles. The discordance in their particular judgments, argues Jonathan Cohen, arises "from the clash of two principles which cannot conceivably co-exist in the moral outlook of anyone but the possessor of a split personality. It is a fundamental disagreement, which is the logical antecedent of an unlimited number of particular disputes about the morality of governmental confiscation of Church property, about whether an obstetric surgeon should save the mother rather than the child, about whether peasants should invest their capital in a new Church or in land drainage, and so on."[38]

A more evident source of this surface disagreement is doctrinal divergence. Without belief in God and in a church established by his Son, Catholics' concern for church property and their interest in building places of worship are not intelligible. Both would strike *them too* as immoral were their factual beliefs identical with Marxists'. So Stuart Hampshire's analysis appears closer to the mark: "The conflicting moral conclusions of a Marxist and a Christian Fundamentalist, or the differences which may arise even between two contemporary and similarly educated liberal unbelievers, will generally (but not always or necessarily) [nor exclusively, I would add] be shown in argument to rest on different empirical or at least corrigible beliefs about the constitution of the universe."[39]

The influence of his beliefs pervades a Christian's life to an extent he seldom attends to. Many a familiar act, held beneath the magnifying glass, reveals multiple links with his faith. Thus "the reality and activity of God, the shaping of a community of faith in consequence of the divine activity, the apprehension of the divine activity and the historical life and destiny of the community of faith — all are involved in the simple act of taking up the Bible to read."[40] Such beliefs not only motivate but also justify Christians' printing and purchasing Bibles, reading them to their children, using them in religious services, and so on.

As a single act may incarnate multiple beliefs, so a single belief may ground multiple actions. Thus "there are significant beliefs," writes Gustafson, "about the nature of man himself. If I believe that man participates in a nature which is directed toward his fulfillment, and if I believe that this nature is not drastically corrupted, I am likely to assess occasions for action differently than if I believe that man is thoroughly disordered. For example, if my convictions are of the latter sort, I might judge that the function of the state is primarily to establish order and exercise power in order to curb the disruptive tendencies among individuals and their relations to each other. If I believe that man naturally moves toward his own and the social good, I am likely to judge the importance of the state to be the coordination of resources toward the fulfillment of certain positive moral values."[41]

Whichever direction a Christian's thinking takes, he or she is likely to have non-Christian company. Indeed when, in a pluralistic society, Christian views diverge on a yes-or-no, pro-or-con issue, at least one of the positions is bound to be shared by others. Hence the temptation recurs to say: "Being a Christian makes no difference to the *content* of morality. It motivates a person to be a good citizen, say, but does not determine what form of government to favor."

However, one might as reasonably survey the occupants of a city bus — a housewife on her way to shop, a girl on her way to dancing lessons, a clerk on his way to the office, a mobster on his way to a payoff, a lover on his way to a rendezvous — and conclude that "being a mobster or a schoolgirl, a housewife or a clerk, is merely a matter of motivation; it doesn't affect one's movements." The answer, naturally, is that the overall pattern of their movements differs, and it differs for a reason. The housewife doing her shopping traces quite a different route than the enforcer making his rounds, or the clerk ensconced in his office, or the girl at her lessons, then visiting friends. And the same is true of Christians, Buddhists, atheistic humanists, Nazis, Sawi, and so forth: their paths may coincide at some points but certainly do not at all, and each life pattern has its inner rationale. The absence of behavior specific to some one group does not prove identity of conduct, actual or prescribed.

Earlier examples illustrate a possible kindred confusion. Given the alternative of building a church or investing in irrigation, a Christian might decide either way. Again, given the choice of devoutly reading Scripture or visiting a sick friend, a Christian might do either. No immediate, sure inference connects even a uniform Christian "is" to a specific Christian "ought." But from this it by no means follows that Christian belief is logically unrelated to Christian moral decision. The relation is unmistakable (after all, a Marxist would neither build the church, nor worship in it, nor devoutly read Scripture) but is complex. And in this, of course, it resembles non-Christian moral reasoning.

A specific feature of this complexity merits special attention. For it has played a key role in negative verdicts on the relevance of Christian faith and so indicates an area where clarification is needed. My approach will be dialogical: suggestion, objection, reply.

G. Christian Horizons

"For Christian ethics," writes Gordon Kaufman, "right and wrong cannot be decided merely in terms of the present situation in history, however impregnated with ideals our situation may appear to be. For the Christian ethic is historical-eschatological: it takes its bearings, not from what seems real and obvious in the present, but from the living past and the hoped for future."[42]

This sounds reasonable enough. But let us consider. The past cannot live in the sense of providing a goal or of weighting the value balance one way or the other. It is not something we can now *achieve* through our action. Nor is heaven. It may at most be merited (I take no side on the question) by doing what, by other criteria than any relation to future bliss, we judge to be right. As for the terrestrial expectations of a Teilhard de Chardin, they appear so distant and vague as to furnish little concrete guidance for present practice. A Christian aspires to brotherhood regardless of whether he believes in Omega, and even if he had detailed knowledge of that final consummation, he would not thereby learn the way to its achievement. He could not infer concretely what present steps to take. For butterfly grows from caterpillar, too, and man from child, but how different the process that engenders them![43]

"Thus the attempt has been made," writes Pierre Antoine, "in order to found morality, to seek from history what it was seen we could no longer ask from nature. This seems to me quite futile, and dangerous. Quite futile because, even were we to accept the risky speculations of a philosophy or theology of history, it is difficult to see how they allow us to attain, in the circumstantial way required for action, the detail or singularity of the situation or event. Dangerous, since there is the risk of thus having only an ideological justification of an interpretation which is in fact arbitrary."[44]

The interest of the following examples is that they answer both these objections and thereby validate Kaufman's claim. A Christian's overall view of salvation history inevitably does have important implications for concrete moral choices.

(1)   Kaufman develops and illustrates his thesis as follows: "The Christian ethic, eschatological to the core, makes sense only from a point of view which does not judge things in terms of the possibilities or probabilities of the present but believes rather in God's ultimate triumph. It is this expectation that enables the Christian ethic to express itself in radical nonresistance. . . . On any short-term view it should be obvious that power, not love, rules human history, that those who love and give themselves are only destroyed. 'Pragmatic pacifism' is thus nonsense. But the Christian ethic is not rooted in any short-term judgments of this sort. It is rooted in an eschatological perspective in which the ultimate overcoming of the world by the power of God's love is expected. From this perspective, absolute self-giving makes sense. For faith, believing that God's purpose will prevail, it is possible, indeed only reasonable, to express that purpose through love, even though this means historical destruction. But this is true only for a faith that lives in this hope, not for any other perspective."[45]

The example suggests the sense of Kaufman's reference to a "living past" as well as to a "hoped for future." In this perspective the paschal mystery of death and resurrection is not a one-time victory but an eschatological reality. Calvary and Easter Sunday were the first act in a continuing drama — an initial realization of the truth Bonhoeffer stated: "The only way to overcome evil is to let it run itself to a standstill because it does not find the resistance it is looking for."[46] Our swords are no more acceptable than Peter's. God's power works in other ways.

This is not the traditional Christian view. Christians have more commonly supposed that God helps those who help themselves and that to renounce all use of force, at every level, would be to tempt God. It is neither reasonable nor Christian to let the Mafia run the country or Hitler run the world. Viewed from this majority standpoint, the pacifist reading of divine intentions and strategy may appear a "risky speculation" (to apply Antoine's phrase). But there is no evading such "speculation." For no airtight case can be made on either side; yet we must decide, one way or the other. Both collectively and individually we are daily faced by the question whether to counter evil with force. Whichever way we decide this issue, the result will be a theological position, and from that position will derive a multitude of very concrete conclusions for our personal conduct and for society.

(2)   Of Jonathan Edwards, whose early scientific efforts showed such promise, Henry Stob writes: "It can hardly be doubted that he refused to devote himself to physical science less from a sense of incapacity for such studies than from a profound conviction that the physical and external is of little weight as compared with the inner and spiritual. On this conviction, expressed in the proposition that 'the things which are seen are temporal and the things which are not seen are eternal,' he built his imposing philosophy of inwardness."[47]

The New England divine's attitude and choice typify the Christendom on which Teilhard de Chardin looked back: "Hitherto, to love God and one's neighbour might have seemed no more than an attitude of contemplation and compassion. Was not to love God to rise above human distractions and passions in order to find rest in the light and unvarying warmth of the divine Sun? And was not to love one's neighbour primarily to bind up the wounds of one's fellow men and alleviate their suffering? Detachment and pity — escape from the world and mitigation of evil — in the eyes of the Gentiles could not those two notes be legitimately regarded as the Christian characteristics of charity?"[48] Such a view, coherently carried through, leaves little room for scientific research. "The more religious-minded the person chosen for such work, the greater the odds that, in line with what he has been taught, he considers, religiously speaking, the advances and achievements of science simply as something inessential added to and subsidiary to the Kingdom of God."[49]

A different vision motivated Teilhard in his life as scientist-priest. He too, like Edwards and Teresa and countless Christians, aspired to the eternal. But he saw it ahead and not just within or above. As biological evolution, through ice age and cul-de-sac and endless aberrations, advanced steadily to Homo sapiens, so the noosphere, through dark age and world war and untold confusion and strife, is progressing just as surely toward the "full stature of Christ" (Eph. 4:13). The second coming, like the first, will be a consummation, an incarnation, not a destruction. Nothing will be lost. "The universe itself is to be freed from the shackles of mortality and enter upon the liberty and splendour of the children of God" (Rom. 8:21).

In a world on its way to Omega all has value. The physical, the social, the political, the scientific — they too have eternal significance. So they weigh more heavily in the balance of decision. To be quite concrete, let us suppose that one of the options confronting a person is linguistic research in a new, promising area in pursuit of personal insights reflecting his background, aptitude, and interests. From a traditional viewpoint such an undertaking would doubtless rate low in comparison with other possibilities. "Feed the poor, preach the Gospel, or praise

God in a life of prayer," would be the likely reaction, "but what good are linguistics to body or soul?" Suppose, though, that growth in knowledge and understanding is an essential dimension of progress toward history's goal. And suppose that language constitutes the central nervous system, as it were, of the evolving noosphere. Then it is inconceivable that an advance in the understanding of language should lack lasting significance. And a Teilhardian decision-maker, viewing the scientific option in that light, would therefore rate it higher among the alternatives open to him. It still might not rise to the top of his list, but if not of his, then of others' in their particular circumstances. Within this optic such research acquires new status.

So does research in general, and much more besides. For without looking beyond the cognitive dimension of human evolution, we can, for instance, say: If Einstein was important for the advancement of human understanding, then so were his parents, his teachers, his publishers, his doctor, and his milkman. More generally, and in abstract Teilhardian terms: Since the myriad forms of "tangential" energy, linking element with element at a given level of advance, form the necessary substratum for the "radial" energy which carries the universe forward, they too have lasting significance.

Here, then, another forced option confronts us, and a momentous one. We cannot avoid the issue. For in decisions like Edwards' and countless others, weights must be assigned, whether heavier or lighter; and a skeptical "Unproved!" helps not a whit. The context of choice, unlike the speculative, obligates us to take Teilhard's serious questions seriously and decide one way or the other, on the basis of available evidence, as he did. And were we to attempt a demonstration that evolution is not continuing, or is not continuing collectively but individually, or does not have the collective terminus Teilhard envisioned, our speculations would look every bit as risky as his, if not considerably shakier. Having formulated our own position, and seen the need to, we might then feel less inclined to speak of "an ideological justification of an interpretation which is in fact arbitrary."

Once we decide, either way, terrestrial values will be weighted accordingly. More precisely, they will be raised or lowered by an affirmative or negative verdict, but more or less according to its strength. Thus, if from a Christian viewpoint the reasons on one side appear markedly superior to those on the other, then the probability factor, operative in all assessments of individual value aspects (see VIII, G), will be proportionately stronger, and the alteration in rating correspondingly increased in one direction or the other.

(3)   According to one conception of the church and its teaching minis-

try, revelation contains the essential truth for man and is complete, having terminated with the apostles. "To the successors of the apostles, sacred tradition hands on in full purity God's word, which was entrusted to the apostles by Christ the Lord and the Holy Spirit. Thus, led by the light of the Spirit of truth, these successors can in their preaching preserve this word of God faithfully, explain it, and make it more widely known."[50] But not make any consequential addition to it, the conception would add, or permit any significant modification.

This "coins-in-a-napkin" model has practical implications. It may not go so far as to say with Pascal that in theology "innovations are infallibly errors." But in general it does not favor inquiry or new ideas. A theologian would mistake his audience were he to justify his research to proponents of this view by saying, "The question I'm exploring is new and of basic importance."[51] From their viewpoint he would have stated strong reasons *against* the investigation. For one thing, in proportion as an inquiry is both new and significant, it is likely to unsettle people's minds. And for that to be legitimate, some notable advantage would have to be envisioned. But it could hardly be truth—not new, important truth. And even apart from the effect on people's faith and peace of mind, serious research must appear a dubious enterprise when at best it can discover second-rate truths, while at worst it undermines essentials. The risks outweigh the hoped-for benefits.

The case of Galileo has special interest as an illustrative example. For more than the position of the earth and therefore man's place in the universe were at issue, more even than the veracity of the Bible as people then read it. In defense of his position Galileo extended his challenge to the underlying conception of Scripture which gave that reading its weight, and in so doing he trespassed on terrain in which basic change seemed still more inconceivable. Theologians and common folk agreed in viewing the Bible as a divine authority on all it touched. And what the whole of Christendom held on a matter of such consequence could hardly be mistaken. So the consultants of the Holy Office declared Galileo's theories formally heretical, and he was silenced.

The Constitution of Vatican Council II already quoted above offers quite a different picture when it says: "This tradition which comes from the apostles develops in the Church with the help of the Holy Spirit. For there is a growth in the understanding of the realities and the words which have been handed down. This happens through the contemplation and study made by believers, who treasure these things in their hearts (cf. Lk. 2:19, 51), through the intimate understanding of spiritual things they experience, and through the preaching of those who have received through episcopal succession the sure gift of truth.

For, as the centuries succeed one another, the Church constantly moves forward toward the fullness of divine truth until the words of God reach their complete fulfillment in her."[52] "Our knowledge and our prophecy alike are partial," wrote Paul, "and the partial vanishes when wholeness comes" (1 Cor. 13:9–10).

This conception — the "seed-in-the-ground" conception, we might call it (Mk. 4:26–29) — has quite other implications than the former view. What is security for coins is death for a seed. The wrappings — Inquisition, index of forbidden books, Syllabus of Errors, rigorous censorship, and the like — must come off if the seed is to grow. True, the initial planting is decisive for all that follows: in a sense all is determined at the start. But the progress from seed to shoot to plant to full maturity is a story of constant newness — important newness. So any policy that systematically discouraged inquiry and the diffusion and discussion of new ideas would be suicidal.

The implications of either model extend well beyond theory. Shall women be ordained? Should divorce and remarriage be permitted under any circumstances? What of intercommunion? Or communal penance without individual confession? Or the retirement of a pope? Or abolition of the college of cardinals? Or election of bishops? In case after case the answer may depend largely on which model one favors — coins in a napkin or seed in the ground or some other.[53] The balance of values is importantly affected by this difference in "horizon."

H. Rules

As we have repeatedly observed, tension between past and present, permanence and change, characterizes recent controversy concerning rules in Christian ethics. Specific norms, say of sexual morality, have long been current in Christendom but now are challenged. In reply Ramsey, Gustafson, Wogaman, and others cite the value of sound, value-based rules as social embodiments of charity and advise that when long tradition and experience speak in their favor, "exceptions to such rules are not made lightly, and the existence of exceptions is hardly evidence for the invalidity of the rule."[54]

Wilhelm Korff provides a complementary analysis, highlighting more explicitly the distinctiveness of Christian norms. "The contemporary crisis in ethics," he writes, "is by no means just a crisis in the churches' ethical teaching, but a crisis of earlier ethical thinking in general. It is an expression of the uncompleted process of modern society's self-discovery."[55] The liberal state, inspired by ideals of rationality and personalized morality, leaves more and more room to individual self-determination (regarding divorce, abortion, homosexual relations, military service, etc.). But the typical recipient of this largesse finds himself taxed beyond his capacities. He is not that mature, unbiased, presuppositionless judge the system supposes, needing no authorities, no tradition, no guidance from without. So ethical uniformity, born of sheer reason, is excluded as surely as is radical individualism. "What on the contrary stand a far better chance of success and in fact operate decisively, are the inner moralities [*Binnenmoralen*] established and maintained by the most diverse institutions, societies, and groups."[56]

The individual chooses, for instance, to become or remain a Christian, or a member of a specific Christian communion. Included in this option is a set of moral standards: "Thou shalt not commit adultery," "Thou shalt not kill," "Thou shalt not steal," "Thou shalt not covet," and so forth — all determining more precisely the single law of love (Rom. 13:9). As a willing member of the community and participant in its life, a Christian will not question these subsidiary norms or envision an exception unless strong evidence intimates a conflict with the supreme rule of charity. In so forming his conscience and ordering his conduct, he does not abdicate his responsibility as a moral agent; he does his *human* best.[57]

I. Conclusion

From viewpoint after viewpoint, therefore — though less notably with respect to its overall criterion of right and wrong — Christian moral reasoning appears distinctive: in its conception of the acts to be judged; in the procedures by which it judges them; in its rules of preference; in the values it weighs and balances; in the beliefs that, directly or indirectly, codetermine the verdicts; in the broad horizons that guide detailed decision-making; in the precepts that ease the burden of analysis. From each of these standpoints, as well as overall, the distinctiveness is global, not atomic. Christian norms, for instance, are not uniquely Christian one by one. They are like the streets we travel in our cars and seldom think of leaving (to invade a sidewalk or cut across a field). Any single road we share with others. But our itineraries differ. Other people live, work, shop, and play in different parts of town, hence take different routes, even to identical destinations. So it is for precepts, so it is for all the other items in our list: they reveal a Christian gestalt, an overall configuration, not a Christian essence.

Nevertheless, the recurring stress of this chapter on Christian distinctiveness may easily appear both elitist and divisive. To the first of these imputations I shall reply by noting that nothing so far said conflicts with John Bennett's admission, which I endorse, "that those who call themselves Christians will often need to learn about the moral conditions for the good life and the good society from those who do not accept the Christian name."[58] As for the appearance of divisiveness, it may be helpful to observe that there are at least three ways, and not just one, in which Christian moral reasoning might become "just like other people's." Once these alternatives are distinguished, it should be evident which is the preferable option.

First, Christians might jettison the values and beliefs which make their deliberations, if not always their verdicts, differ from other people's. They would then resemble everyone else in the sense that they would cease to be Christians and would become laissez-faire liberals, Moslems, hedonistic utilitarians, disciples of Ayn Rand, or what have you. They would not become mythical "average persons," devoid of beliefs and values. The same decisions would remain to be made, in keeping with whatever alternative values and beliefs they had adopted. And their new premises would be as distinctive as those they abandoned. They would just cease to be Christian.

Second, while retaining their distinctive beliefs and values, Christians might keep them theoretical and refuse or neglect to relate them coherently to their moral decisions. This by itself, and regardless of the judgments reached, would associate them importantly with the majority of mankind, who, as Sidgwick observed, do not consistently follow any one logic in their moral reasoning. Add mass conformity in verdicts, and Wordsworth's description would be verified anew:

> ". . . There is a dark
> Inscrutable workmanship that reconciles
> Discordant elements, makes them cling together
> In one society. . . ."[59]

Third, Christians might associate themselves with those, of whatever creed or metaphysic, who seek coherence in their lives, and then opt for the value-balancing approach, which in humanity at large as in Christendom may not have dominated moral reasoning, yet is the dominant single pattern. Within this framework they would endeavor to harmonize and integrate their distinctive aspirations, ideals, beliefs, customs, institutions, and ethical norms. "This notion of homogeneity," wrote Teilhard, "is without doubt of central importance in intellectual, moral and mystical life. Even though the various stages of our interior life cannot be expressed strictly in terms of one another, on the other hand they must agree in scale, in nature and tonality. Otherwise it would be impossible to develop a true spiritual unity in ourselves — and that is perhaps the most legitimate, the most imperative and most definitive of the demands made by man of today and man of tomorrow."[60]

Retrospect

THE MOMENT HAS COME to survey where we have been and why.

In first approximation the course of the preceding discussion may be compared to that of a broad beam of light, which converges, passes through a focus, then diverges again till it reaches it original breadth. Thus part one was not specifically Christian; part two was but still encompassed widely divergent lines of thought; part three focused on the crucial question of criterion and from among several candidates made its selection; part four then developed the logical and procedural implications of this option, first broadly, yet within a Christian perspective; then more widely still, in relation to moral reasoning generally. In somewhat greater detail the movement went as follows.

Part one defined the task. We would study prospective Christian moral reasoning, attending specially to the criteria of right and wrong, since they are decisive for both the logic and the conduct of such reasoning. And our aim would be to learn how Christians should form their moral judgments, more than how they have.

However, norms cannot be excogitated without reference to Christian practice and then be labeled "Christian." So part two furnished historical materials and did some initial winnowing, first of varied value-balancing, then of prominent countercases, apparent or real.

With this preparation, both descriptive and analytic, part three could focus rapidly and render a verdict: If Christian moral reasoning is to be both consistent and true to its past, it must be based on the balance of values; value-maximization must be its logic and its law. Thereupon a broad procedural issue had to be faced: In determining a course of action should we have recourse to a systematic hierarchy of values, or should we attend more directly to the concrete values and disvalues present on each occasion or in each area of decision?

Had our verdict favored the hierarchy, its elaboration would have been our first concern in part four. As it was, we turned instead to large

questions of logic (chapter 8) and procedure (chapter 9) within the perimeters set by part three. Then, having examined Christian moral reasoning both descriptively (part two) and normatively (part three and
the first chapters of part four), we could view it finally within a broader
setting and consider to what extent it is and should be distinctive (chapter 10). The inner scrutiny permitted external comparison.

The discussion was therefore ordered and in a sense systematic,
but not "scientific." It did not proceed via precise definitions to construct some coherent, tight-knit system. For in my judgment that was
not what our genuine needs required nor what the realities of the situation allowed. To grasp at least the sense of this verdict, consider the following allegory.

Back at a time when the region is still uncharted, a man decides to
trap in the Cascade Mountains; so he consults first a theoretician, then
an experienced frontiersman, to learn the lay of the land. The theoretician gives him an exact definition. "The Cascades," he says, "are the
mountains situated between latitudes M and N and longitudes X and Y."
The merits of this definition he then expounds as follows: "Any feature
of the landscape or any trip by land or water you can now map precisely
in relation to these parameters — so many miles from the northern
boundary, so many miles from the southern, etcetera. Indeed, your
whole trapping enterprise, from start to finish, may be systematically
charted within this uniform framework. True, the requisite calculations
may be complex, even for the most familiar valley or the simplest canoe
trip; and in the absence of special instruments and training they may be
impossible to perform. But at least you have a system. A theory has been
found."

This theory, alas, meets the fate of all its kind. "Why on earth have
you drawn the boundaries there," someone is sure to object; "in the
north and east you've encroached on the Rockies, and in the south and
west you've overlapped the coastal range. Your lines are completely arbitrary!" To this the theoretician would doubtless reply that he had no
intention of being governed by common terminology, vague and fluctu-
ating as it is; his scientific purposes required conceptual refinement.
And this reply might appear halfway plausible. After all, we have in
fact developed instruments which permit such exactness and use them
to fix longitudes and latitudes, which we mark on our maps or report,
for instance, in ships' logs. However, if the trapper really needed to determine longitude and latitude, and had the wherewithal, he would of
course do so directly and ignore the definition; to estimate his position,
then his distance from those theoretical borders, would be a needless
complication. So the conceptual revision has no justification, and the

overall proposal makes no sense, despite its surface clarity and precision. "Ramsey was quite right," wrote Wittgenstein of a kindred theoretician, "that in philosophy we must be neither 'woolly' nor scholastic.
But I don't think he saw how that is to be achieved, for the solution is
not: to be scientific."[1]

Of his own procedure, followed here, Wittgenstein wrote: "I
strive *not* after *exactness*, but after a synoptic view."[2] To see what this
means, let us return to our allegory and note how the second informant
(the frontiersman) answers the trapper's request. Were the Cascades
laid out like central Manhattan, he might simply describe that uniform
pattern: valleys north and south, valleys east and west, arranged at regular intervals. But as it is, he sketches a rough map, with special attention to rivers and streams, and notes how to travel them. For such are
the trapper's needs, and such the terrain. "This is the Columbia River,"
he observes," and here are some vicious rapids. Avoid them. The portage is easiest on this side, and you'd better start at the top of this big
loop. After that the cliffs get too steep." His account makes no scientific
pretensions. The words are all familiar ones — "loop," "rapids," "big,"
"cliff," "river" — with their familiar, fuzzy meanings. But somehow
they do the job. The trapper knows just where to portage.

My strategy is similar. I have drawn a rough map of the landscape, as it were, noting key features, marking major obstacles, sketch-
ing alternative routes, and assessing their merits. "Values are decisive,"
I suggested, "but they should not be understood narrowly or lead to
narrowness. In the determination of acts, institutions, programs, and
goals, the values to be consulted embrace both act and result, both
lower and higher, both here and hereafter. Charity will then have full
scope in its service of the other, especially the needy and least advan-
taged. Procedurally, too, no narrowness should result. The unique criterion of maximal value is best satisfied when rules supplement case-by-
case deliberation, when communal wisdom aids personal reflection,
when the Spirit speaks and reason listens."

The hard part, however, lies ahead. For a sketch makes no portages
and shoots no rapids. Nor does it indicate exactly what turns to take, by
land or water, to avoid a frothing boulder or an impassable thicket. It
just warns us away from certain routes and rapids; it does not assure
success in the ones we take. Thus the present guidelines warned, for example, against the use often made of "nature" in moral reasoning, of
the ban on "evil" means, and of "absolute" rules and values (in the sense
of rules to be obeyed irrespective of consequences, and values judged inviolable regardless of circumstances). But think of all the turns not
taken in advance and of all the white water to be threaded on our own:

1)   Values, we said (IV, F; X, H), are often served most surely if enshrined in rules, and rules are most effective when not questioned or transgressed. But a balance must be struck. How numerous should the rules be, and how rigid? Theory teaches and experience confirms that it is easy to exceed in either direction: too many and too rigid, or too few and too lax.

2)   An analogous balance must be sought with regard to obedience, whether civil or religious. Obedience should not be stone-blind, but neither should it reduce to following one's own lights. Where does the just mean lie? (IV, H)

3)   Where too does the proper balance fall between the claims of the world's destitute on the one hand and those of one's immediate circle — family, friends, clients, students, dependents, employees — on the other? Who can state precisely the order of precedence? (V, G)

4)   The better nourished the heart (symbol of altruism), the more powerful and sure its beat for the benefit of the whole body. Up to a certain limit, therefore, the more blood the heart itself receives, the better, provided a proportionate amount goes elsewhere. But where nature is sure, man is perplexed. Who knows the formula of a healthy altruism, concerned about self because concerned for others? What is imprudence and what self-indulgence? (VIII, A)

5)   For human moral sight panoramic vision tends to blur, while atomization tends to blind. Somewhere in between, clarity is optimal. But where? (VIII, E, F)

6)   With regard to specific values we should be neither too trusting nor too critical. Our "intuitions" may be mere custom and upbringing; yet we cannot probe forever. We must know where to stop. Yet where is that? (VIII, F)

7)   The narrower our factual focus, the less reliable our verdict; we must take the larger view. But the broader our factual focus, the more conjectural our calculations, so the less reliable once again our verdict — unless we manage the delicate adjustment of insisting that thought be thorough while recognizing that it never is. (IX, B; X, G)

8)   The more deliberation the better, up to a certain point; thereafter it becomes disproportionate to the importance or urgency of the matter at hand. But where is that point? (IX, B)

9)   Without clear standards we cannot discern the Spirit's promptings; with them we would seem to fix limits for his guidance. Thus between credulity on the one hand and incredulity on the other, discernment treads a tenuous path. (IX, C)

10)   For Christ to be our model and Scripture our guide requires a difficult blend of sameness and difference, docility and discernment. We

must read out of Scripture the local, the temporal, the culturally contingent, without reading in ourselves and our own biases. We must follow Christ along our own very personal paths; resemble him, yet remain ourselves. (IX, D, E)

11)   With respect to church guidance, like dilemmas arise: my personal *experience* versus the fact that it is *mine* (hence narrow, one-sided); the reasons I *see* versus the fact that *I* (single, fallible, sinful) see them. How awkward that I, so partial, am the one who must decide! (IX, F, G)

12)   Those who offer the guidance face dilemmas of their own. For one thing, abstract directives are surer but less helpful; concrete directives more helpful but riskier. Similarly, the thorniest problems are those for which guidance is most needed, yet at the same time those for which guidance is most difficult to formulate and (since most contestable, divisive, and likely to bring discredit) least prudent to give. (IX, H)

13)   In Christian value ethics Christian beliefs are basic (X, C, E, F, G), and so are Christian values (X, D). But which are they? (VII, A, B) And how are they ranked? (VII, C) And on any given occasion which ones are at stake, how importantly? (VIII, G) Question after question remains to be answered.

So the sketch is just a sketch and can be nothing more. It might be made more detailed but cannot become a systematic science. These queries suggest why. They also indicate the direction to take from here — not to reliance on autonomous reason, as the tale of the trapper might suggest, but toward Christian humility and trust. Johnson was so largely right: "To prefer one future mode of life to another, upon just reasons, requires faculties which it has not pleased our Creator to give us." A Christian should therefore recall that in addition to our faculties he gives us himself and that for his grace to lead us, we need not know it has. If we sincerely petition our Father for the guidance we need, and are open and attentive to receive it, and make full use of the means at our disposal, then — perceived or unperceived, recognized or not — guidance will be given us (Mt. 7:7–11).

"Do not be childish, my friends," Saint Paul advised some enthusiastic but unreflective Christians. "Be as innocent of evil as babes, but at least be grown-up in your thinking" (1 Cor. 14:20). Weigh the value of what you are doing or intend to do. Recognize the need for such balancing. But acknowledge also the limits of your powers; cherish no illusions of self-sufficiency. Thus the serpent and the dove, surprisingly paired (Mt. 10:16), form an appropriate symbol of Christian moral reasoning.

Notes

1. The Need for Moral Reasoning

1. Zoé Oldenbourg, *The Crusades*, trans. A. Carter (New York, 1966), p. vi.

2. E. Clinton Gardner, *Biblical Faith and Social Ethics* (New York, 1960), p. 68.

3. Christopher Dawson, *The Historical Reality of Christian Culture: A Way to the Renewal of Human Life* (New York, 1960), pp. 21–22.

4. On these latter, strategic considerations, see e.g. John C. Bennett, "Christian Ethics and Forms of Economic Power," in J. Bennett et al., *Christian Values and Economic Life* (New York, 1954), pp. 235–57. On the analytic difficulties, see Antony Flew, "The Profit Motive," *Ethics*, 86 (1975–1976), 312–22.

5. John Dewey, *Human Nature and Conduct: An Introduction to Social Psychology* (New York, 1922), p. 171. On the topic of this section, see also Carl Wellman, "The Justification of Practical Reason," *Phil. and Phen. Research*, 36 (1975–1976), 531–46.

6. James Boswell, *Boswell's Life of Johnson*, ed. G. B. Hill, rev. L. F. Powell, 6 vols. (Oxford, 1934), vol. 2, p. 22. For corroboration, see Irving L. Janis and Leon Mann, *Decision Making: A Psychological Analysis of Conflict, Choice, and Commitment* (London-New York, 1977), pp. 22–29; Alan Donagan, *The Theory of Morality* (Chicago, 1977), pp. 200–9.

7. Henry Sidgwick, *Outlines of the History of Ethics for English Readers* (London, 1886), p. 224.

8. Joseph Butler, *Works*, 2 vols. (Oxford, 1849–1850), vol. 2, pp. 31–32.

9. W. Norris Clarke, "The Mature Conscience in Philosophical Perspective," in *Conscience: Its Freedom and Limitations*, ed. W. Bier (New York, 1971), p. 361. An important, complementary explanation of knowledge by connaturality, less germane to our present purposes, might be developed from the conclusion of VIII, F.

10. Clarke, "Mature Conscience," pp. 366–67.

11. Karl Barth, *Church Dogmatics*, eds. G. W. Bromiley and T. F. Torrance (Edinburgh, 1957), vol. II/2 (*The Doctrine of God*), pp. 669–70.

12. Ibid., p. 671.

13. H. D. Lewis, *Morals and Revelation* (New York, 1951), p. 6.

14. John Dewey, *Reconstruction in Philosophy,* 2d ed. (Boston, 1948), p. 164.

15. *Summa theologica,* II–II, q. 50, a. 1, ad 1.

16. Austin Fagothey, *Right and Reason: Ethics in Theory and Practice,* 3d ed. (Saint Louis, 1963), p. 63.

17. C. D. Broad, *Five Types of Ethical Theory* (London, 1930), pp. 284–85.

18. *Summa,* II–II, q. 51, a. 3.

19. Irving M. Copi, *Introduction to Logic,* 3d ed. (London-New York, 1968), pp. 3–4.

20. Fagothey, *Right and Reason,* pp. 200–1.

2. The "Acts" to Be Assessed

1. Viktor Cathrein, *Philosophia moralis,* 17th ed. (Freiburg, 1935), pp. 76–77.

2. T. E. Jessop, *The Christian Morality* (London, 1960), p. 67.

3. See W. David Ross, *The Foundations of Ethics* (Oxford, 1939), pp. 114–24.

4. Joseph Fletcher, *Situation Ethics: The New Morality* (Philadelphia, 1966), p. 54.

5. Broad, *Five Types of Ethical Theory,* p. 143.

6. Henry Sidgwick, *Methods of Ethics,* 7th ed. (New York, 1907), p. 201. Cf. Edward Westermarck, *The Origin and Development of the Moral Ideas,* 2d ed., vol. 1 (London, 1912), pp. 205, 214–15. On Kant's similar view, see Gerard Hughes, *Authority in Morals* (London, 1978), pp. 40–42.

7. Anthony Kosnik et al., *Human Sexuality: New Directions in American Catholic Thought* (New York, 1977), p. 89.

8. Ibid., p. 90.

9. Ibid., p. 97.

10. As has often been noted, preoccupation with one's subjective rightness may be positively harmful. See e.g. W. G. Maclagan, *The Theological Frontier of Ethics* (London-New York, 1961), pp. 135–36; Helen Oppenheimer, *The Character of Christian Morality* (London, 1965), pp. 23–25; T. E. Jessop, *The Christian Morality,* p. 76: "The Christian is not, in his moral aspect, to devote himself to an ideal of self, but to the individual persons within his reach; not to make his mind of a certain sort for its own sake, not to cultivate it in order to make it virtuous, not to be always feeling his own pulse, but to become interested in his 'neighbours'; and the forms which this outward-looking interest takes *are* the virtues."

11. John Giles Milhaven, "Towards an Epistemology of Ethics," *Theological Studies,* 27 (1966), 238.

12. The difficulty of objective generalization is similarly obscured when

one combines the objective and the subjective in norms such as "Abortion is never justifiable *to avoid* interruption of one's professional career" (see F. Scholz, cited by Richard McCormick, "Notes on Moral Theology: 1978," *Theological Studies*, 40 [1979], 61).

13. See, for instance, Bernard Häring, *Morality Is for Persons* (New York, 1971), pp. 134–35, where samples such as these are listed with others of the previous variety and still others of neither category under the common label "absolutes" in answer to situationists.

14. See Richard McCormick, "Notes on Moral Theology," *Theological Studies*, 39 (1978), 93–94.

3. The Central Question to Be Answered

1. G. E. Moore, *Principia Ethica* (Cambridge, 1922), p. 2.

2. Ibid., p. 6.

3. Ibid., p. 7. Cf. Max Scheler, *Formalism in Ethics and Non-Formal Ethics of Values: A New Attempt toward the Foundation of an Ethical Personalism*, trans. M. Frings and R. Funk, 5th ed. (Evanston, 1973), pp. 14–15, 25.

4. See Alexander Sesonske, *Value and Obligation: The Foundations of an Empiricist Ethical Theory* (Berkeley, 1957), p. 2.

5. A. J. Ayer, *Language, Truth and Logic*, 2d ed. (London, 1946), p. 107. See Richard B. Brandt, "Emotive Theory of Ethics," in *The Encyclopedia of Philosophy*, ed. P. Edwards, 8 vols. (London-New York, 1967), vol. 2, pp. 493–96; William P. Alston, "Emotive Meaning," ibid., pp. 486–93.

6. Rudolf Carnap, *Philosophy and Logical Syntax* (London, 1935), p. 24. On "The Imperative Mood," see part one of R. M. Hare, *The Language of Morals* (Oxford, 1952).

7. Charles Stevenson, *Ethics and Language* (New Haven, 1944), p. 13; italics omitted.

8. Joel Kupperman, *Ethical Knowledge* (London-New York, 1970), p. 36.

9. G. E. Moore, *Philosophical Papers* (London, 1959), pp. 89–90. Cf. Alan R. White, *G. E. Moore: A Critical Exposition* (Oxford, 1958), pp. 118–19.

10. On the divers uses or senses of "good," see Georg Henrik von Wright, *The Varieties of Goodness* (New York, 1963), e.g. pp. 8–12; Patrick Nowell-Smith, "The Meaning of 'Good'," in *Readings in Ethical Theory*, ed. W. Sellars and J. Hospers, 2d ed. (New York, 1970), pp. 302–17; F. E. Sparshott, *An Enquiry into Goodness* (Chicago, 1958), pp. 169–202.

11. Hampshire, "Fallacies in Moral Philosophy," *Mind*, 58 (1949), 480–81.

12. See Ludwig Wittgenstein, *Philosophical Investigations*, trans. G. E. M. Anscombe, 2d ed. (Oxford, 1958), §77.

13. Ibid., §80. See Hampshire, "Fallacies in Moral Philosophy," p. 472.

14. For a fuller treatment of some of these points, see Garth Hallett, *Dark-*

ness and Light: The Analysis of Doctrinal Statements (New York, 1975), chap. 3
("Moral Meaning"). Concerning Moore's handling of "good" in *Principia Ethica*,
see e.g. *Broad's Critical Essays in Moral Philosophy*, ed. D. Cheney (London,
1971), chap. 5; H. J. Paton, "The Alleged Independence of Goodness," in *The
Philosophy of G. E. Moore*, ed. P. Schilpp, 2d ed. (New York, 1952), pp. 113–34;
and Moore's reply, ibid., pp. 615–20.

    15. Wittgenstein, *Philosophical Investigations*, §353.

    16. Moore, *Philosophical Papers*, p. 313.

    17. In the philosophy of science fuller, more detailed distinctions may be
appropriate, for instance, Peter Achinstein's (*Concepts of Science: A Philosophical Analysis* [Baltimore, 1968], chap. 2), between logically necessary or sufficient
properties on the one hand and relevant properties on the other; then between se-
mantically and nonsemantically relevant properties, positively and negatively
relevant, centrally and noncentrally relevant. Here, however, such refinements,
even if applicable, would excessively complicate the discussion.

    18. Norman Malcolm, *Knowledge and Certainty: Essays and Lectures*
(Englewood Cliffs, N. J., 1963), p. 113. Anthony Kenny takes issue with Malcolm's exegesis of Wittgenstein (but misses some important distinctions) in the
useful article "Criterion," in Edwards, *The Encyclopedia of Philosophy*, vol. 2,
pp. 258–61.

    19. See Ilham Dilman, *Matter and Mind: Two Essays in Epistemology*
(London, 1975), pp. 88–89.

    20. R. Harré, "Concepts and Criteria," *Mind*, 73 (1964), 353; H. G. Hub-
beling, "The Logic of Criteria in Ethics and Philosophy of Religion," *Mind*, 79
(1970), 59; compare Richard Swinburne, "The Objectivity of Morality," *Philosophy*, 51 (1976), 8–9.

    21. D. A. Lloyd Thomas, "A Note on Hare's Analysis of 'Good'," *Mind*, 72
(1963), 562–67; C. D. MacNiven, "Strong and Weak Descriptivism in Ethics,"
Mind, 81 (1972), 161–78.

    22. Ludwig Wittgenstein, *The Blue and Brown Books* (Oxford, 1958), p. 5.

    23. The same distinction might be drawn in terms of intrinsic and extrin-
sic "reasons." Compare William Frankena, "Obligation and Motivation in
Recent Moral Philosophy," in *Essays in Moral Philosophy*, ed. A. I. Melden
(Seattle, 1958), pp. 44–45.

4. Value-Balancing

    1. Sidgwick, *Methods of Ethics*, p. xix.

    2. Jacques Maritain, *Moral Philosophy: An Historical and Critical Sur-
vey of the Great Systems* (New York, 1964), p. 448.

    3. Bernard Lonergan, *Insight: A Study of Human Understanding* (New
York, 1956), p. 601.

    4. Nicholas Rescher, *Introduction to Value Theory* (Englewood Cliffs,
N. J., 1969), pp. 5–6.

5. Without a further distinction this declaration may appear to conflict with the correlation between meaning and criteria in chapter 3. There I had moral reasoning in view, that is, the discussion of cases, not the discussion of moral reasoning, as here. And what figures as criterion (partial or total) in the one context may not in the other. For the moment some criterion or defining trait is challenged, its criterial or defining status tends to be suspended. Thus, were someone to question whether water is H_2O, that trait would drop from water's definition for the duration of the debate (for the reasons I have suggested), and the disputants would fall back on the prescientific notion ("the stuff that falls from clouds, runs in our rivers, etc."). This same explanation, notice, forestalls objections that might be raised (and sometimes are) against including such expendable items in the meaning of terms, as in III, A and B, and indicates a possible extension of the list in III, A. For fuller development, see Peter Achinstein, *Concepts of Science*, p. 42, and "On the Meaning of Scientific Terms," *Journal of Philosophy*, 61 (1964), 500–1.

6. C. H. Dodd, *Gospel and Law: The Relation of Faith and Ethics in Early Christianity* (New York, 1951), pp. 42–43.

7. Bruno Schüller, *Die Begründung sittlicher Urteile: Typen ethischer Argumentation in der katholischen Moraltheologie* (Düsseldorf, 1973), p. 99.

8. Schüller, "Typen ethischer Argumentation in der katholischen Moraltheologie," *Theologie und Philosophie*, 45 (1970), 529.

9. See Roland de Vaux, *Ancient Israel: Its Life and Institutions*, trans. J. McHugh (New York, 1961), p. 483.

10. See Asher Finkel, *The Pharisees and the Teacher of Nazareth* (Leiden, 1964), p. 75.

11. W. D. Davies, "Law in First-Century Judaism," in *The Interpreter's Dictionary of the Bible*, 4 vols. (New York, 1962), vol. 3, p. 93.

12. Joseph Bonsirven, *Exégèse rabbinique et exégèse paulinienne* (Paris, 1939), p. 13.

13. Davies, "Law in First-Century Judaism," p. 92.

14. See Peter Noll, *Jesus und das Gesetz* (Tübingen, 1968), p. 5.

15. *Dictionary of Moral Theology*, ed. F. Roberti and P. Palazzini, trans. H. Yannone (Westminster, 1962), p. 339.

16. Ignatius Loyola, *Spiritual Exercises*, 4th rev. ed. (Westminster, 1943), pp. 56–57.

17. Ibid., p. 58.

18. Garth Hallett, "Training in Practical Wisdom: The Decision Seminar," *Gregorianum*, 52 (1971), 789–90. The number ratings and total have been omitted.

19. *Summa*, II–II, q. 64, a. 7.

20. Ibid., q. 66, a. 7.

21. Ibid., q. 31, a. 3, ad 3.

22. See also *Summa*, I–II, q. 94, a. 4 and 5; *Quodl.* 6, q. 7, art. unic.; *In V Eth.*, lect. 16; John Mahoney, "The Spirit and Moral Discernment in Aquinas," *Heythrop Journal*, 13 (1972), 291–97.

23. *Summa*, I–II, q. 94, a. 4, in *Basic Writings of Saint Thomas Aquinas*, ed. A. Pegis, 2 vols. (New York, 1945), vol. 2, p. 778. See *Summa*, II–II, q. 51, a. 4; q. 120, a. 1; *In II Eth.*, lect. 2.

24. See I. M. Crombie, "Moral Principles," in *Christian Ethics and Contemporary Philosophy*, ed. I. Ramsey (New York, 1966), p. 258.

25. See Jonathan Bennett, "Acting and Refraining," *Analysis*, 28 (1967–1968), 30. It is sometimes suggested that the explanation has more to do with moralists' concern to lay down minimal conditions for salvation (cf. George Regan, *New Trends in Moral Theology* [New York, 1971], pp. 131–32). But why should that require mainly negative norms? Matthew 25 achieves the same purpose without citing a single action to avoid. The blessed are commended and the wicked condemned for the good they did or failed to do.

26. Paul Ramsey, "The Biblical Norm of Righteousness," *Interpretation*, 24 (1970), 425. Notice that there is question here of "binding moral practices," not of practical norms like driving on one side of the street, which have a somewhat different rationale. On both, see Rolf Sartorius, "Individual Conduct and Social Norms: A Utilitarian Account," *Ethics*, 82 (1971–1972), 200–18.

27. James Gustafson, *Theology and Christian Ethics* (Philadelphia, 1974), p. 116.

28. William Frankena, *Ethics*, 2d ed. (Englewood Cliffs, N. J., 1973), p. 40. For a good discussion of these alternatives, see Richard B. Brandt, "Toward a Credible Form of Utilitarianism," in *Contemporary Utilitarianism*, ed. M. Bayles (Garden City, 1968), pp. 143–86. A brief survey of utilitarianism can be found in J. J. C. Smart, "Utilitarianism," in Edwards, *The Encyclopedia of Philosophy*, vol. 8, pp. 206–12. For broader coverage see (in addition to Bayles) David Lyons, *Forms and Limits of Utilitarianism* (Oxford, 1965) or J. J. C. Smart and Bernard Williams, *Utilitarianism: For and Against* (Cambridge, 1973).

29. Jonathan Bennett, "'Whatever the Consequences,'" in *Situationism and the New Morality*, ed. R. Cunningham (New York, 1970), p. 145. See Benedetto Croce, *Philosophy of the Practical*, trans. D. Ainslie (London, 1913), pp. 110–20.

30. Bennett, "'Whatever the Consequences,'" p. 145.

31. Basil Mitchell, "Ideals, Roles, and Rules," in *Norm and Context in Christian Ethics*, ed. G. Outka and P. Ramsey (New York, 1968), p. 359. See also Geoffrey Warnock, *The Object of Morality* (London, 1971), pp. 31–34.

32. Wittgenstein, *The Blue and Brown Books*, p. 178.

33. Cathrein, *Philosophia moralis*, p. 365.

34. Ibid., p. 366.

35. Paul Ramsey, *The Patient as Person: Explorations in Medical Ethics* (New Haven, 1970), pp. 8–9. Cf. Donagan, *The Theory of Morality*, p. 207. For discussion of a variant form of "domino" argument, citing the effect on others than the agent, see e.g. Daniel Maguire, *The Moral Choice* (New York, 1978), pp. 245–49.

36. Karl Rahner, "Christ as the Exemplar of Clerical Obedience," in K. Rahner et al., *Obedience and the Church* (Washington, 1968), pp. 12–13.

37. Karl Rahner, *Christian in the Market Place*, trans. C. Hastings (New York, 1966), pp. 177–79.

38. J. P. Mackey, "Faith and Morals," *The Furrow*, 19 (1968), 703–4.

39. Reinhold Niebuhr, *The Children of Light and the Children of Darkness: A Vindication of Democracy and a Critique of Its Traditional Defense* (New York, 1960), pp. xiii–xiv.

40. Jacques Maritain, *Some Reflections on Culture and Liberty* (Chicago, 1933), p. 18.

41. G. K. Chesterton, *Orthodoxy* (London, 1912), p. 80.

42. Pierre Teilhard de Chardin, *The Future of Man*, trans. N. Denny (New York, 1964), p. 40.

43. Ibid., p. 41.

44. Ibid., p. 47.

45. Ibid., pp. 49–50.

5. Alternative Approaches

1. Frankena, *Ethics*, p. 14. Alan Donagan's observations apply to the word "produce," as well as to "consequence," in Frankena's usage and in mine: "Colloquially, the word 'consequence' is sometimes used as a synonym for 'causal consequence'; but it is also used in a far wider sense, now common in academic philosophy, according to which the distinction between a causal consequence and a foreseeable outcome is obliterated. One event is the consequence of another, in this wider sense, if it happens after it but would not have happened had certain alternatives to that other event happened" (*The Theory of Morality*, p. 51).

2. Sidgwick, *The Methods of Ethics*, p. 14.

3. Peter Knauer, "La détermination du bien et du mal moral par le principe du double effet," *Nouvelle Revue Théologique*, 87 (1965), 367. For similar accusations, see Edward A. Westermarck, *Ethical Relativity* (New York, 1932), pp. 140–41; Alfons Deeken, *Process and Permanence in Ethics: Max Scheler's Moral Philosophy* (New York, 1974), pp. 51–52; J. N. Findlay, *Values and Intentions: A Study in Value-Theory and Philosophy of Mind* (London, 1961), pp. 425–26. Knauer's reference to "higher" values can be understood in relation to twentieth-century German thought. In particular, "Max Scheler described four levels of material (i.e. not formal) values. At the bottom are the pleasant and unpleasant; next come life values; above these are mental values; and at the top are the absolute objects of religious experience, the holy and unholy. Morally speaking, an action or attitude is preferable to the extent that it shares in a higher rather than lower value" (Vernon Bourke, "Value Scales and Today's Morality," in *Human Values in a Secular World*, ed. R. Apostol [New York, 1970], p. 29).

4. Fletcher, *Situation Ethics*, p. 82. See also John Glaser, "Commands-Counsels: A Pauline Teaching?" *Theological Studies*, 31 (1970), 275–87; Bernard Häring, *The Law of Christ: Moral Theology for Priests and Laity*, trans. E. Kaiser, 3 vols. (Westminster, Md., 1961–1966), vol. 1, pp. 300–1; Gordon Kaufman, *The Context of Decision: A Theological Analysis* (New York, 1961), pp. 54–55; Rudolf Liechtenhan, *Gottes Gebot im Neuen Testament* (Basel, 1942), pp.

28–29; Oppenheimer, *Christian Morality*, pp. 66–71; John Knox, *The Ethic of Jesus in the Teaching of the Church* (London, 1962), e.g. pp. 50–51.

5. Paul Ramsey, *Basic Christian Ethics* (New York, 1950), p. 79.

6. Compare Hughes, *Authority in Morals*, pp. 43–45; J. O. Urmson, "Saints and Heroes," in Melden, *Essays in Moral Philosophy*, pp. 202–4. Frankena (*Ethics*, p. 67) turns this reluctance into a theory: "Often such moral ideals of personality go beyond what can be demanded or regarded as obligatory, belonging among the things to be praised rather than required, except as one may require them of oneself." See also ibid., p. 47, and A. Donagan, "Is There a Credible Form of Utilitarianism?" in Bayles, *Contemporary Utilitarianism*, pp. 194–96. Moral criteria do not switch for the first person. But what we call obligatory is what we might demand, and we would not, in practice, demand of another to do what is highest. And, of course, what we do in practice has an effect on what we are inclined to say when we theorize.

7. I shall not discuss the finer distinctions alleged by philosophers, say between "what, morally speaking, one ought to do, and what one has an obligation to do" (Warnock, *The Object of Morality*, p. 94). For one thing, the distinctions are often badly drawn and badly applied. For another, though there are contexts in which, having made no promise or otherwise committed ourselves, we would say we had no duty or obligation yet *should* do this or that, the question of precept versus counsel generally arises in different contexts, where no such distinctions are drawn by either side. And even in the cases where we do so distinguish, between what we "ought" and what we are "obliged" to do, it is often not clear that both expressions then have a moral sense.

8. Here I can appropriate the words of Richard Brandt (*Ethical Theory: The Problems of Normative and Critical Ethics* [Englewood Cliffs, N. J., 1959], p. 360): "This explanation of 'moral obligation' permits us to speak of different stringencies of duty or obligation. Furthermore, we do speak in this way: Sometimes we say our duty is very compelling, whereas at other times we regard it as fairly slight." So too some acts are seriously sinful, others less so.

9. "From this it follows that where the 'better means' is offered in the concrete, and really recognised as such [and] as possible in the here and now, this entails not merely a moral possibility but a moral *demand* for the individual concerned, a demand which is not merely posited but at the same time made possible of achievement, even though the alternative course may in itself have a positive moral value of its own. To refuse the better means offered in the concrete would be an explicit denial of the will to a greater increase in the love of God, and therefore culpable and a sin" (Karl Rahner, *Theological Investigations*, trans. D. Bourke, vol. 8 [London-New York, 1971] p. 146). See also Hughes, *Authority in Morals*, pp. 69–70.

10. See e.g. Kenneth Stern, "Testing Ethical Theories," *Journal of Philosophy*, 63 (1966), 237.

11. Ignatius, *Spiritual Exercises*, p. 56. On the closing sentence Karl Rahner comments: "There should be no doubt in the first place that the two experiences referred to are not simply juxtaposed without connection. The second, concerning the discernment of spirits, is the means of interpreting the first. For these

consolations and desolations are not as mere facts a means of recognizing the will of God, but only through their origin being recognized." See "The Logic of Concrete Individual Knowledge in Ignatius Loyola," in Rahner, *The Dynamic Element in the Church*, trans. W. O'Hara (London, 1964), p. 157. On the other hand, see note 19 below.

12. Autograph Directory, chapter 1, ##11–12. In the *Spiritual Exercises*, see the first "Rules for the Discernment of Spirits."

13. Autograph Directory, chapter 3, #18 (#2 in editions which number anew for each chapter).

14. Eusebio Hernández García, *La elección de los Ejercicios de San Ignacio* (Comillas, 1956), p. 27. Cf. Ignatius, in *Monumenta Ignatiana*, vol. 2 (Rome, 1919), p. 781.

15. Piet Penning de Vries, *Discernment of Spirits according to the Life and Teachings of St. Ignatius of Loyola*, trans. W. D. Van Heel (New York, 1973), p. 56.

16. Cf. Ignatius Loyola, *The Spiritual Journal of St. Ignatius Loyola*, trans. W. Young (Woodstock, Md., 1958), p. 4.

17. An analogous hypothesis, susceptible of similar treatment (step by step), might be envisaged with regard to communal discernment: third-time evidence leading an individual to one conclusion, while signs of the Spirit moving in the community seem to point another way. Contrast this statement of the hypothesis, and the suggested line of solution, with those in John C. Futrell, "Communal Discernment: Reflections on Experience," *Studies in the Spirituality of Jesuits*, 4 (1972), 165.

18. José Calveras, "Buscar y hallar la voluntad divina por los tiempos de elección de los Ejercicios de S. Ignacio," *Manresa*, 15 (1943), 270.

19. See the rules of discernment for the second week, ##4–5, in the *Spiritual Exercises*. Thus, in his description of the second time Ignatius cites, not a single source of "light and knowledge," but two: the experience of consolations and desolations itself as well as the discernment of various spirits. Discernment takes such movements as its objects, but the movements themselves may enlighten, prior to discernment. Cf. Rahner, *Dynamic Element*, p. 103; Leo Bakker, *Freiheit und Erfahrung: Redaktionsgeschichtliche Untersuchungen über die Unterscheidung der Geister bei Ignatius von Loyola* (Würzburg, 1970), pp. 51–53.

20. H. Wheeler Robinson, "Law and Religion in Israel," in *Judaism and Christianity*, vol. 3, *Law and Religion*, ed. E. Rosenthal (New York, 1969), p. 61.

21. J. Duncan Derrett, *Law in the New Testament* (London, 1970), p. 334. "Often in the case of midrash the connection with the original text consists of hardly more than a play on words but this verbal connection would be quite sufficient" (Addison G. Wright, "The Literary Genre Midrash," *Catholic Biblical Quarterly*, 28 [1966], 133).

22. Cf. David Daube, *The New Testament and Rabbinic Judaism* (London, 1956), pp. 59–60, and (for a point of contrast) Robert Banks, *Jesus and the Law in the Synoptic Tradition* (Cambridge, 1975), p. 150 ("pre-Mosaic Torah, like the Noachian precepts, was never regarded as lessening the authority of Mo-

Notes to Pages 82–85

saic legislation"). The closest parallel is with a text of Qumran, which cites the same passage of Genesis in behalf of monogamy; see Hugh Anderson, *The Gospel of Mark*, New Century Bible (London, 1976), p. 242. Though here as in IV, A, and for similar reasons I shall not attempt to identify Jesus' original words, it is good to keep in mind that "since . . . the hand of the Church and of the Evangelist is in evidence here it is difficult to ascertain with any precision how much of the teaching reproduced actually goes back to Jesus himself" (ibid., p. 240).

23. Milhaven, "Towards an Epistemology of Ethics," p. 236. Milhaven furnishes the following references: Saint Thomas, *Summa*, II–II, q. 110, a. 3, c, and 4 ad 4; H. Davis, *Moral and Pastoral Theology* (New York, 1952), p. 114; E. Elter, *Compendium philosophiae moralis*, 3d ed. (Rome, 1950), pp. 151–54; E. Genicot and J. Salsmans, *Institutiones theologiae moralis*, 14th ed., vol. 1 (Buenos Aires, n. d.), p. 340, n. 415; H. Noldin and A. Schmitt, *Summa theologiae moralis*, 27th ed. (Barcelona, 1951), vol. 2, p. 578, n. 638; A. Sabetti and T. Barrett, *Compendium theologiae moralis*, 34th ed. (New York, 1939), p. 300, n. 312.

24. John T. Noonan, Jr., *Contraception: A History of Its Treatment by the Catholic Theologians and Canonists* (Cambridge, Mass., 1966), pp. 239–40.

25. See e.g. Edward Stevens, *The Morals Game* (New York, 1974), p. 92.

26. On this diversity Charles Curran provides numerous references in "Absolute Norms in Moral Theology," in Outka and Ramsey, *Norm and Context*, pp. 140–49.

27. *Summa*, I–II, q. 94, a. 2.

28. Ibid.

29. Ibid., q. 1, a. 7; q. 2, a. 1, ad 1; q. 82, a. 1.

30. Ibid., q. 14, a. 2.

31. Ibid., q. 3, a. 8.

32. E.g. *Summa*, I–II, q. 1, a. 4. Within a Christian perspective though, as Aquinas apparently realized (ibid., q. 18, aa. 4–8), the final end is right-motivating, not right-making, as it is for Aristotle.

33. *In IV Sent.*, d. 33, q. 1, a. 1, ad 4.

34. *Summa*, I–II, q. 94, a. 2.

35. See Charles Curran, "Absolute Norms and Medical Ethics," in *Absolutes in Moral Theology?* ed. Charles Curran (Washington, 1968), p. 116.

36. *Summa*, I–II, q. 91, a. 2.

37. E.g. *In II Sent.*, d. 24, q. 2, a. 4.

38. E.g. *Summa*, II–II, q. 47, a. 3.

39. Noonan, *Contraception*, p. 243.

40. Compare the manner in which "Epictetus (I, 16) for his part tries to prove that men are not permitted to shave, since God (nature) endows them with a beard so as to avoid all confusion and distinguish them visibly from women" (Bruno Schüller, "La théologie morale peut-elle se passer du droit naturel?" *Nouvelle Revue Théologique*, 88 [1966], 469).

41. Joseph Arntz, "Lo sviluppo del pensiero giusnaturalistico all'interno del tomismo," in *Dibattito sul diritto naturale*, ed. F. Böckle, trans. A. Fabbio and G. Fogliazza (Brescia, 1970), p. 118.

42. Gisbert Sölch, "Verpflanzung menschlicher Organe: Was Die Sitten-lehre dazu sagt," *Die neue Ordnung*, 8 (1954), 379. The article summarized is Bender's "Organorum humanorum transplantatio," *Angelicum*, 31 (1954), 139–60. Bender treated the same theme, similarly, in *Perfice munus*, 30 (1955), 209–14; 31 (1956), 89–91, 483–84. For references to those who took a similar position, see Martin Nolan, "The Principle of Totality in Moral Theology," in Curran, *Absolutes in Moral Theology?* p. 308 (note 28). For historical background, see Häring, *Morality Is for Persons*, pp. 168–70.

43. See Schüller, *Die Begründung sittlicher Urteile*, pp. 182–98.

44. Bender, "Organorum humanorum transplantatio," p. 149.

45. Ibid., p. 150.

46. Sölch, "Verpflanzung menschlicher Organe," p. 379.

47. Bender, "Organorum humanorum transplantatio," p. 147.

48. Curran, "Absolute Norms and Medical Ethics," p. 136.

49. Cornelius J. van der Poel, "The Principle of Double Effect," in Curran, *Absolutes in Moral Theology?* p. 194.

50. See Josef Fuchs, "The Absoluteness of Moral Terms," *Gregorianum*, 52 (1971), 444–47.

51. Richard A. McCormick, *Ambiguity in Moral Choice* (Milwaukee, 1973?), p. 1. Cf. McCormick's "Notes on Moral Theology," *Theological Studies*, 39 (1978), 104–16; and R. McCormick and P. Ramsey, eds., *Doing Evil to Achieve Good: Moral Choice in Conflict Situations* (Chicago, 1978). The recent, rarer type of argument Germain Grisez deploys, for instance against artificial contraception, is basically similar to this and so susceptible of a similar critique. See e.g. Germain Grisez, *Contraception and the Natural Law* (Milwaukee, 1964), p. 91: "Not to seek that the good be realized is compatible with fundamentally loving it, for such nonintention merely is permission that the good not be. But to choose by our very action that the good not be realized is incompatible with fundamentally loving it, for such a choice is identically an unwillingness to permit the good to be. And man's basic obligation with regard to all of the essential goods is that he should be open to them, that he should be willing that they be." Here too I would say, as I shall in a minute, faulty psychology intrudes on and vitiates accurate objective assessment.

52. See Giacomo Perico, "Il problema dei trapianti umani," *Aggiornamenti sociali*, 6 (1955), 349.

53. Ewing, *Ethics* (New York, 1953), p. 38.

54. Ibid.

55. Schüller, *Die Begründung sittlicher Urteile*, pp. 74–75. See Kaufman, *Context of Decision*, pp. 103–4; Gene Outka, *Agape: An Ethical Analysis* (New Haven, 1972), pp. 273–74.

56. Sidgwick, *The Methods of Ethics*, p. 243. For good remarks on this question, see also Hastings Rashdall, *The Theory of Good and Evil: A Treatise on Moral Philosophy*, 2d ed., 2 vols. (London, 1924), vol. 2, pp. 124–28; Bennett, "Christian Ethics and Forms of Economic Power," pp. 254–56.

57. John T. Noonan, Jr., "Responding to Persons: Methods of Moral Argument in Debate over Abortion," *Theology Digest*, 21 (1973), 300–1.

58. J. F. Donceel, "Immediate Animation and Delayed Hominization," *Theological Studies*, 31 (1970), 76.

59. Noonan, "Responding to Persons," p. 298.

60. Ibid., p. 301.

61. Ibid., p. 302.

62. Compare Wittgenstein, *Philosophical Investigations*, §486.

63. See Noonan, "Responding to Persons," pp. 304–5.

64. John T. Noonan, Jr., "Abortion and the Catholic Church: A Summary History," *Natural Law Forum*, 12 (1967), 129.

65. John G. Milhaven, "The Abortion Debate: An Epistemological Interpretation," *Theological Studies*, 31 (1970), 110.

66. Noonan, "Abortion," p. 85.

67. Joseph Fletcher, "Four Indicators of Humanhood — the Enquiry Matures," *The Hastings Center Report*, December 1974, 4. Referring to an earlier article in the same journal, Fletcher comments: "In substance I contended that the acute question is what is a *person;* that rights (such as survival) attach only to persons; that out of some twenty criteria one (neocortical function) is the cardinal or hominizing trait upon which all the other human traits hinge; and then I invited those concerned to add or subtract, agree or disagree as they may." I disagree, not merely with the answer, but with the question and its supposed significance.

68. Stevens, *The Morals Game*, p. 110.

69. See, for instance, Hallett, *Darkness and Light*, pp. 97–101, 109–14.

70. For further illustration of these remarks, in relation to abortion, see Garth Hallett, "The Plain Meaning of Abortion," *America*, June 19, 1971, 632–33.

71. Richard McCormick, "Notes on Moral Theology: April-September 1974," *Theological Studies*, 36 (1975), 95. For prior treatment of the example, see H. J. McCloskey, "An Examination of Restricted Utilitarianism," in Bayles, *Contemporary Utilitarianism*, p. 121. For a survey of the discussion, see Dan W. Brock, "Recent Work in Utilitarianism," *American Philosophical Quarterly*, 10 (1973), 265–66. For an analysis like Schüller's in kindred cases, see Brand Blanshard, "'Good,' 'Right,' 'Ought,' 'Bad,'" in *Readings in Ethical Theory*, ed. Wilfrid Sellars and John Hospers (New York, 1970), pp. 228–31.

72. Jonathan Harrison, "Utilitarianism, Universalisation, and Our Duty to Be Just," in Bayles, *Contemporary Utilitarianism*, p. 32.

73. H. J. McCloskey, "A Non-Utilitarian Approach to Punishment," ibid., p. 248. T. L. S. Spriggs makes counterobservations about "the likelihood that the facts will become known" in "A Utilitarian Reply to Dr. McCloskey," ibid., pp. 277–78. See also Kai Nielsen, "Against Moral Conservatism," *Ethics*, 82 (1971–1972), 223–27.

74. For similar analyses, see Robin Attfield, "Toward a Defence of Teleology," *Ethics*, 85 (1974–1975), 130; A. C. Ewing, *Ethics*, pp. 47, 76–77; Lyons, *Forms and Limits of Utilitarianism*, p. 173; Brand Blanshard, "The Impasse in Ethics — and a Way Out," in Sellars and Hospers, *Readings in Ethical Theory*, pp. 291–92.

75. For a similar one, see Germain Grisez and Russell Shaw, *Beyond the*

New Morality: The Responsibilities of Freedom (Notre Dame-London, 1974), p. 132.

76. Ibid.

77. Lyons, *Forms and Limits of Utilitarianism*, p. 12.

78. See McCormick, "Notes, 1974," p. 96.

79. Ewing, *Ethics*, p. 15.

80. Cf. Andrew Oldenquist, "Rules and Consequences," *Mind*, 75 (1966), 183; idem, "Choosing, Deciding, and Doing," in Edwards, *Encyclopedia of Philosophy*, vol. 2, pp. 100–2; and C. I. Lewis, *The Ground and Nature of the Right* (New York, 1955), pp. 45–46.

81. Moore, *Principia Ethica*, p. 25.

82. Ibid., pp. 146–47.

83. Gerard Manley Hopkins, "The Candle Indoors."

84. This suggested reconciliation is not new. Cf. e.g. J. N. Findlay, *Axiological Ethics* (London, 1970), pp. 45–46.

85. Broad, *Critical Essays*, p. 43.

86. Ibid., pp. 43–44.

87. See Edna Ullman-Margalit, "The Generalization Argument: Where Does the Obligation Lie?" *Journal of Philosophy*, 73 (1976), 511–22.

88. Smart, "Utilitarianism," p. 206.

89. See Ullman-Margalit, "The Generalization Argument," p. 517.

90. See Marcus Singer, *Generalization in Ethics: An Essay in the Logic of Ethics, with the Rudiments of a System of Moral Philosophy* (New York, 1961). For criticism and references to other criticism, see, for instance, Michael Robins, "The Fallacy of 'What Would Happen If Everybody Did That?'," *Southwestern Journal of Philosophy*, vol. 6, no. 2 (1975), 89–108.

91. Immanuel Kant, *Critique of Practical Reason and Other Writings in Moral Philosophy*, trans. L. W. Beck (Chicago, 1949), p. 63.

92. Cf. e.g. (recent and fuller) Thomas G. Higgins, *Man as Man: The Science and Art of Ethics*, rev. ed. (Milwaukee, 1958), pp. 202–4; (briefer) Saint Thomas, *Summa*, II–II, q. 64, a. 5, c.

93. See Schüller, *Die Begründung sittlicher Urteile*, pp. 182–90.

6. The Christian Criterion of Right and Wrong

1. James Gustafson, "Context versus Principles: A Misplaced Debate in Christian Ethics," *Harvard Theological Review*, 58 (1965), 171.

2. Ibid., p. 173.

3. Brock, "Recent Work in Utilitarianism," p. 257.

4. Nicholas Crotty, "Conscience and Conflict," *Theological Studies*, 32 (1971), 221–22.

5. Ibid., p. 223.

6. Noonan, *Contraception*, p. 243.

7. See e.g. Francis Simons, "The Catholic Church and the New Morality," *Cross Currents*, 16 (1966), 434.

8. Germain Grisez, *Contraception and the Natural Law* (Milwaukee, 1964), chap. 2. For further difficulties of sense, see Hallett, *Darkness and Light*, pp. 90–92, 125–34. For a critique of Grisez's revised argument, see e.g. John G. Milhaven, "Contraception and the Natural Law: A Recent Study," *Theological Studies*, 26 (1965), 425–27.

9. *Summa*, I–II, q. 94, a. 2.

10. Ibid., II–II, q. 50, a. 1, ad 1.

11. Ibid., q. 53, a. 5. See also e.g. *Summa*, I–II, q. 100, a. 8; q. 105, a. 2, ad 1.

12. *Summa contra gentiles*, 3, 122. On the other hand, see e.g. *In II Sent.*, d. 24, q. 2, a. 4.

13. Peter Geach, "Why Logic Matters," in *Contemporary British Philosophy*, 4th series, ed. H. D. Lewis (London, 1976), p. 97.

14. Mircea Eliade, *Myths, Dreams and Mysteries: The Encounter between Contemporary Faiths and Archaic Realities*, trans. P. Mairet (New York, 1960), p. 23.

15. Sidgwick, *Outlines*, p. 109. Cf. James Gustafson, *Protestant and Roman Catholic Ethics* (Chicago, 1978), pp. 15–17, 27–28.

16. Gerald Kelly and John Ford, *Contemporary Moral Theology*, 2 vols. (Westminster, Md., 1962–1963), vol. 2, *Marriage Questions*, p. 272.

17. Sidgwick, *The Methods of Ethics*, p. 102.

18. Barth, *Church Dogmatics*, vol. II/2, p. 542.

19. Jean Piaget, *The Moral Judgment of the Child*, trans. M. Gabain (Glencoe, Ill., 1960), p. 1.

20. Joseph Fletcher, "What's in a Rule?: A Situationist's View," in Outka and Ramsey, *Norm and Context*, p. 335.

21. Compare, for example, Bernard Häring's manner of speaking, in *The Law of Christ*, vol. 1, pp. 287–88, e.g.: "Since all created values are situation-centered (this means that they are relative, conditioned by changing circumstances), the acts related to them are not good under any and all circumstances."

22. My handling of the sheriff case and of that of the lazy voter indicates why I eschew the term "utilitarianism"—even "ideal utilitarianism." As Dan Brock remarks ("Recent Work in Utilitarianism," p. 265): "To meet objections to utilitarianism from justice and fairness in this way is, in effect, to grant the force of these objections. The result of incorporating a principle independent of utility in any of its ordinary senses is a theory which, though probably more defensible, is distinctly non-utilitarian."

23. Hallett, *Darkness and Light*, p. 86.

7. The Search For a Guiding Hierarchy of Values

1. Nicolai Hartmann, *Ethics*, trans. S. Coit, 3 vols. (New York, 1932), vol. 1, p. 16.

2. For example F. Compagnoni writes: "It seems to me that the need for a hierarchy of values is not dictated by a blind conservatism nor by a tendency to

reify morality, but by the fact that otherwise practical reason would be left without any criterion by which to judge" ("Dalla specificità formale alla specificità d'insieme della morale cristiana," *Rivista di teologia morale*, 6 [1974], 233).

3. Walter Everett, *Moral Values: A Study of the Principles of Conduct* (New York, 1918), p. 182.

4. Peter A. Bertocci and Richard M. Millard, *Personality and the Good: Psychological and Ethical Perspectives* (New York, 1963), p. 332.

5. Clyde Kluckhohn, quoted in Milton Rokeach, *The Nature of Human Values* (New York, 1973), p. 24.

6. See Garth Hallett, "'Happiness'," *Heythrop Journal*, 12 (1971), 301–3.

7. Häring, *The Law of Christ*, vol. 1, pp. 324–25.

8. See Sidgwick, *The Methods of Ethics*, p. 240, and idem, *Outlines*, p. 45; Hartmann, *Ethics*, vol. 2, pp. 30–36; Blanshard, "'Good,' 'Right,' 'Ought,' 'Bad,'" pp. 233–34. This analysis explains why I have not joined those Christian teleologists who define right and wrong in terms of just nonmoral values and disvalues, and why, accordingly, I attach little importance to the distinction between moral and nonmoral values (no more than to the equally vague distinction between social and nonsocial, say, or aesthetic and nonaesthetic).

9. See e.g. Daniel Callahan, "Doing Well by Doing Good: Garrett Hardin's 'Lifeboat Ethic'," *The Hastings Center Report*, December 1974, 1–4; Laurence Simon, "The Ethics of Triage," *The Christian Century*, Jan. 1–8, 1975, 12–15.

10. Such "pleasures of satisfaction" G. H. von Wright contrasts with "passive pleasures" and "active pleasures." See his *The Varieties of Goodness*, pp. 64–65.

11. Such disparities — force-rating disparities for one value versus another, or my good versus others', or immediate good versus long-range — go far toward explaining sin: both its prevalence (from the strength) and its wrongness (from the rating). Unless we turn all lesser values into mere means, it is not true to say, "Sin is to make a means an end" (Ildefons Lobo, "Toward a Morality Based on the Meaning of History: The Condition and Renewal of Moral Theology," in *Understanding the Signs of the Times*, ed. F. Böckle, vol. 25 of *Concilium* [New York, 1967], p. 38). Rather, we are often snared by a lesser good. Compare and contrast the analysis in J.-M. Pohier, "Recherches sur les fondements de la morale sexuelle chrétienne," *Revue des sciences philosophiques et théologiques*, 54 (1970), 11–15.

12. Hartmann, *Ethics*, vol. 2, p. 177. See e.g. Blanshard, "'Good,' 'Right,' 'Ought,' 'Bad,'" pp. 239–40.

13. Ignatius, *Spiritual Exercises*, 4th ed., p. 12. For historical background, see John Passmore, "Attitudes to Nature," in *Nature and Conduct*, ed. R. S. Peters (London, 1975), pp. 252–55; Aquinas, *Summa*, II–II, q. 25, a. 3.

14. John Laird, *Morals and Western Religion: A Discussion in Seven Dialogues* (London, 1931), p. 106. For the historical background of such reductive thinking, see Stephen Clark, *The Moral Status of Animals* (Oxford, 1977), pp. 15–16.

15. Paul W. Taylor, *Normative Discourse* (Englewood Cliffs, N. J., 1961),

p. 23. See also Frankena, *Ethics*, pp. 81–82; and John Locke, *An Essay concerning Human Understanding*, bk. 2, chap. 20, §§1–5.

16. W. David Ross, *The Right and the Good* (Oxford, 1930), p. 70.

17. C. I. Lewis, *The Ground and Nature of the Right* (New York, 1955), p. 64; see also pp. 68–69; and Sidgwick, *The Methods of Ethics*, p. 401.

18. Moore, *Principia Ethica*, p. 188.

19. I do not use this term to caricature the Puritan movement or to "concentrate the antipathies" of this particular user — as Gordon Wakefield puts it in his foreword to Geoffrey F. Nuttall, *The Puritan Spirit: Essays and Addresses* (London, 1967), p. 5 — but because puritans of the kind Knappen describes, here and later, were sufficiently numerous and the consequent public perception is sufficiently widespread to make "puritan" a natural, suggestive label for the tendency I am describing. The scare quotes serve as a reminder that puritans were not all of a piece.

20. Marshall Knappen, *Tudor Puritanism: A Chapter in the History of Idealism* (Chicago, 1939), p. 341.

21. Cf. Augustine, *De moribus ecclesiae catholicae*, xxi, 38.

22. Keith Ward, *Ethics and Christianity* (London, 1970), p. 79.

23. Rashdall, *Good and Evil*, vol. 2, p. 299.

24. Fagothey, *Right and Reason*, p. 182.

25. Ibid., p. 183. See Bertrand Russell to the same effect: "The Elements of Ethics," in Sellars and Hospers, *Readings in Ethical Theory*, p. 25; and Fletcher, *Situation Ethics: The New Morality*, p. 61.

26. Knappen, *Tudor Puritanism*, pp. 350–51.

27. *Inst.*, III, 9.4 (quoted by Kenneth Kirk, *The Vision of God: The Christian Doctrine of the* Summum Bonum [London, 1931], p. 426).

28. *Summa contra gentiles*, iii, 37 (translation from Kirk, *The Vision of God*, p. 382); cf. *Summa*, I–II, q. 3, a. 8.

29. *Summa*, I–II, q. 3, a. 7, ad 3.

30. Maurice Giuliani, "Respect de Dieu et 'indifférence'," *Christus*, 7 (1960), 508.

31. Maurice Giuliani, "Se vaincre soi-même pour trouver Dieu," *Christus*, 9 (1962), 23. For the tradition behind such declarations, see E. Portalié, "Augustin (Saint)," in *Dictionnaire de théologie catholique*, 15 vols. (Paris, 1903–1950), vol. 1, part 2, col. 2433. On this final restriction see Aquinas, *Summa*, I–II, q. 2, a. 7.

32. *Summa*, I–II, q. 108, a. 4.

33. *In duo praecepta caritatis*, prol. Concerning love for human beings, see *Summa*, II–II, q. 44, a. 3, c.

34. *Summa*, II–II, q. 24, a. 8, trans. R. J. Batten (London-New York, 1975).

35. Dietrich von Hildebrand, *Christian Ethics* (New York, 1953), pp. 80–81.

36. John Haughey, *The Conspiracy of God: The Holy Spirit in Us* (New York, 1976), p. 104.

37. Norbert Rigali, "Christian Ethics and Perfection," *Chicago Studies*,

14 (1975), 234. Cf. Compagnoni, "Dalla specificità formale," p. 233; René Le Senne, "Ethics and Metaphysics," in *Contemporary European Ethics*, ed. J. Kockelmans (New York, 1972), pp. 135–36.

38. Frederick Copleston, "Ethics and Metaphysics: East and West," *Proceedings of the American Catholic Philosophical Association*, 51 (1977), 77–78.

39. Scheler, *Formalism in Ethics*, pp. 94–96, 104–10. See my note 3 in chapter 5. Like remarks apply to the three-tiered scheme in Maurizio Flick and Zoltan Alszeghy, *Metodologia per una teologia dello sviluppo* (Brescia, 1970), pp. 74–77, and to "the classical hierarchy among the goods that love can pursue: first come the supernatural, then the natural goods of the soul, the intrinsic goods of the body, and finally all external goods" (Gérard Gilleman, *The Primacy of Charity in Moral Theology*, trans. W. Ryan and A. Vachon [Westminster, Md., 1959], p. 308).

40. Rigali, "Christian Ethics and Perfection," p. 234.

41. Ibid., p. 238.

42. Ibid., p. 239.

43. Except in the sense indicated by A, 6, above.

8. Problems of Analysis

1. G. E. M. Anscombe, "Modern Moral Philosophy," *Philosophy*, 33 (1958), 10.

2. Fletcher, *Situation Ethics: The New Morality*, pp. 164–65. Compare Augustine, *De sermone domini in monte*, P.L. vol. 34, col. 1254.

3. Max Rieser, "An Outline of Intellectualistic Ethics," *Journal of Philosophy*, 55 (1958), 367.

4. It should be noted, however, that the perspective is often broader, so less manageable, than here: self-regard and other-regard are made to cover both attitude and rule of action, as for instance in Gene Outka, *Agape: An Ethical Analysis* (New Haven, 1972).

5. See Ramsey, *Basic Christian Ethics*, pp. 99–100.

6. See e.g. 2 Cor. 8:9. I realize that such spotty evidence and rapid argumentation are not fully convincing, so I am presently embarked on a thorough study of this basic but little-explored issue.

7. See Outka, *Agape*, pp. 276–77. It is also sometimes maintained, though not convincingly, that self-sacrificing altruism might on occasion not work out for the common good. See e.g. Nicholas Rescher, *Unselfishness: The Role of the Vicarious Affects in Moral Philosophy and Social Theory* (Pittsburgh, 1975), pp. 41–43. For other objections, see David Pugmire, "Altruism and Ethics," *American Philosophical Quarterly*, 15 (1978), 75–80.

8. See Garth Hallett, *A Companion to Wittgenstein's "Philosophical Investigations"* (Ithaca, 1977), p. 220.

9. Frankena, *Ethics*, p. 47.

10. For some I shall not mention, see H. B. Acton, "Negative Utilitarianism," *Proc. Arist. Soc.*, supplem. vol. 37 (1963), 83–94.

11. Ross, *The Foundations of Ethics*, p. ix; see also p. 272. For fuller development, see A. D. M. Walker, "Negative Utilitarianism," *Mind*, 83 (1974), 424–28.

12. Frankena, *Ethics*, p. 46.

13. Rescher, *Introduction to Value Theory*, p. 9 (apparent misprint corrected).

14. John Rawls, *A Theory of Justice* (Cambridge, Mass., 1971), p. 3.

15. Ibid., p. 303.

16. Ibid., pp. 103–4.

17. Kai Nielsen, "On Philosophic Method," *International Philosophical Quarterly*, 16 (1976), 361.

18. Rawls, *A Theory of Justice*, p. 75.

19. Ibid., p. 105.

20. Ibid., p. 64.

21. Ibid. For a concrete illustration, see Frank C. Sharp, *Good Will and Ill Will: A Study of Moral Judgments* (Chicago, 1950), pp. 227–28.

22. Rawls, *A Theory of Justice*, p. 302.

23. Hans Reiner, *Pflicht und Neigung: Die Grundlagen der Sittlichkeit* (Meisenheim/Glan, 1951), pp. 168–69.

24. Richard McCormick, "Notes on Moral Theology: April-September, 1971," *Theological Studies*, 33 (1972), 88.

25. Dewey, *Reconstruction in Philosophy*, p. 171.

26. Cf. C. I. Lewis, *An Analysis of Knowledge and Valuation* (La Salle, Ill., 1946), pp. 494–95; Joseph Mayer, "Comparative Value and Human Behavior," *Philosophical Review*, 45 (1936), 479; Blanshard, "Impasse," pp. 291–92; Moore, *Principia Ethica*, p. 149; L. J. Russell, "Is Anthropology Relevant to Ethics?" *Proc. Arist. Soc.*, supplem. vol. 20 (1946), 61–72.

27. See John Laird, *The Idea of Value* (Cambridge, 1929), p. 364.

28. Michael Keeling, *What Is Right?* (London, 1969), p. 28.

29. For further illustrations of culture-conditioned judgments, see H. Richard Niebuhr, *Christ and Culture* (New York, 1956), e.g. pp. 125, 145, 146.

30. St. Augustine, *De moribus manichaeorum*, i. 1 (P.L. vol. 32, col. 1345).

31. Pierre Teilhard de Chardin, *The Phenomenon of Man*, trans. B. Wall (New York, 1961), p. 218.

32. Bertrand Russell, *The Analysis of Mind* (London, 1933), p. 140. Cf. Brock, "Recent Work in Utilitarianism," p. 245.

33. Frankena, *Ethics*, p. 111.

34. Donagan, *The Theory of Morality*, p. 221. Cf. Monroe Beardsley, "Intrinsic Value," *Phil. and Phen. Research*, 26 (1965–1966), 11–12; or in Sellars and Hospers, *Readings in Ethical Theory*, p. 408.

35. Arthur and Eleanor Sidgwick, *Henry Sidgwick: A Memoir* (London, 1906), p. 68.

36. P. Wheelwright, quoted in Donald Davidson, J. C. C. McKinsey, and Patrick Suppes, "Outlines of a Formal Theory of Value, I," *Philosophy of Science*, 22 (1955), 149.

37. Ross, *The Foundations of Ethics*, p. 180.

38. Ibid., p. 181.

39. Ibid., p. 182.

40. Mayer, "Comparative Value and Human Behavior," p. 476. See Rashdall, *Good and Evil*, vol. 2, p. 5. Similar objections are sometimes urged, not just against the use of cardinal numbers but against value-maximization generally, e.g. in John Finnis, *Natural Law and Natural Rights* (Oxford, 1980), pp. 112–15 ("none can provide a common denominator or single yardstick").

41. On the wide variations in the logic of measurement, see Davidson, McKinsey, and Suppes, "Outlines," p. 151.

42. See Rashdall, *Good and Evil*, vol. 2, pp. 23–24; Morris R. Cohen and Ernest Nagel, *An Introduction to Logic and Scientific Method* (London, 1934), pp. 293–98 (intensive versus extensive qualities).

43. Kurt Baier, *The Moral Point of View: A Rational Basis of Ethics* (Ithaca, 1958), p. 71.

44. See e.g. F. J. Connell, "Morality, Systems of," in *New Catholic Encyclopedia*, 15 vols. (London-New York, 1967), vol. 9, pp. 1131–34.

9. Questions of Procedure

1. Brock, "Recent Work in Utilitarianism," p. 257.

2. Sidgwick, *The Methods of Ethics*, p. 121. Cf. David P. Gauthier, *Practical Reasoning* (Oxford, 1963), p. 26.

3. Karl Stern, *The Pillar of Fire* (New York, 1959), p. 216.

4. For concrete illustration and development, see James Gustafson, *Can Ethics Be Christian?* (Chicago, 1975), pp. 1–2, 18.

5. Jerome Stolnitz, "Notes on Ethical Indeterminacy," *Journal of Philosophy*, 55 (1958), 363–64.

6. Hampshire, "Fallacies in Moral Philosophy," p. 476.

7. See Lars Bergström, *The Alternatives and Consequences of Actions. An Essay on Certain Fundamental Notions in Teleological Ethics* (Stockholm, 1966), p. 30.

8. Ibid., pp. 45–55.

9. Janis and Mann, *Decision Making*, p. 342.

10. Ibid.

11. John Bennett, *Christian Ethics and Social Policy* (New York, 1946), p. 67.

12. C. O'Donnell, ed., *Freedom and Community* (New York, 1968), p. 10.

13. Ibid., pp. 10–11. For concrete illustration, see Maguire, *The Moral Choice*, pp. 131–32.

14. Lewis, *Nature of the Right*, p. 32. See Keeling, *What Is Right?* chaps. 1 and 5.

15. Daniel Maguire, *Death by Choice* (Garden City, N.Y., 1974), pp. 89–90. For a similar example of sensitive synthesis, see Maguire, *The Moral Choice*, pp. 253–54.

16. Peter Berger, *Pyramids of Sacrifice: Political Ethics and Social Change* (New York, 1974), pp. 127–28. Cf. Bennett, *Christian Ethics and Social Policy*, pp. 29–31; Maguire, *The Moral Choice*, pp. 154–56.

17. Berger, *Pyramids of Sacrifice*, p. 163.

18. David A. J. Richards, *A Theory of Reasons for Action* (Oxford, 1971), p. 46.

19. This popular version differs from the Ignatian saying in *Acta Romana Societatis Iesu*, 12 (1951–1955), 138: "Trust in God as though all success depended on him and none on you; yet work as though you alone are to do everything and God nothing."

20. Yet see, for instance, Dietrich Bonhoeffer, *Letters and Papers from Prison*, ed. E. Bethge, trans. R. Fuller, rev. ed. (New York, 1967), pp. 178–79. For contrast, see e.g. Kaufman, *Context of Decision*, pp. 27–28.

21. See Geoffrey Warnock, *Contemporary Moral Philosophy* (London, 1967), pp. 69–70; Aquinas, *Summa*, II–II, q. 52, a. 1, ad 1.

22. Rahner, *Dynamic Element*, p. 118.

23. Ignatius, *Spiritual Exercises*, pp. 111–12 (rules of discernment for the second week, #2).

24. Cf. Bakker, *Freiheit und Erfahrung*, pp. 173–83; W. W. Meissner, "Psychological Notes on the *Spiritual Exercises*, III," *Woodstock Letters*, 93 (1964), 178–88.

25. Ignatius, *Spiritual Exercises*, pp. 112–13 (rules of discernment for the second week, #5).

26. Ibid., p. 114 (rules of discernment for the second week, #8); translation slightly altered.

27. *Confessions*, bk. 8, chap. 12.

28. Its rules, for instance, suggest "to place before my eyes a man whom I have never seen or known, and to consider what I, desiring all perfection for him, would tell him to do and choose for the greater glory of God our Lord, and the greater perfection of his soul" (*Spiritual Exercises*, p. 59).

29. J. L. Houlden, *Ethics and the New Testament* (Baltimore, 1973), p. 13. For a broad treatment, see E. J. Tinsley, *The Imitation of God in Christ: An Essay on the Biblical Basis of Christian Spirituality* (London, 1960).

30. Houlden, *Ethics and the New Testament*, pp. 13–14.

31. Immanuel Kant, *Foundations of the Metaphysics of Morals*, in Beck, *Writings on Moral Philosophy*, pp. 68–69. Cf. A. Campbell Garnett, *Religion and the Moral Life* (New York, 1955), p. 13.

32. Cf. Wittgenstein, *Philosophical Investigations*, §§65–78; Garth Hallett, "'Light Dawns Gradually over the Whole'," *Heythrop Journal*, 18 (1977), 316–19. For an alternative, complementary line of response, compare Basil Mitchell, *Law, Morality, and Religion in a Secular Society* (London, 1967), p. 43.

33. James Gustafson, *Christ and the Moral Life* (New York, 1968), p. 161.

34. See note 7 in chapter 8.

35. The role of Scripture in moral decisions has been treated so frequently and fully elsewhere that I can be brief. In addition to the references below, see for instance: Hughes, *Authority in Morals*, pp. 11–19; Edward LeRoy Long, Jr.,

"The Use of the Bible in Christian Ethics," *Interpretation*, 19 (1965), 149–62; Gustafson, *Protestant and Roman Catholic Ethics*, pp. 21–29.

36. Bruce C. Birch and Larry L. Rasmussen, *Bible and Ethics in the Christian Life* (Minneapolis, 1976), p. 193.

37. James Gustafson, "The Place of Scripture in Christian Ethics: A Methodological Study," *Interpretation*, 24 (1970), 444.

38. See Hughes, *Authority in Morals*, pp. 11–16.

39. Birch and Rasmussen, *Bible and Ethics*, p. 69, citing Brevard S. Childs, "Biblical Theology's Role in Decision-Making," in *Biblical Theology in Crisis* (Philadelphia, 1970).

40. See Garth Hallett, "Whatever You Loose Shall Be Loosed," *America*, October 4, 1975, 188–90.

41. J. Philip Wogaman, *A Christian Method of Moral Judgment* (London, 1976), pp. 40–41.

42. Ibid., p. 43.

43. Ibid., pp. 166–67. See Hughes, *Authority in Morals*, pp. 19–21.

44. Wogaman, *A Christian Method*, pp. 168–69.

45. Birch and Rasmussen, *Bible and Ethics*, p. 134.

46. Yves M.-J. Congar, *Tradition and Traditions: An Historical and a Theological Essay*, trans. M. Naseby and T. Rainborough (London, 1966), p. 295. Cf. Vatican Council II's Dogmatic Constitution on Divine Revelation, chap. 2.

47. Haughey, *The Conspiracy of God*, p. 101.

48. Quoted in Karl Rahner, "Magisterium," in *Sacramentum Mundi: An Encyclopedia of Theology*, ed. K. Rahner et al., 6 vols. (London-New York, 1968–1970), vol. 3, p. 357.

49. See Bruno Schüller, "Bemerkungen zur authentischen Verkündigung des kirchlichen Lehramtes," *Theologie und Philosophie*, 42 (1967), 534–51; and Avery Dulles, *The Resilient Church: The Necessity and Limits of Adaptation* (New York, 1977), chap. 5 ("Doctrinal Authority for a Pilgrim Church"), which cites in turn "McCormick's fuller discussions of the magisterium and dissent in *Theological Studies*, 29 (1968), 714–18; 30 (1969), 644–68; and 38 (1977), 84–100; and in *Proceedings of the Catholic Theological Society of America*, 24 (1969), 239–54."

50. See Hallett, *Darkness and Light*, chap. 5.

51. Pohier, "Recherches," pp. 218–19.

52. James Gustafson, *The Church as Moral Decision-Maker* (Philadelphia, 1970), p. 92.

53. Charles Curran, *Ongoing Revision in Moral Theology* (Notre Dame, 1975), p. 50.

54. Note the parallel with positive precepts, as analyzed in IV, E.

55. Bennett, *Christian Ethics and Social Policy*, p. 79.

56. Ibid., p. 81.

10. The Distinctiveness of Christian Moral Reasoning

1. Fletcher, *Situation Ethics: The New Morality*, p. 156.

2. Dionigi Tettamanzi, *Temi di morale fondamentale* (Milan, 1975), p. 141, quoting A. Valsecchi.

3. Jacques Vallery, *L'identité de la morale chrétienne. Points de vue de quelques théologiens contemporains de la langue allemande* (Louvain-la-Neuve, 1976), p. 192.

4. Gerard Hughes, "A Christian Basis for Ethics," *Heythrop Journal*, 13 (1972), 41.

5. Josef Fuchs, *Human Values and Christian Morality* (Dublin, 1970), pp. 121–22.

6. Peter Berger, "For a World with Windows," in *Against the World for the World*, ed. P. Berger and R. Neuhaus (New York, 1976), p. 10.

7. See Richard A. McCormick, "Notes on Moral Theology: 1976," *Theological Studies*, 38 (1977), 59.

8. Norbert Rigali, "On Christian Ethics," *Chicago Studies*, 10 (1971), 240.

9. Laird, *Morals*, p. 27.

10. See Compagnoni, "Dalla specificità formale," pp. 226–29.

11. Wittgenstein, *Philosophical Investigations*, §66.

12. Taylor, *Normative Discourse*, p. 113.

13. Gustafson notes that, for reasons soon to be mentioned, "many Protestants prefer to write about Christian discipleship, about *Nachfolge Christi* (following of Christ) rather than *imitatio Christi*" (*Can Ethics Be Christian?* p. 115).

14. Dodd, *Gospel and Law*, pp. 52–53.

15. Wittgenstein, *Philosophical Investigations*, §130. See Hallett, *Companion*, pp. 56–57, and idem, *Darkness and Light*, pp. 11–19.

16. Wittgenstein, *Philosophical Investigations*, §131.

17. Cf. Avery Dulles, "Finding God's Will," *Woodstock Letters*, 94 (1965), 152; Jessop, *The Christian Morality*, pp. 54–55; Barth, *Church Dogmatics*, vol. IV/2, §§67–68.

18. Warnock, *Contemporary Moral Philosophy*, pp. 57–58. In like vein, see MacNiven, "Descriptivism," p. 176, and Kai Nielsen, "Ethics, Problems of," in Edwards, *Encyclopedia of Philosophy*, vol. 3, p. 131.

19. Friedrich Nietzsche, *Beyond Good and Evil: Prelude to a Philosophy of the Future*, trans. H. Zimmern (London, 1967), p. 240. See Outka, *Agape*, p. 262.

20. Nietzsche, *Beyond Good and Evil*, p. 229.

21. Edward Gibbon, *The Decline and Fall of the Roman Empire*, quoted in Peter Quennell and Hamish Johnson, *A History of English Literature* (London, 1973), p. 283.

22. Don Richardson, *Peace Child*, 3d ed. (Glendale, Calif., 1976), pp. 177–78.

23. Ibid., pp. 74–75, 178–80, 185–87, 190–91, 206.

24. Dwight M. Donaldson, *Studies in Muslim Ethics* (London, 1953), pp. 10–11. Compare Westermarck, *Origin and Development*, vol. 1, p. 291; Richard Brandt, *Hopi Ethics: A Theoretical Analysis* (Chicago, 1954), pp. 138–39.

25. W. R. Rucker, "A Value-Oriented Framework for Education and the

Behavioral Sciences," in *Human Values and Natural Science*, ed. E. Laszlo and J. Wilbur (London-New York, 1970), p. 82. The list is Harold Lasswell's.

26. Gill, "An Abstract Definition of the Good," ibid., p. 227.

27. Ignatius Loyola, *The Spiritual Exercises of St. Ignatius*, trans. L. Puhl (Westminster, Md., 1963), p. 69.

28. Ibid.

29. C. S. Lewis, *Christian Behaviour* (London, 1943), p. 42.

30. James Brodrick, *Saint Ignatius Loyola. The Pilgrim Years 1491–1538* (New York, 1956), pp. 131–32.

31. Robert Faricy, "Population and the Quality of Life: A Theological View," *Homiletic and Pastoral Review*, Feb. 1974, 51.

32. Paolo Valori, *L'esperienza morale: saggio di una fondazione fenomenologica dell'etica* (Brescia, 1971), p. 33. For similar, equally massive illustrations, see Heinrich von Stietencron, "Moral im zyklischen Denken: Die Auswirkung der Wiedergeburtslehre auf soziale Werte und Normen," in *Religion und Moral*, ed. B. Gladigow (Düsseldorf, 1976), pp. 129–34.

33. This case tends to merge with one we shall consider shortly (G, 2), illustrating a different configuration.

34. Wogaman, *A Christian Method*, p. 80. For trenchant, complementary remarks, see G. K. Chesterton's introduction to Owen Francis Dudley, *Will Men Be Like Gods?: Humanitarianism or Human Happiness* (New York, 1931), pp. viii–x. See also Wilhelm Korff, *Theologische Ethik: Eine Einführung* (Freiburg im Breisgau, 1975), pp. 38–39.

35. Gerard Manley Hopkins, "That Nature Is a Heraclitean Fire and of the Comfort of the Resurrection."

36. Wogaman, *A Christian Method*, pp. 81–82.

37. Stephen Toulmin, *An Examination of the Place of Reason in Ethics* (Cambridge, 1958), p. 219.

38. Jonathan Cohen, "Three-Valued Ethics," *Philosophy*, 26 (1951), 221.

39. Hampshire, "Fallacies in Moral Philosophy," p. 475. For further concrete illustration, see, for instance, the long quotation in VII, D, and Donagan, *The Theory of Morality*, pp. 34–35.

40. Paul L. Lehmann, *Ethics in a Christian Context* (New York, 1963), p. 26.

41. James Gustafson, "What Ought I to Do?" *Proc. Amer. Cath. Phil. Assoc.*, 43 (1969), 62.

42. Kaufman, *The Context of Decision*, p. 62.

43. See Sidgwick, *The Methods of Ethics*, pp. 22 and 470.

44. Pierre Antoine, *Morale sans anthropologie* (Paris, 1970), pp. 24–25.

45. Kaufman, *The Context of Decision*, pp. 62–63.

46. Dietrich Bonhoeffer, *The Cost of Discipleship*, trans. R. Fuller, 2d ed. (London, 1959), p. 127.

47. Henry Stob, "The Ethics of Jonathan Edwards," in *Faith and Philosophy: Philosophical Studies in Religion and Ethics*, ed. A. Plantinga (Grand Rapids, Mich., 1964), pp. 112–13.

48. Pierre Teilhard de Chardin, *Science and Christ*, trans. R. Hague (New York, 1968), p. 169.

49. Ibid., p. 216.

50. The Doctrinal Constitution on Divine Revelation, Vatican Council II, §9.

51. See e.g. Hallett, *Darkness and Light*, pp. 4–8.

52. The Doctrinal Constitution on Divine Revelation, §8.

53. See Dulles, *The Resilient Church*, pp. 31–35, and chap. 3. Dulles seems to overlook pine trees, say, which shed their lower limbs year by year, or trees in general, whose cambium layer one year is dead wood the next, when he writes: "On the second [organic] theory, the authentic developments that occurred in postapostolic times would likewise be irreformable, in the sense of irreversible, since they had been inspired by the Holy Spirit" (p. 34).

54. Gustafson, quoted in IV, F.

55. Wilhelm Korff, "Reale Chancen zur Versöhnung. Gesellschaftliche Binnenmoralen und freiheitliche Rechtsordnung," in Gladigow, *Religion und Moral*, p. 136.

56. Ibid., p. 139.

57. And he proceeds here as he does elsewhere, say in jurisprudence and executive decision-making. "In both these areas," notes Wogaman (*A Christian Method*, p. 41), "people have learned to live with uncertainties and still to arrive at the kind of judgments which permit unambiguous action," by adopting the approach he labels "methodological presumption" (see IX, F).

58. Bennett, *Christian Ethics and Social Policy*, p. 123.

59. William Wordsworth, *The Prelude*, bk. 1.

60. Teilhard de Chardin, *Science and Christ*, p. 221. Cf. Robert H. Dailey, *Introduction to Moral Theology* (New York, 1970), p. 15.

Retrospect

1. Manuscript 163.

2. Ludwig Wittgenstein, *Zettel*, ed. G. E. M. Anscombe and G. H. von Wright, trans. G. E. M. Anscombe (Oxford, 1967), §464.

Index